LOUIS AND THE PRINCE

About the author

Geordie Greig, the grandson of Sir Louis Greig, was
born in 1960, and educated at Eton and St Peter's
College, Oxford. He was the New York correspondent of *The Sunday Times* for five years until 1995
when he was appointed literary editor. Geordie
Greig is now the editor of *Tatler* magazine. He lives
in London with his wife and son.

Louis and the Prince

*A Story of Politics, Intrigue
and Royal Friendship*

Geordie Greig

CORONET BOOKS

Hodder & Stoughton

First published in Great Britain in 1999 by Hodder and Stoughton
First published in paperback in 2000 by Hodder and Stoughton
A division of Hodder Headline

A Coronet Paperback

10 9 8 7 6 5 4 3 2

A CIP catalogue record for this title is available
from the British Library.

ISBN 0340 72883 3

Printed and bound in Great Britain by
Clays Ltd, St Ives plc.

Hodder and Stoughton
A division of Hodder Headline
338 Euston Road
London NW1 3BH

For Kathryn

Contents

List of Illustrations

Louis Greig and Prince Albert at the Oxford and Cambridge boat race in 1922. (Illustrated London News)

Louis Greig and Prince Albert at RAF Cranwell in 1918.

Louis Greig and the Prince of Wales share a cigarette.

Louis Greig, his son Carron and his sister Jean, in Barnes in 1932. (Topham)

Louis Greig and family at Ladderstile, Kingston Hill.

Louis Greig and Prince George, the Duke of Kent in 1941.

Louis Greig and King Farouk on his diplomatic mission in 1943.

A cartoon of Louis.

The fixer in his final years.

Louis Greig and Prince Albert at Wimbledon in 1926. (Topham)

Wimbledon's royal box.

Prince Henry and Prince Albert with Bridget and Jean at Cambridge in 1920.

The Deputy Ranger: enjoying his royal residence.

Prince Albert and Louis Greig preparing for their flight to France in 1918. (Hulton & Company)

Cartoon of Louis Greig.

The future King on HMS Cumberland.

Marjorie Gordon introduced to Prince Albert by Louis Greig. (Hulton Getty/Rita Martin)

Another gaiety girl: Phyllis Monkman. (Hulton Getty/Sasha)

Madge Saunders with Leslie Henson, whom she eventually married. (Hulton Getty/Brooke)

Acknowledgements

I am most grateful to Her Majesty Queen Elizabeth II for permission to quote from previously unpublished letters by King George VI and from material in the Royal Archives. I am also most grateful to Her Majesty Queen Elizabeth the Queen Mother for permission to quote from her previously unpublished letters and for talking to me about my grandfather; and also to HRH The Duke of Kent for permission to quote from his father's unpublished letters.

I wish to thank the following other people for generously giving interviews, information, advice and permission to quote from copyright material: Sir John Aird, Jon Barratt, Antony Beevor, Sarah Bradford, Anna Brüning, Jean Buckberry at RAF Cranwell, Lord Callaghan of Cardiff, Dame Barbara Cartland, Ann and Mike Bemis, Adrienne Connors, Artemis Cooper, Joseph Cooper, Lord Charteris of Amisfield, Lady Margaret Colville, Lady Cromer, Roseanne Cuninghame, Captain North Dalrymple-Hamilton, Caroline Donald, Caroline Erskine, Sir Edward Ford, Jack Fitch, Caroline Gascoigne, Martin Gilbert, Vanessa Green, David Greig, Susan Greig, John Grigg, Blyth Harvey, Humphrey Hawksley, Lady Pamela Hicks, Vice-Admiral Sir Ian Hogg, Anthony Howard, James Ireland, Chris Jakes, Lt Col Sir John Johnston, Iain Johnstone, Peter Kemp, Lord Laing of Dunphail, Mrs Derek Lawson, Lord and Lady Longford, Nancy, Lady Maclay, Caroline Marçal, Emily Monson, Tessa Miller-Stirling, The Hon Lady Murray, Dame Felicity Peake, Lady Penn, The Hon Laura Ponsonby, The Hon Caroline Ponsonby, Pamela Ramsay, Michael Reynolds, the late Sir Robert Rhodes-James, Mrs Michael Ritchie, Kenneth Rose, Gordon Sinclair, John Scrimgeour, Pam Snagge, John Stourton, The Earl of Strathmore, The Hon Mrs Charles Strutt, Viscount Stuart of Findhorn, Sir Michael Thomas, Michael Thornton, Major Peter Verney, Lord Wigram, Philip Williamson, Cheryl Younson, Philip Ziegler.

Two books stand out as models of biography and were essential guides during my research: *King George V* by Kenneth Rose and *King George VI* by Sarah Bradford. Both are scholarly, popular, and authoritative, capturing the broad sweep as well as the fine details of the lives of the monarchs and their reigns. I am indebted to both authors.

Copyright material from the Ramsay MacDonald Papers is reproduced by permission of the executrix of the late Malcolm MacDonald. The letters written by Edward, Prince of Wales, are reproduced by permission of L'institut Pasteur, Paris. Verses from Osbert Sitwell's Rat Week are reproduced by kind permission of his literary executor Frank Magro; Winston Churchill's letters by kind permission of C & T Publications Ltd; extracts from Cecil Beaton's diaries by kind permission of the literary executors of the late Cecil Beaton.

The staff of the following organisations and institutes were always helpful: The Bodleian Library, Oxford University; Birmingham University Library; The Eisenhower Library, Abilene, Texas; Cambridge University Library; Glasgow Academy; Merchiston Castle School, Edinburgh; Columbia University, New York; The Theatre Museum; News International Library; Lambeth Palace Library; the Wimbledon All-England Lawn Tennis Club; Glasgow Academy; Glasgow University; The Cabinet War Rooms; Churchill College, Cambridge; The Imperial War Museum; the Public Record Office, Kew. I would especially like to thank the Royal Archives at Windsor Castle where Lady de Bellaigue, the Registrar, and Oliver Everett, the Assistant Keeper of Archives, were wonderfully patient, resourceful and generous with their time.

David Mills read all my early drafts and was always encouraging and supportive. Philip Williamson read my chapters on Ramsay MacDonald and Julian Thompson read the first world war chapters; both helped eliminate errors. James Adams provided a much needed fresh sense of perspective. Two others have also closely read the manuscript but prefer to remain unacknowledged. They know who they are and I am most grateful. Hugo Vickers was also extremely generous with his time and knowledge. For any errors which remain, the blame rests solely with me.

This book would not have been written without the energy and enthusiasm of my agent Ed Victor and my publisher Roland Philipps. I also thank Roseanne Boyle and Karen Geary of Hodder & Stoughton.

Finally, I wish to thank my family, especially my mother and father, who trepidatiously watched this book develop from my initial perusals through cobweb-covered boxes and files in their attic.

Most of all I want to thank my wife Kathryn, to whom I owe more than I can say.

Prologue

'The sporting side of the London Season has presented features of unusual interest this year. The Wimbledon Lawn Tennis Championships are always an important social fixture . . . and the Duke of York's interest in lawn tennis has this year resulted in H.R.H. entering the doubles at Wimbledon with Wing Commander Greig – a partnership which won the RAF Doubles in 1920. The fact that a Prince of the Reigning House is competing adds tremendously to the Wimbledon interest.'

Illustrated London News, 19 June 1926

In the year of the General Strike a lesser wind of change blew through Buckingham Palace. Louis Greig and Prince Albert, the Duke of York, entered the 1926 doubles competition at Wimbledon, which was the first time a member of the royal family had played in the All-England tennis tournament.

King George V's second son was thirty-one years old and cut an elegant, athletic figure in his long white trousers and short-sleeved flannel shirt when he strolled on to Number Two Court on Friday, 25 June, in the golden jubilee year of the lawn tennis championships. He was slightly built, his short brown hair slicked back and divided in a sharp parting. His movements were wooden, and he radiated a sense of anxiety. Louis Greig was fourteen years older, but extraordinarily fit for a forty-five-year-old. The taller, broad-shouldered Scot had a monkish pate, a weathered and tanned face framing intensely focused blue eyes. Usually they glinted with humour or mischief, but, on this occasion, they were locked on to his partner. Louis had taught the Prince how to play tennis, and felt responsible for his protégé's performance in so public a forum.

Albert feared that they might be completely outclassed by their opponents in the world's most famous tennis tournament, as they never had played in front of such a large crowd. He had forbidden the publicity-conscious Wimbledon committee from scheduling the match on the Centre Court, instead asking for a discreetly placed outer court. Number Two Court had been the compromise. Not only was Albert apprehensive about his game, but he was, also, nervous about the recent political and industrial unrest. The preceding weeks had been marked by the long-drawn-out coal strike that had divided the nation. The miners had been told to accept a pay cut or face the sack. When confronted with a national lock-out, the Trades Union Congress called a General Strike which started on 3 May and lasted twelve days. It collapsed after extraordinary interventions, voluntary work and a loss of nerve by the TUC, but it had still established a new political climate, and Albert did not want to seem too light-hearted or frivolous at such a sensitive time.

On that warm June afternoon, newspaper photographers and reporters at Wimbledon focused their attention on Albert's wife, the Duchess of York. She was small and dark-haired with a winning smile. Unfettered by fashion, she wore her hair in an unbecoming fringe and dressed 'picturesquely' in her own distinctive style. The trademark fox fur round her neck caught the attention of the novelist Muriel Spark, who used it in *The Prime of Miss Jean Brodie* to denote the sartorial superiority of the English mother of her Edinburgh teacher's cleverest pupil, Sandy Stranger, who 'had a flashy winter coat trimmed with fluffy fox fur like the Duchess of York's while the other mothers wore tweed, or at the most musquash that would do them all their days'.[1]

From a wooden bench in the front row she smiled and enthusiastically applauded when her husband and Louis, wooden racquets under their arms, walked on to the court with anxious, earnest expressions. They were facing two veteran players, A. W. Gore and H. Roper Barrett, who had previously won Wimbledon titles, Gore the men's singles title in 1901, 1908 and 1909, and Roper Barrett the doubles in 1909, 1912 and 1913. Just eight weeks earlier, Elizabeth herself had been the focus of much press attention after the birth of their first child, Princess Elizabeth. It would have been hard to believe that just ten years later, in 1936, her husband would leapfrog his eldest brother to be crowned King George VI, or that their two-month-old baby would eventually become Queen Elizabeth II.

Almost as soon as the match started it went badly for Louis and his partner. In the crowd was Frank Pakenham, the present Earl of Longford, then a twenty-year-old undergraduate at Christ Church, Oxford, who saw them outplayed and made to look amateurish and uncoordinated as a pair. 'Louis Greig was a champion player, and he helped the Duke through the match, but the crowd made it very difficult as they were so close and so intense. The Duke got on very badly. He was left-handed, and the crowd tried to encourage him by calling out, "try the other hand, Sir". He could not get his game going at all, at times simply lashing out wildly with his racquet. The Duke was clearly overcome by the whole experience.'[2] The only time Pakenham met Albert face to face was years later, when he was King. 'Why did you join?' asked George VI. Unclear if he was referring to the Catholic Church, the Labour Party or for that matter anything else, Pakenham replied: 'Because I like to be on the side of the underdog.' To which the King replied, 'So do I.' In 1926, on Number Two Court, Albert and his partner were very much in that category.

Their defeat pained the Duchess, who shared her husband's anguish at every lost point. Her sweet demeanour masked an iron core of ambition and strength on which Albert was to rely so much in later years. 'Elizabeth was very much unlike the cocktail-drinking girls who came to be regarded as typical of the 1920s,' wrote Lady Airlie, an influential lady-in-waiting to Queen Mary. Elizabeth always knew what she wanted, and usually got it. She hated watching her husband endure such a public panning.

Albert fought to control his frustration; he possessed a fiery temper, sometimes grinding his teeth in rage, which some courtiers referred to as his 'gnashes'. The match tested his patience to the full as Louis darted all over the court, trying to return as many of their opponents' shots as possible. It sometimes amounted to blatant poaching, which, in turn, put Albert off his stroke, and muddled their game. The final score was a devastating 1–6, 3–6, 2–6. The *Sunday Times* afterwards rubbed home the full extent of the defeat, pointing out that the winners had a combined age of 110. It was a piece of royal and sporting history that stayed in many people's memories. More than seventy-three years after the match, James Callaghan, the former Labour Prime Minister – even though he had not witnessed it – remembered Wing Commander Louis Greig as the man who played at Wimbledon with the Duke of York. 'He was someone in the news and it stuck in my mind.'[3]

The friendship between the two men had begun seventeen years earlier when Prince Albert was a thirteen-year-old boy cadet and Louis was a naval surgeon. Louis became the Prince's single most trusted confidant and mentor during his early adulthood. George V always encouraged their relationship and arranged for Louis to be in the same ships in the Navy, and afterwards a courtier. He called Louis 'The Tonic' because of his irrepressible enthusiasm and good humour. The King passionately believed that the forthright Scottish naval surgeon would benefit his hesitant second son; and that was exactly what happened. 'He is the man who made the Duke of York,' pronounced Sir Bryan Godfrey-Faussett, seasoned courtier and one of George V's closest friends.[4]

Louis was no typical courtier. What stood out was his

confidence, energy and ability to put people at their ease. He was equally at home in the back streets of Glasgow as at a colonial grande dame's cocktail party in some distant port of the Empire. He was not an intellectual, but he was clever and blessed with plenty of practical common sense. He was more curious than sophisticated in his cultural tastes; he enjoyed Christina Rossetti's poetry as much as the popular novelists of the day. Quick-witted, charming and focused, his humour warm and infectious, Albert's father had nicknamed him 'The Tonic' with good reason.

Albert and Louis liked each other from the start of their friendship. The Prince had always needed parental approval, and when his mother and father became admirers of Louis, Albert felt good about forging the friendship. Yet it was an unlikely alliance. Not only was Louis more than twice Albert's age when they first met, but their starting points in life could hardly have been more different. When Louis was born in 1880 in the upstairs bedroom of a terraced house in Glasgow, his advent did not even make the births announcements in the *Herald*. News of Albert's birth, in 1895, in a royal household with palace doctors in attendance, was telegraphed to his great-grandmother Queen Victoria, and became a subject for national celebrations.

Louis never appeared for a second to doubt his ability to succeed; Albert, at times, feared he never would. Sir John Wheeler-Bennett, George VI's official biographer, was convinced theirs was the most influential friendship of Albert's early years. 'He gave to Lieutenant Greig his confidence, his affection and his admiration, and a friendship was engendered between them which was to play a highly important part in the development of his personality and character.'

The relationship eventually spanned more than forty-five years. Louis saw Albert at his lowest ebb when his life was threatened by illness and his career was in tatters. He played a critical supporting role in his courtship of Elizabeth

Bowes-Lyon. Albert asked Louis to be by his side when he
went to the King to ask for permission to marry the woman
who would eventually become his queen. The friendship was
to change both their lives for the better. That was what George V
intended; he felt strongly that Albert needed The Tonic.

Chapter One

'Strike Sure'

Greig family motto

Louis Leisler Greig was born on 17 November 1880, the ninth of eleven children, in the west end of Glasgow. His father, David, was a successful Scottish merchant, whose trading company, Greig, Leisler & Co., had offices in Glasgow and Hamburg. Louis was given the German middle name in honour of his father's German business partner, who was also made his godfather. His mother, Jessie Thomson, the daughter of a shawl and fancy dress manufacturer, was a robust religious woman with a particular interest in homeopathic medicine. She served on the board of management of the Western Infirmary and the Houldsworth homeopathic hospital in Glasgow.

No one doubted that the family roost was ruled by this severe, formidable woman with a ramrod-straight back and puritanical dress sense. She habitually wore long black skirts and had her hair scraped back tightly into a bun. Yet she was elegant and carefully attired; her clothes were modest, but never dowdy on her tall, statuesque figure. A high forehead, a patrician nose and a firm gaze marked her out as a woman whose word was not to be questioned. Her hair was a luxurious dark brown, and when unwound – only when she got into bed – it reached halfway down her back. Even though she was no great beauty she was striking, and her clear, sharp vision of what was right and wrong made her a powerful matriarch.

Her life was dominated by her children. On average she gave birth every eighteen months for a period of twenty-four years. Her tastes were conventional, as were her conservative politics, except when it came to a staunch belief in better conditions for women and children and, in particular, her support of the suffragettes. Her other unorthodox interest, in homeopathy, and her work with hospitals in Glasgow, brought medicine to those who could not afford it, or were too ignorant to ask for the right help.

She ran a strict household, but also one filled with much laughter and a great deal of chatter from her large brood of children, who seldom drew breath and spilled out of every corner of the family house in Lynedoch Crescent. And none of the Greig sons or daughters was ever backward in coming forward with their views. Jessie always maintained she had no sense of humour. 'Granny Greig only made jokes which she had not intended,' remembered her granddaughter, Nancy Maclay, the daughter of Louis's eldest brother Robert. Louis liked to tease her affectionately to combat her sometimes unintentional humour or sharp rejoinders.

Louis's father was a gentler, quieter character who was pleased to let his wife run the household. Rarely did he raise his voice, but when he did it was to thunderous effect, most often to quell the din of his many children. Lean and dark-haired, even in his fifties he gave the appearance of being fit and athletic. Serious in his work and in his Christian faith, he was also, unlike his wife, intentionally witty. He would let slip little one-line ripostes or put-downs, often quite ironical and seldom unoriginal. Laughter always seemed to be about to break on his face. Family life was a somewhat exhausting trial for David Greig, who at heart just wanted a peaceful life at home. When Jessie took the children up to him to get his approval after persuading them into hand-me-down clothes, he would scarcely look up from his newspaper except to mutter approvingly 'first class, first class'.[1] His business, buying and selling commodities, occasionally took him to Frankfurt, but mostly he was content to stay home. His children were to be far more adventurous travellers, making long and exhausting journeys to India, Singapore and New Zealand. David was a comfortably-off merchant who was able to afford to send his boys to the best private schools in Glasgow and provide governesses for his daughters. His one luxury was to take a holiday house in the Orkneys, a large stone-built farmhouse where there were shooting, fishing and other traditional pursuits for a country gentleman.

It was difficult to grow up in the centre of Glasgow without feeding off the city's energy. Louis's childhood was firmly rooted at No. 18 Lynedoch Crescent in the heart of the city, which remained the family home until his mother's death in 1915. His father died at the age of sixty-two in 1900 when Louis was nineteen. It was a substantial sandstone house, four storeys high. Inside, its most impressive features were an ornate grape-and-barley cornice in the drawing room and a sweeping wrought-iron staircase which dominated the hall. It was somewhat gloomy and dark and a tight squeeze for all eleven children.

Kelvinside was a prosperous area for generally well-to-do Glasgow families. The houses were solid and well built in elegant gaslit streets. The crescent-shaped garden outside the Greigs' house, enclosed by iron railings, was carefully looked after, providing a welcome patch of green for the children to play on. The house has changed hands many times since the Greigs lived there. It was at one time a boarding house and now holds the offices of Douglas Laing & Co., whisky blenders and bottlers.

Although Louis's home was far from grand, it was not that dissimilar to York Cottage, where Prince Albert was brought up. Harold Nicolson, George V's biographer, described Albert's childhood home on the Sandringham estate as 'a glum little villa in which the rooms inside with their fumed oak surrounds, their white over-fanlights, are indistinguishable from those of any Surbiton or Upper Norwood home'. It was like thousands of other middle-class homes. Prince George passed up the opportunity to live in great extravagance, but instead chose to live in a style similar to that of a great many of his subjects. Queen Victoria always had an uncannily instinctive ability to be sympathetic to what her fellow countrymen thought and felt. It was not exactly the common touch, but an ability to judge and assess wisely their mood or taste. Prince George also inherited this tendency and, to a certain extent, so did Albert when he eventually came to the throne.

Lynedoch Crescent contained features similar to those in many a well-to-do Edwardian household. An Alexandre fourteen-stop walnut-cased harmonium stood in the dining room. A white marble clock and classical bronze figures were on the mantelpiece, all lit by five gaselier globes, visible through the street window. In the drawing room, a polished rosewood grand piano took centre position alongside walnut-inlaid bookshelves, a tapestry-covered sofa, a copper coal scuttle and an assortment of walnut, bamboo and wicker chairs. The books, according to an insurer's inventory, included the life of the Prince Consort in five volumes, the complete works of Dickens, and several hundred others on general literature. Three pairs of deer antlers hung in the hall, trophies of beasts shot by the Greigs on Orkney. A mahogany barometer and exotically painted Chinese ceramic jars were displayed on a tallboy on the landing. Outside at the rear was a washhouse in a small walled garden.

Louis's childhood was defined by his noisy, omnipresent brood of ten brothers and sisters. Almost exactly a year after his parents were married in Glasgow on 25 March 1864, Agnes Ethel was born on 3 March 1865, at their then home in Fitzroy Place. Robert Coventry followed in 1867; Jessie Constantine in 1869; George Thomas in 1871; David Herbert in 1873; John Edwin, known as Jack, in 1875; Anna Blyth in 1877; and Marjorie Frances in 1879. Louis Leisler was born the next November at their new home in Lynedoch Crescent, with

Arthur and Kenneth following in 1883 and 1888. There were more than twenty-four years between the birth of the oldest and the youngest child. Kenneth and Robert were practically from different generations; the one could have been the other's father. In a group portrait of all the Greig children, Robert stands very much defined as a grown-up with his moustache, formal suit and distinctly adult bearing, while Louis is a boy who has not yet reached puberty. It was, on the whole, a very happy childhood with a prominent role being taken by the elder children in the running of the household. Jessie's favourite was Robert, whom she called 'young husband' because she relied on him so much. David was happy to leave his eldest son to sort out minor domestic disputes or problems. The other children called Robert 'Coffee', a shortening of his middle name, Coventry, and also because he turned a mild brown tan when hot rather than red. One advantage of having such a spread of brothers and sisters of all ages was that Louis and the younger ones were not intimidated by older people. Differences of age never really bothered them, and this made them appear more confident with other people than most of their contemporaries. But then, none of the Greig children was shy. They were known for their easy charm, larky humour and noisy chatter. Louis was one of the more mischievous. The roof over their house was steep and high, overlooking the whole of the city. It was a tempting place to explore, and Louis was never allowed to forget how once he was caught dashing naked over the eaves, as a dare with another brother in tow.

Photographs of Louis, aged eleven, show a scruffy rough-and-tumble little boy wrestling with friends in the street, playing pavement cricket, his crudely cut hair and blunt-nosed features surrounding a cheeky grin. His shirt is untucked, his hair is tousled and untidy, his cheeks are flushed, and he often looks slightly breathless or as if he has been caught doing something forbidden. He was a ragamuffin of a child, who was not mollycoddled by his parents. While extremely proud of her children, Jessie did not bathe them in compliments. She once exhorted Louis to remember that 'he had the sort of unflattering visage which was best framed by a hat'.[2] Louis just laughed when he heard this; very little dented his self-confidence, not even his father's sometimes stern letters extolling him to work hard at school, which he took seriously, winning several prizes for Latin and history. David and Jessie Greig both instilled in their children the importance of a Christian family and community. It was a message that sank in, and from an early age Louis was a fixer and facilitator for others – helping in the house, liking to play the role of negotiator or go-between, but always displaying a sense of independence.

Louis came from a long line of optimists. According to family papers, his paternal grandfather, Robert Greig, was 'a cheery hospitable soul, fond of good company' who was a skilled horseman and a trooper in the Lothian Yeomanry for twenty years. He was described by his colonel as 'the gayest man in the regiment' because he extravagantly appeared at nearly every parade drill on a different horse. He was also a city elder of Edinburgh and a member of the University Council, and used to boast that he had been one of the first people to recognise the ability of Professor James Simpson, the scientist who discovered chloroform, and had voted for him when he was an applicant for a university chair long before his famous scientific breakthrough. Robert Greig smoked, took snuff and chewed tobacco, and was reckoned to be the best judge of grain in Edinburgh market. Stories survive of one particularly unscrupulous farmer being seen talking to him one day in the Grassmarket; when asked about it afterwards, he confessed to Greig: 'I just wanted to be seen with an honest man before I sold my corn.' He made a comfortable living with a grain and bakery business in Edinburgh's Canongate, but farming was his real delight, and he bought a small estate called Glen Park, just outside Edinburgh.

For all the Greig children to thrive and prosper was a triumph of parenting particularly in Glasgow, where infant mortality was high. But then Louis's family was always strong on survival. A pair of wooden candlesticks took pride of place on the dining-room sideboard as testimony to their ability to beat the odds. They were made from a piece of wood salvaged from the wrecked steamer *Orion*, which had sunk off Port-Patrick on 18 June 1850. George Thomson and his wife Agnes, Louis's maternal great-grandparents, had clung to that makeshift raft, which eventually took them to safety. Louis's uncle, George Greig, had not been so lucky, drowning in 1882 in New Zealand in quicksand while working there for a shipping firm. Louis's great-grandmother on his father's side, Ann Coventry, was reckoned to be 'the prettiest girl in Kinross', and Jessie Blyth, his grandmother on his father's side, also cut a fine figure, although in her latter years she 'became a religious maniac and lost her sense of proportion and humour. This might have been due to the worry of bringing up a large family with seven children as a widow.'[3]

The most celebrated member of the Greig family was Sir Samuel Greig, born in Inverkeithing in November 1735, who emigrated to Russia in 1764 to join the Russian Navy and within six years had been promoted to Rear Admiral commanding the Russian fleet in the Mediterranean, which annihilated the Turkish Navy at the Battle of Chesme Bay off the coast of Asia Minor in 1770. Catherine the Great appointed him Grand Admiral in 1782, and, six years later, he became the commander-in-chief of the Russian fleet which defeated the might of Sweden at the Battle of Hogland. When he died, he was accorded a state funeral and a magnificent monument in Reval Cathedral. Sir Samuel Greig's son was also a Russian admiral, but the family line petered out just over a century later with the Russian Revolution. Some starved, others fled or were killed. The last survivor directly in line to the great admiral, Baron Johan von Greig, contacted Louis in desperate straits in the 1940s. Louis arranged for money to be sent to him every month in Austria, where he had become stateless, penniless and in danger of starving.

Louis was proud of his ancestry, and as a child was dressed in a MacGregor kilt because the first traceable Greig was a MacGregor who, with his wife, settled at Kennoway, Fife, in 1611. They were two members of the feisty MacGregor clan which was broken up after it had achieved a resounding victory over the rival Colquhouns, who then sneakily retaliated with a Royal Commission, which decreed that the MacGregors' attack had been an act of rebellion. The clan was outlawed and the name proscribed for 170 years, until 1775. Many had been forced to take refuge with other clans or had changed their names to Greig, Green, White, Black; in fact almost anything but their actual name. The government drove them out of Balquidder in Perthshire, and settled them in pairs mainly in the east of Scotland. They were also forbidden to wear the tartan, carry weapons or to meet. The punishment for any three clansmen found together was for all three to lose their heads. The Kennoway pair took the name of Greg, which subsequently became Greig.

Exact details of the Greig line are hazy, as a fire destroyed parish records at Markinch in the early nineteenth century. The Christian name of the first Kennoway Greig is not even known, but his wife was called Bessie and both were born before 1600. The family kept itself fairly aloof, and they were perceived as outsiders, inventing their own particular family customs, such as having three witnesses to a child's, baptism rather than one.

Glasgow, however, provided the essential ingredients for the making of Louis. He enjoyed what J. B. Priestley called 'the merriment, the innocence and the aspirations of the small business and professional families' when looking back on his own childhood in Yorkshire. At the age of eight, Louis went to Glasgow Academy, one of the city's oldest private schools, where he did well, winning several prizes for Latin and history as well as the Victor Ludorum. Every day he bicycled from Lynedoch Crescent to the imposing classical building of polished sandstone on Colebrooke Street. He was remembered, according to the school records, as an outstanding athlete, 'a quarter who jinks well, and is very good at making openings for his halves . . . a good tackler and fair kick'.[4]

Aged thirteen, he progressed to Merchiston Castle School in Edinburgh, where he boarded. The school is famous as the home of John Napier, the mathematician who invented logarithms in 1614 and Napier's Bones, an early mechanical calculating device used for multiplication and division. Once again, Louis was an outstanding athlete as well as a smart scholar. The urge to succeed was strong, his large family making him very competitive. At home, as the third youngest boy, he was never the centre of attention for long and so always had to fight to get noticed. This drive to do well, to be seen to prosper and to please others, stayed with him throughout his life and is one of the defining qualities of his whole career.

Louis chose to study medicine at Glasgow University because it was the only means available for a young man of his age to join the Navy. He was too old to join as a cadet, having spent so many of his early years diverted by sport. Rugby played a substantial part in his school and university days, the high point being his captaincy of the prestigious Glasgow Academicals, after which he was spotted by the selectors as a potential member for the Scottish team. Although his elder brother Robert had earlier also been selected to play for Scotland, Louis was the player who was to make more of a mark. He was a wing forward who was not only aggressive but also extremely fast and difficult to stop. He was determined to lead the Scottish team. Louis began to see beyond his family and Glasgow to a wider world with greater opportunities.

Medicine was an ambitious career move; six years of study were needed to graduate as a Bachelor of Medicine and a Bachelor of Surgery from Glasgow University. Louis started in 1898, studying Latin and chemistry; in 1899 he took a course in zoology and entered the faculty of medicine in 1900 to learn physiology, anatomy and dissecting; advanced dissecting followed in 1901; pathology, surgery and midwifery in 1902;

and then studies in throat and nose surgery in 1903. He worked hard and won a prize for systematic physiology with second-class honours.

Like all his family Louis had a gentle Scottish accent, which he was eventually to lose when he moved south. But what changed his life and influenced him more than anything else was a year training as a junior doctor in the Gorbals, one of the most deprived inner-city areas in Britain. He was aghast at the wretched conditions, with so many people trapped in poverty, misery and ill health without much hope of a way out of the stinking, ill-ventilated tenements that were all piled up on each other. All his life, Louis would remember treating the most vulnerable members of society. The Gorbals provided his most formative experience, as he saw how desperate people's lives could become.[5] He found the trust placed in his profession humbling; his black doctor's bag acted as a passport, a guarantee of free passage without fear of being robbed.

Yet Louis recognised that Glasgow also had a bright, prosperous side that offered great opportunities. The city was constantly expanding; its population rose from 83,000 in 1801 to almost ten times that with 784,000 in 1911. The middle classes had moved further out when the Highlands were cleared and the new Glaswegians moved in. In the 1820s the city had been colonised by Gaelic-speaking Highlanders and later, when the Irish potato crop failed, even more immigrants piled in. The Glasgow economy was able to provide jobs, but often at a terrible human cost when it came to the state of its housing and health facilities. The economy boomed as cotton mills, bleaching factories, dye works, iron foundries and ship-building prospered. Louis saw how Scotland's merchant and professional classes remained upwardly mobile. It was a path he determined to follow.

There were essentially two worlds in late nineteenth century and early twentieth century Glasgow; prosperity and poverty were found side by side. There was a vibrant economy, growing richer and more splendid as it built magnificent public and residential buildings. There was plenty of high culture and a ready generosity and humility as well as a sense of public service from many of those who made their fortune there. The prosperous lived comfortable, even luxurious lives. But the flip-side was hideous. 'I have seen human degradation in some of the worst phases, both in England and abroad, but I can advisedly say that I did not believe until I visited the wynds of Glasgow that so large an amount of filth, crime, misery and disease existed in any civilised country,' wrote an employee of the West of Scotland Handloom Weavers' Commission.[6]

In 1886, when Louis was six years old, one-third of Glasgow's families lived in single-room flats. Three years later the Royal Commission on Housing found that there were more than four people per room in one in ten of Glasgow's houses; more than three people in almost a third and more than two in over half. In 1902 the city's medical Officer of Health, Dr Chalmers, noted that 30 per cent of infantile deaths occurred among the 14 per cent of the population accommodated in single-room dwellings.[7]

Another doctor was shocked to discover a meek acceptance of death and disease, especially in children. 'Their little bodies are laid on a table or on a dresser so as to be somewhat out of the way of their brothers and sisters, who play and sleep and eat in their ghastly company. From beginning to rapid ending, the lives of these children are short. One in five of all who are born there never see the end of their first year.' Throughout his life Louis would again and again remark that his time in Glasgow as a young doctor had changed his view of politics and society. But it did not make him want to stay. He never had any desire to make his life in Scotland's second city.

An important moment in Louis's early life was the marriage of his elder sister, Connie, to John Scrimgeour, a brilliant young stockbroker, whose father had founded J. & A. Scrimgeour, one of the City's leading stockbrokers. 'It changed the whole family's outlook. The Greigs all went to stay with Connie in London and saw a grander, bigger life; new horizons were opened,' remembered Louis's nephew, David Greig. John Scrimgeour was so successful in the City that he bought Stedham, a large country estate in Sussex. Every summer he rented stretches of Scottish salmon rivers and grouse moors on which to fish and shoot, always asking Louis to stay. It set the Greig children thinking that there were a great many opportunities beyond Glasgow and, like so many enterprising Scots, almost all of them saw their future elsewhere.

Louis was a free-spirited, dashing bachelor who always seemed to be enjoying himself, forever talking, rushing about, and not afraid to express his views forcefully and candidly, without hesitation. He had joined the Navy only three years before Albert, on 10 February 1906, after his year working in the Gorbals. He initially was assigned to HMS *Victory*, but four months later, in July, he was picked for fast-track promotion to Haslar, the Navy hospital training school. At Haslar, he specialised in tropical medicine, winning the prestigious Haslar Gold Medal. Seniority on the Navy List was decided from the results of this exam, with prizes to the value of £20 being awarded for the first three places[8] (an inscribed gold medal being the first prize; a microscope and a silver medal for the runners-up). Even at that early stage, Louis was determined to succeed. He was a sailor-surgeon who also played hard – gambling, drinking, dancing and filling every other spare moment of his day with sport.

His first voyage was aboard HMS *Hibernia*, a West Country battleship of the Channel fleet, which toured the Mediterranean. When *Hibernia* was in port, Louis's social life was very full. He was often out until the early morning, complaining in his diary of being 'up the pole' after too much drink. He was confident and successful in romance. In May 1907, Louis fell for a girl he identifies only as Mollie. After treating the Admiral's orderly for measles he had gone ashore in Ireland to play cricket for his ship against Dublin University, but also to meet Mollie, who was 'no whit changed except that she is, if possible, more charming'. He later confessed to 'a disgraceful evening'. In the memorandum space in his Boots Home Diary and Note Book, his hedonistic approach to romance is hinted at from the aphorisms he wrote out, such as: 'A man who wants to make love but is withheld by a sense that he aught not, is at his dullest.' He adds:

> *If in this shadow-land of life*
> *Thou hast found one true heart to love thee*
> *Hold it fast, love it again*
> *Give all to keep it thine*
> *For love like nothing in this world can last.*

A month later he confided to his diary that he is 'practically e——d', but, after that close brush with marriage, Mollie is never mentioned again and by August he had moved on ('met a charming lass of Derbyshire'). Subsequently a girl called PL attracted his attention ('took her for a long walk in afternoon'), but the path to true love for him was far from smooth, and he 'received some strenuous epistles' from her, and The romance was over.

Louis was a young man in the prime of his life when he met Albert at the Royal Naval College of Osborne on the Isle of Wight in 1909. This was his next posting after HMS *Hibernia* and, understandably, the Prince, an apprehensive naval cadet, looked up to the dashing elder officer. It was the start of an innocent and old-fashioned friendship between a young pupil and his teacher, which should not be seen as anything more at this stage. Albert felt strongly that he had met someone who not only understood him, but with whom he could talk easily. Louis saw that he could be of help to a boy who needed encouragement and nurturing, and he took him under his wing.

Chapter Two

'Louis Greig may be "getting on" in football years, but this season his game has become quite young again; we saw the old Scottish national war horse on Saturday at the top of his game.'

The Morning Post, 11 November 1909

Cadet HRH Prince Albert of Wales, as he was registered in Osborne's entry book in 1909, had one unique disadvantage to his contemporaries; he had never been in a class with more than three pupils. He was suddenly placed on an equal footing with about seventy other thirteen-year-old boys all better equipped to deal with naval life, having boarded at private schools for the past three or four years. He had had barely any contact with children outside royal circles except for twice-weekly dancing lessons with the offspring of a few of his father's aristocratic friends, and his lack of sophistication and guile showed. He quickly gained the nickname 'Sardine' thanks to his slight physique, and a terrible stammer led some staff to dismiss him as bone-headed. He floundered around at the bottom of his class, often too scared to speak for fear of mockery. The usual teasing and minor bullying took their toll. On one occasion he was heard screaming in protest when members of his own term, Grenville (each was named after a famous admiral), tied him up.

Just ten days into his first term, Albert stoically wrote to his mother proclaiming all was fine. The stiff-upper-lip façade was maintained by his brother Edward, who reassured his family that 'Bertie is getting on well'. It did not, however, fool his father, the Prince of Wales, who had himself trained as a naval cadet and knew of the initial tribulations. 'No doubt it will take a term or two for Bertie to settle down,' he wrote to Henry Hansell, the boys' well-meaning but ineffective former private tutor at Sandringham. Having an elder brother at Osborne at the same time provided little comfort; strict segregation of classes and age groups mostly kept them apart. Unfortunately, this did not prevent unkind comparisons being made. 'One could wish,' wrote Hansell, 'that he had more of Prince Edward's application and keenness.' One contemporary later made the damning and haunting judgement that it was like comparing an ugly duckling with a cock pheasant.[1] It was hardly surprising that Albert felt unsure of himself, after being whisked away from the cocooned home environment at York Cottage with all its pampering paraphernalia of a royal household in Edwardian England.

Albert had not even been taken to school by his parents, as his brother had been two years earlier. Hansell took him. His parents were too busy to spare the time for their second son. It was a frightened little boy who waved goodbye to Frederick Finch, his nursery footman, and the other servants of York Cottage as he set off for his new home. The following day his parents were diverted by a demonstration in Downing Street involving thousands of women and many men, who were there supporting the demands for women's suffrage. While this early feminist battle for votes for women was being waged, Albert could not have been introduced to a more all-male establishment. As he and Hansell sat in their carriage with the crunching sound of horses' hooves on the gravel drive resounding in their ears, Albert caught his first glimpse of the imposing Italianate villa that was to be home for the next two years.

He lacked the supreme confidence of his grandfather, King Edward VII, the stout, bronchial bon viveur who had been on the throne for eight years, enjoying his reign over the largest empire on earth. Albert also lacked the instinctive enthusiasm that his father, the Prince of Wales, held for the Navy. The strait-laced and duty-bound former naval officer with a tobacco-stained beard always maintained a sober approach to family life and public duties, and expected his sons automatically to enter the Navy as lowly cadets just as he had done at their age. Albert found it all a terrible shock to his delicate sensibility, and on his first night he was pitifully homesick.

It was of little comfort that his new home had once been a royal residence. The college was housed in the stable block of Osborne House, where his great-grandmother, Queen Victoria, had died eight years earlier. She had loved her summer retreat, describing it to her uncle, King Leopold of the Belgians, just before she purchased it as 'so snug & nice'.[2] The villa was later so disliked by Edward VII that he ignored Queen Victoria's will and his sisters' wishes by giving it to the nation as a convalescent home for officers.[3] By the time Albert arrived, the buildings that housed the cadets had seen better days; some parts had so deteriorated that the boys could push their feet through the walls.[4]

Everything was performed at the double as soon as the cadets were woken by a 6 a.m. bugle-call reveille. When a gong was struck, they knelt down to say their prayers. At strike two, they brushed their teeth; on strike three, they hurriedly plunged into a green-tiled pool full of icy water at the end of their dormitory.[5] 'It seemed pretty cold, but it didn't take us long to get used to it, and nobody could afford to be known as a water-funk!' remembered one of Albert's contemporaries.[6] Albert's father had insisted that he was to be treated just like every other cadet. Gieves, the naval outfitters in Savile Row, slipped through the only concession, substituting cashmere for the rough blue wool of Albert's 'rug of uniform pattern', which he had to fold neatly at the end of his bed. It was a small comfort during a brutal baptism of fire.[7] Osborne was far from being either snug or nice for the Prince in his cavernous, unheated dormitory, alongside twenty other boys shivering in iron bedsteads. Draughty, cathedral-scale sash windows afforded little protection from the cold. It was a forbidding, frosty and frightening place for any new boy, and Albert felt isolated and vulnerable.

What he needed at Osborne was a sympathetic friend and mentor for his first uncertain steps towards adulthood. He found them in Lieutenant-Surgeon Louis Greig, the assistant medical officer, then aged twenty-eight, who stood out from the other members of staff because of his reputation as an international sportsman. He was one of the most prominent and colourful sportsmen of his generation. He had won five caps for Scotland at rugby, first playing against the All Blacks in 1905. The following year he had been made captain, and led his country against South Africa in 1906, Wales in 1907 and 1908, and against Ireland in 1908. Albert was not alone in singling Louis out from the other twenty-seven officers at Osborne for a generous amount of hero-worship.

By the time Albert arrived at Osborne, Louis had been there two years. As a ship's doctor he was outside the traditional hierarchy, his decisions on medical matters overriding all ranks. Sooner or later, everyone got to know the medical officer, and Albert was no exception. Louis was a tall, charismatic naval officer with intense blue eyes, sandy hair and an outstanding athlete's physique. He was 'a ready talker, knowledgeable and thoroughly alert – nothing ever escaped his quick eye'.[8] He was 'incessantly on the move', his face memorable for its cheerful expression. He was not exactly handsome, but attractive in a somewhat rugged seafarer's way, and certainly memorable. Well turned out in his blue-braided uniform and peaked cap, he never looked sleek but 'always as if his clothing was too loose for his restless figure'.[9] He was an officer to whom the cadets turned if in trouble. 'Prince Albert took a strong liking to this tough, debonair older man, whose gaiety cheered him.'[10] Kindness was a quality often noted. 'Louis was always a man who went out of his way to help, and if a lame duck was in need of a leg up, he was always the first to step in,' remembered one fellow officer.[11]

Albert needed friends among the staff as his academic progress was disastrous. He was nearly always bottom – sixty-eighth out of sixty-eight – in the examination lists. Osborne was, in effect, a technical college, and he did not find it easy to learn the mathematics, navigation and science after the risible education he had received under Hansell at Sandringham. Years later Albert told a friend how he would not answer questions in maths classes at Osborne because his stammer did not allow him to pronounce the 'f' of the word fraction.[12] Yet there were signs that he had pluck and also the social skills to prosper outside the classroom; he was remembered by his fellow cadets as 'likeable' and 'generally popular'. Yet it was sometimes an uphill struggle; he had never played a team sport like rugby or hockey. To have a famous former rugby international as one of your supporters in such a hearty institution provided Albert with a welcome sense of security.

Louis was more than twice the Prince's age – twenty-eight to Albert's thirteen – but the seeds of a lifelong friendship were sown during the next two years during which they saw each other most days – even if neither quite understood the depth of the connection made at the time. After all, students often don't realise exactly when a charismatic schoolmaster becomes such a lasting influence. As a sign of affection, Albert presented Louis, at the end of his first term, with a signed photograph of himself in naval uniform, a typically royal present. There was more than a slight sense of adulation in such a gesture.

Prince Albert's progress to Osborne had been after a privileged but somewhat unsettling childhood. He had been born at the apogee of the British Empire, two years before Queen Victoria's Diamond Jubilee in 1897, an occasion of imperial pomp and celebration unseen since the age of the Roman Empire. Sandringham, where he was born, and where one day he would die, was the place he regarded above all the other royal houses as home. But the actual day of his birth – 14 December 1895 – did not bring the undiluted joy that might have been expected; he was born on 'Mausoleum Day', the anniversary of the death from typhoid of his German great-grandfather after whom he was named, Prince Albert of Saxe-Coburg and Gotha, thirty-four years earlier, and also the anniversary of the death from diphtheria of Queen Victoria's third child, Princess Alice of Hesse.

The shadow of Queen Victoria loomed large, terrifying her brood, who were all made the more nervous by the inauspicious timing of young Albert's arrival. But they need not have been so fearful, as this seventy-six-year-old, diminutive widow was quickly appeased and delighted by the tactful suggestion that her grandson Prince George, the proud father, should name the newborn infant Albert and that Queen Victoria should be godmother. The Queen wrote to 'Darling Georgie', 'It is a great satisfaction to us that it should be a second boy & I need not say how *delighted* I am that my great wish – viz that the little one born on that sad anniversary shld have the dear name of Albert – is to be realised'. To underline her pleasure, she somewhat unhelpfully sent a bust of her Prince Albert to baby Albert at Sandringham as a christening present.

Albert's somewhat ambivalent welcome was an indication of the nature of family life in a royal household. Duty, tradition, deference and the continuity of the line were the overriding priorities. It was significant, in his family's eyes, that he was only the second son of the grandson of the Queen-Empress, and so unlikely to succeed to the British Crown, which William Gladstone had optimistically classified as 'the greatest inheritance a man can have'. As in many upper-class households, there was little emphasis on the cosy, comforting aspects of home life. And this lack of demonstrative affection was something of which Albert's parents were both acutely aware, but also apparently impotent to change. Both habitually repressed their emotions. Shortly before her marriage to Prince George on 6 July 1893, Princess May wrote to her future husband, the future King George V: 'I am very sorry that I am still so shy with you, I tried not to be so the other day, but alas failed. I was angry with myself! It is so stupid to be so stiff together, & really there is nothing I would not tell you, except that I *love* you more than anybody in the world, & this I cannot tell you myself so I write it to relieve my feelings . . .' Prince George replied: 'Thank God we understand each other, & I think it really unnecessary for me to tell you how deep my love for you my darling is & I feel it growing stronger & stronger every time I see you; although I may appear shy & cold . . .'[13]

This inability to show the love they felt was to have inevitable consequences in their relationship with their children. It was a distinctly naval household into which Albert was born, with his father a seasoned officer in the Senior Service. He 'retained a gruff, blue-water approach to all human situations, a loud voice and also that affliction common to Navy men, a damaged eardrum'.[14] It was a strict and disciplined childhood. Albert's father was an explosive, sometimes intemperate character whose orbit was somewhat Olympian and remote and for the young prince, as for so many upper-class children, it was a darkly observed adult universe. Albert's real world was the nursery and the governesses, tutors, nurses and other servants who looked after him. At times, the adult world must have seemed even rather surreal, with a stuffed baboon holding a tray for visitors' cards inside the hall at Sandringham. The Big House on the family's Norfolk estate was like some fantasy hotel with its saloon, the principal reception room with its Elizabethan-style fireplaces and blue and red upholstered sofas. Edged with stone and boasting tall, decorated Elizabethan chimneys and stone portes-cochères in the style of a French château, it was the sort of imposing edifice that Henry James might have taken as a model for his opulent country house, Matcham, in *The Golden Bowl*.

Although Albert was born on the Sandringham estate, it was not at the Big House, but instead at York Cottage, where his parents lived far more modestly. He was born in this ordinary house decorated throughout by Maples, the Tottenham Court

Road upholsterers, at the specific request of Prince George while he and his bride were on honeymoon. The cottage was in the shadow of other royal houses and was an appropriately unostentatious setting for this timid, nervous second son to be born into. He arrived eighteen months after the birth of Prince Edward, known to his family as David. Princess Mary, his only sister, followed in 1897, Prince Henry in 1900, Prince George in 1902 and finally the sickly Prince John in 1905. Albert's early existence was dominated by the nursery: a swing-door divided the passage on the first floor from the bedroom of his parents and other members of the household. There was a day nursery where they played (too cramped for many toys) and a night nursery where the three eldest children slept with a nurse. There they had their bath in round tin tubs filled with hot water brought by maids. The setting was idyllic, with views of the park with the exotic Japanese deer and, of course, the thousands of pheasants that Albert's father and grandfather loved to shoot.

It was an upbringing characterised by sudden unannounced change. Albert's early childhood effectively ended, along with the nineteenth century, when Queen Victoria died. The Coronation of Edward VII in 1902 ushered in the true start of the twentieth century. Albert's father had become Prince of Wales in November 1901, in recognition of the fact that he was the next heir to the throne. More immediate to the children's lives was the removal of Lalla Bill, their childhood nurse and surrogate mother, who was suddenly transferred. They were left in the charge of Finch, the nursery footman. The next dramatic change was the abrupt introduction of their tutor. '"This is Mr Hansell," my father said coldly, "your new tutor", and with that he walked out of the room, leaving us alone with Mr Hansell, who was no doubt as embarrassed as we were,' remembered Prince Edward.[15] Kind, loyal and dull, Hansell was not the inspiring teacher they needed.

Edward was glamorous, handsome and loquacious. His golden hair, quick tongue and effortless ability to switch on a beguiling charm made Albert appear awkward, slow and less interesting. Albert stammered, catching on words, agonisingly trying to force a syllable, reddening in the face when he could not get his tongue round a particular sound. Prince George's approach was far from helpful. 'Get it out,' he would bark,[16] which would have the reverse effect. It was not the young prince's only physical disability. Albert's legs were crooked, giving him knock-knees for which he was treated with a set of splints for several hours a day. It was no easy regime, but there were happy moments, especially visits to his more ebullient and fun-loving grandparents at the Big House.

The most dramatic change in Albert's childhood was being dispatched, aged thirteen, to board at Osborne. The Prince of Wales had robustly cast aside any suggestion of sending his two eldest sons to a traditional public school, insisting that the Navy would teach them all they needed to know.

Coming from the restricted environment of York Cottage, Albert's only contact with people outside his immediate family had been the courtiers who worked for his father or grandfather. Most came from narrow social backgrounds and were, almost by definition, deferential, cautious and often craven. Albert quickly found that Louis played a considerable part in the formation of the cadets' character through their physical education. 'He forcefully coached the college teams and was a spectacle to see and hear, as even at Osborne he was renowned for a wealth, ferocity and lucidity of language which left no illusions to his meaning.'[17] Louis was a passionate keep-fit enthusiast, running every day, and always performing his Müller exercises, a series of keep-fit routines, specified by J. P. Müller, a Danish physical educationalist, which became fashionable at the turn of the century after he had published a series of pamphlets. At his surgeries, Louis saw the cadets on a daily basis, routinely inoculating them, keeping their medical history sheets up to date, and occasionally issuing Hurt certificates (unchanged since Nelson's day) for injuries or wounds inflicted while on duty. *In extremis*, this enabled ratings to claim a pension if their health deteriorated.

Albert desperately needed someone to believe in him. Even at the end of his schoolroom days at York Cottage, Hansell had described him as a 'scatter brain . . . who cannot get on without a bit of a shove . . . and must have a certain amount of individual help and encouragement, especially encouragement'.[18] Louis was to provide that help.

There was intense pressure from his family for Albert to succeed. His father was insistent that the Navy would provide the blueprint for a model life. Ten years earlier, in July 1899, Prince George had specifically addressed an audience of boys on board the training ship *Conway* to define the qualities required of a sailor: '(1) Truthfulness, without which no man can gain the confidence of those below him; (2) Obedience, without which no man can gain the confidence of those above him; and (3) Zest, without which no seaman is worth his salt.'

Fortunately, Louis was an effective and charismatic teacher, who liked helping young people; Albert soon learned to lean on him, and also on his term officer, Lieutenant William Phipps, who became a minor courtier to the Prince almost thirty years later after he had become King. Louis always tried to put into practice his philosophy that life should never be boring, scribbling down spirited doggerel in his diary to reinforce his can-do attitude:

> *I'd rather be a 'has been'*
> *Than a 'might have been' by far*
> *For a 'might be' is a 'never was'*
> *But a 'has been' was once an 'are'*

Louis always dared to win, but what made him stand out was his language. Curses would spew forth in explosive outbursts, both on and off the rugby pitch. His performance during a game was peppered with colourful expressions which, at times, left his team-mates, not to mention the opposition, open-mouthed. The legend in the bars and pubs of

Glasgow and Edinburgh was that rugby fans had not gone to Murrayfield to *see* Louis Greig play, but to *hear* him.

What Louis self-mockingly referred to as his 'Elizabethan turn of phrase' worried his elder brother Robert, who was a member of the National Rugby Selection Committee. It was not that he personally minded his brother's blue-tinted curses, but he feared they might offend other more prurient selectors. During one international match, at which the Prince of Wales was a spectator, there was a pregnant silence after Louis had failed to catch a ball that had been kicked high into the air, right in front of where the Prince sat in the stadium. Some feared Louis would embarrass himself with his usual curses, but he stopped in his tracks, and with both hands defiantly on his hips, turned towards the royal spectator; slowly and exaggeratedly, he mouthed in silence the word 'bother'. Prince George was amused; he liked the bluff rugby captain's self-parodying gesture and admired the sheer strength of personality with which he led the Scottish team. The Prince of Wales took a shine towards Louis and did all he could to encourage his friendship with his second son.

Louis first met the Prince of Wales a few weeks into Albert's first term, when he was captain of the Navy rugby team for its annual match against the Army at Queen's in south-west London. Such inter-service matches were extremely popular, attracting considerable national newspaper coverage and large crowds. Prince George went to great efforts to attend, driving through a blizzard from his London residence, Marlborough House, accompanied by Derek Keppel, the Master of his Household. Both were formally attired in dark greatcoats and top hats to protect them against the icy temperatures, and they witnessed a triumphant day for Louis. Not only did he score both tries, but he led his team to an impressive victory, beating the Army by four goals and two tries. Louis's sister received a letter from a Glaswegian friend, impressed by her brother's tenacity on the pitch. 'Louis played so well that it's impossible to pick holes. He spoiled their halves time & again & marked his man like a knife.'[19]

The newspapers not only praised his performance, but noted that the Prince of Wales had singled out Louis for a private word after the game. Among the spectators was Louis's younger brother, Arthur, who had travelled down from Glasgow. 'The football was very good, especially on the Navy side. Louis was in great form and running about like a two-year-old. He is really in with the royals. He had quite a long chat with the Prince of Wales, who said, "I have heard about you from my son",' Arthur wrote overexcitedly to his older sister Anna.[20] This turned out to be more than simply small talk on the sidelines. Louis had made an impression and caught the imagination of Prince George. He was impressed by the burly rugby star who had spoken with such authority and affection about his sons.

In many ways Louis was an unlikely person to have appealed to the Prince of Wales. He could be quite irreverent and wild. He was so brimful of energy that his friends doubted if anything or anyone could control him. He was sharp, witty and always on the lookout for some fun or for adventure. The royal family, by contrast, has never been famous for its capacity to laugh at itself or, indeed, other people. If they were seen chortling in public, it was as if they felt that someone had stolen their dignity, as Prince Albert's great-aunt Augusta had observed, writing to his mother. 'Did you see that ridiculous Photo of them all *laughing*, Lilly grinning, no, too funny & not royal.'[21]

The day after the match the staff and cadets avidly read the reports in the newspapers. 'Dr Greig, who is again being considered as a candidate for a Scottish cap, now seems able to go on for ever,' declared the *Sporting Life*. Prince Edward quizzed Louis about the game and passed on his version of events in a letter to his father at Sandringham: 'Dr Greig told me that Army were quite weak compared with the Naval team . . .', before enquiring after the health of Queen Alexandra. 'I hope grannie's cold will soon be all right,' he wrote.[22] The Prince's doctor and sports coach was slowly becoming a figure known at court. His friendship with both the princes, but more particularly Albert, was taking root.

Louis's family was surprised by his close contact with the royal family. Before the television age, they were really very remote from most people's lives, and as a result more mysterious and potent. They were distant, dignified and removed. Of course, they were also extremely rich. While the bulk of their wealth and possessions were inalienable Crown property, many of the pictures, jewellery and some of their houses, such as Balmoral and Sandringham, were privately owned. The lives of the royal family were administered by a band of utterly devoted courtiers, mainly drawn from the aristocracy or well-connected upper-class families who considered court appointments almost a hereditary profession. Louis was more impressed by their aura than by their wealth; it was a huge social leap for him to be merrily chatting away to the heir to the throne and his children. Louis's brother Robert teased him about his dizzy social rise, asking if he would still deign to speak to his lowly family in Glasgow. How had he managed to avoid cursing in front of the Prince of Wales, he jokingly enquired. The Greig siblings could not resist ribbing Louis, whom they still saw as their pug-faced, cheeky baby brother, despite his rising fortune.

Louis had read Walter Bagehot's classic work *The English Constitution*, and was familiar with its thesis that it was essential for the royal family not to become overfamiliar or overexposed in order to preserve a sense of mystique. When Louis casually passed the time of day with the Prince of Wales and other members of this powerful dynasty, whose empire stretched over more than a quarter of the known surface of the globe, it was for him like meeting the unmeetable.

At school Louis had learnt that Europe was woven together by a web of Queen Victoria's children and grandchildren, who sat on major and minor thrones. When Albert was born there were twenty reigning monarchs in continental Europe, and he was related to most of them. He was related through his great-grandmother, Queen Victoria, and her nine children to the German Emperor, the Tsar of Russia and the Kings of Belgium, Spain, Portugal, Bulgaria and Romania. And through his grandmother, Alexandra, he was connected to the royal families of Greece and Denmark. On top of that there was what Queen Victoria referred to as the 'royal mob' – all her German relations from Wurtemberg, Hanover, Saxe-Coburg and Gotha, and other mini-states. The map of Europe was mainly defined by kingdoms of Victoria's offspring. It was a time when monarchies still prospered, from the great heartlands of Europe to rather less important territories such as Mecklenburg-Strelitz, where Adolphus-Friederich II reigned. But while the British Empire and the throne appeared so unassailable, it and other regal dynasties were more vulnerable than anyone realised as a more modern democratic age was ushered in. During George V's reign five emperors, eight kings and eighteen minor dynasties lost their thrones. The seeds were also sown for India's emergence as an independent republic. From his earliest schooldays, Albert was acutely aware that his father and his brother were destined to succeed to the throne of the oldest dynasty in Europe, directly linked back to Egbert, who ascended the throne of Wessex in 809. With a short break, occasioned by Oliver Cromwell during the dozen years of the Commonwealth in the seventeenth century, Egbert's direct descendants had reigned in England for 1,100 years. The significance and burden of history on these royal princes was not lost on Louis or his family.[23]

In August 1909, Louis was called to serve the royal family in a formal capacity – even though there were plenty of other palace doctors available – when he treated Albert for a persistent hacking cough during a visit to Britain by the Tsar's children. The Russian Empress had arrived at Spithead in the imperial yacht *Standart* with the young Grand Duchesses and the Tsarevitch, who were thought suitable playmates for the

English princes. Nicholas was an urbane, well-educated monarch who spoke English like an Oxford professor, as well as French and German. His cousin, the Grand Duke Alexander, had dubbed him the 'most polite man in Europe'. But he was badly lacking in the practical knowledge and leadership necessary to run a country as vast and troubled as Russia. Prince George and the Tsar looked almost identical, with their beards and naval bearing, but the similarities ended there. While George V turned out to be a model constitutional monarch, Nicholas could not forget that he was Autocrat of all the Russias until it was too late and the Bolsheviks threw him out, massacring him and his entire family. In 1909, the health of Alexei, the heir to the Romanov throne, was a matter of some concern owing to his haemophilia. Albert was pulled out of Osborne by his father for a few days to get to know his cousins, but while staying with his parents at Barton Manor, another royal house on the Osborne estate, what at first appeared to be a cold passed on by his fellow cadets turned out to be whooping cough. He was put in quarantine, principally because of the obvious fears for the Tsarevitch. Louis was called to monitor Albert's health. He examined him in quarantine, and then, after a convalescent period, in Scotland at Allt-na-giubhsaich, another royal estate some ten miles from Balmoral, where Albert stayed until the end of September.

Shortly afterwards Albert's health was threatened by an outbreak of flu, and once again Louis's medical skills and his winning manner with Albert attracted the attention of his parents. Earlier this century influenza was a serious condition which could often kill. The significant worry it caused is perhaps best judged by the panic measures taken a few years later when the German High Command almost postponed its July offensive, in 1918, owing to an outbreak that proved far more lethal. One million American soldiers were in Europe when influenza struck; one in fifteen died of it.[24]

Albert's family was delighted when he pulled through under Louis's charge, 'cheered' by him 'during the tedium of his confinement'.[25] The Prince and Princess of Wales sent a message of appreciation to Louis via Arthur Bigge – later to become Lord Stamfordham – perhaps the most influential courtier of this century. Appointed as Queen Victoria's assistant private secretary in 1880, the year Louis was born, he had become her private secretary in 1895, the year Albert was born. He continued in the same influential position under George V and was very much His Majesty's voice; the sovereign's wishes and commands were carried out through his letters, written in a flowing script and using ink as thick and black as tar. This time his letter was simply to tell Louis 'how very grateful [the Prince and Princess of Wales] are for the kind and unremitting attention which you have given to Prince Albert during his serious illness. Their Royal Highnesses have learnt from Sir Francis Laking that the treatment and nursing have been in every way admirable and they rejoice to think that the Prince is now on the high road to convalescence. They trust that you and your colleagues are not being overworked, and that the epidemic of influenza may gradually be stamped out.'[26]

Louis made his mark at Osborne. The Prince of Wales admired his sporting prowess and the robust enthusiasm of his teaching and his encouragement of Albert. His medical skills also singled him out. Louis was a calm, authoritative figure with a light touch, who stood firmly by his opinion. Working with the royal family was to open up a whole new vista of opportunities. Louis was a 'born helper'[27] who gained pleasure in pulling strings on behalf of others. He was intrigued to have one foot tentatively inside court, however fleetingly and informally. It was a memorable and significant introduction to the royal family for the man who was to be their most improbable courtier.

Chapter Three

'Greig made the students giddy dancing round him.
He was the hero of the occasion & kept them at it for
about ½ an hour!'
                    Diary entry by Freddie Dalrymple-Hamilton
                                    aboard HMS *Cumberland*

George V shadowed every move in Albert's personal and professional life, and three years into his reign, on 17 January 1913, he arranged for Albert to be assigned to HMS *Cumberland*, where Louis Greig was the ship's surgeon. Louis had joined the ship two years earlier after completing three years as assistant medical officer at Osborne. The 9,800-ton county-class cruiser was used for taking cadets on six-month cruises of the high seas in the final stage of their training before they qualified as midshipmen. Albert was aged seventeen, and had come on by leaps and bounds since his first days at Osborne, although he was still introspective and awkward compared to his more nimble-minded brother. Francis Lambert, a junior officer on board, was not impressed when he encountered Albert. 'He runs the picket boat, and the other evening after dinner when I was on watch he brought her alongside. He is a small red-faced youth with a stutter and when he reported his boat to me he gave a sort of stutter and an explosion. I had no idea who he was and very nearly cursed him for spluttering at me.'[1]

Albert's status had dramatically changed following the

death of his grandfather, King Edward VII, in 1910 and his father's succession to the throne. His parents inherited the invisible but powerful aura of reigning sovereigns; they also had charge of all the royal palaces. Buckingham Palace, the most potent symbol of the British monarchy, was now their principal home. Far more attention inevitably was focused on a king's son than on a grandson; Albert was, after all, just two heartbeats away from being king. He was heir presumptive while Edward became Prince of Wales, pledging his oath to the King at the Coronation in the ancient words of homage. Edward – even aged sixteen – was always more glamorous than the hesitant, awkward Albert. He was enormously popular, even though those at court could already see petulant signs of impatience with the pomp and circumstances of his destiny. With his flaxen hair, china-blue eyes and finely drawn features he was undoubtedly handsome, which tended to make sycophantic courtiers fawn on the boy who would be King. Many chose to ignore the obvious signs of vanity and irresponsibility in this thoroughly spoilt young man who was used to getting his own way. 'The boy is a darling. Backward but sweet,' swooned Lord Esher, one of the homosexual courtiers in Edward VII's court, while barely giving Albert the time of day in his diaries, except to note that he is a 'commonplace character'.[2] At the Coronation, Edward grumbled at having to wear a 'preposterous rig' of white satin breeches and a surcoat of purple velvet edged with ermine.[3] Albert, in the shadow of his brother, was always the more diligent, dutiful boy. Both were kept on a tight leash by their domineering father.

Two years earlier, in 1911, Albert had not known if he would see Louis again when he progressed from Osborne to the senior naval college at Dartmouth and they bade each other farewell. Both teacher and pupil hoped their paths would cross again. It took George V to make sure that they did. Louis Greig was familiar to him by the time Albert was ready to graduate, by reputation, name and sight. He welcomed both his sons' appreciation of, and affection for, this naval doctor. It was no coincidence that when the time came for Albert to join a ship the King chose one where Louis was also on board.

George V endured an extraordinary reign of unparalleled restlessness. He was to lead his nation through the horrors of the First World War and to die in 1936 under the shadow of another global war. While he held his own empire together, the great empires of Russia, Germany and Austro-Hungary fell. Great Britain was besieged by demands for Irish Home Rule and Indian independence. He had to cope with increasing unrest at home, including a fierce constitutional battle to reform, or even abolish, the House of Lords. In 1912, a coal strike lasted five weeks and cost the country thirty million working days.[4] The King also witnessed the rise of the Labour Party as a new and dynamic social force, representing a seismic shift in British politics. This was all difficult for a man who succeeded to the throne on his forty-ninth birthday with horizons that did not appear to stretch beyond the limitations of a Norfolk squire. Yet he rose to the challenges with surprising thoughtfulness, deftness and generosity. He was far-sighted in his muted reaction to the proposed changes to the Lords, listening and reacting carefully to plans to dismantle the Constitution. He was a sure-footed and courageous figurehead in the Great War – even giving up alcohol at every royal table until the conflict was over.

The shadows of that war were looming, although few people saw the warning signs. The balance of power depended on naval strength and Albert was aware of the political symbolism of his service in his father's imperial fleet. After the Coronation, a naval review of 167 British warships had gathered together as a public demonstration of loyalty to the new sovereign and a display of Britain's supremacy at sea. They had passed in front of the Royal Yacht at Spithead while the King took the salute. But even this was a fragile boast, as a thousand miles to the south the Germans sent a gunship, the *Panther*, to the Moroccan port of Agadir, sparking an international crisis. They claimed that it was needed to protect the German subjects in the Atlantic coastal port against Berber attacks. The *Panther* was provocatively replaced by a larger warship, the *Berlin*, and this resulted in indignation from the French, who saw it as a breach of their rights in Morocco. Rumours of war between Germany and France spread, and France called on Britain for support in what became known as the Agadir crisis.

The world seemed to have several other buried powder kegs threatening to explode. As early as 1910, many men and women in Britain were unconvinced that the Liberal government would improve their pay and conditions sufficiently. Violence broke out in Wales during a dock strike, and troops were called in by the local police. Winston Churchill, then Home Secretary, diverted the soldiers and ordered the train with them on board to be halted before it reached the scene of the riots, as he did not wish the British Army to be used to intervene in industrial matters. The Tories rounded on him for being lily-livered. There was no respite in the undermining of imperial power. In Spain, in 1912, two prime ministers were assassinated within a week of each other. The confidence of everyone at sea was irrevocably shattered when the ocean liner *Titanic*, the largest vessel afloat, disappeared beneath the waves with the loss of 1,635 lives, including that of J. J. Astor, one of the world's richest men, whose estate was valued at more than $85 million.

As Louis and Albert headed for the high seas, fundamental changes were taking place in technology, transport, power and politics as the gentle horse-drawn days of the Edwardian era drew to a close. The very day on which Albert joined the *Cumberland* on 17 January 1913, the last horse-drawn omnibus carried its passengers through the streets of Paris for the final time. It was an extraordinary year for progress; the era of hand-crafted manufacturing was being systematically snuffed out with Henry Ford's introduction of the conveyer-belt system of mass assembly. The Victorian and Edwardian eras were moving into the modern age, although nothing seemed very modern for Albert, slinging his hammock aboard the noisy coal-fuelled vessel. There was no favouritism to protect the King's son, who had to haul coal along with the rest of the crew, leaving him covered in soot after heaving the filthy bags to stoke the engine. Albert 'became like all the rest, "a red-eyed demon with flashing teeth" labouring in the pitch-black hold of a dingy collier, where the bags were sent down in slings to be filled and shot skyward again before the next lot came down'.[5] While he was performing this back-breaking labour, the internal combustion engine was being simultaneously heralded as the transport of the new age.

Thomas Cook could hardly have improved on their itinerary in terms of glamorous locations, as Louis and Albert left Devonport on a blustery wintry day. They headed towards the Canary Islands, before steaming across the Atlantic towards the West Indies, island-hopping between St Lucia, Trinidad, Barbados, Martinique, San Domingo, Puerto Rico, Jamaica, Havana and Bermuda. The ship then navigated to the colder clime and large open spaces of Canada – to Halifax, Quebec, Gaspé, and St John's, Newfoundland – before the long voyage back to Plymouth. It was a delightful trip with few mishaps; the only memorable disruption, Louis recorded in his diary, was a dinner when dozens of plates and glasses were sent crashing to the floor after the ship's cable snapped, jerking the vessel forward. There was a brief crisis as the *Cumberland* drifted free for almost two hours until the crew raised enough steam to haul her back into position.

Officially in charge of Albert on board *Cumberland* was Lieutenant-Commander Henry Spencer-Cooper, a young officer known to all as Scoop, who was one of Louis's close friends. Scoop had been Albert's Term Officer at Dartmouth, where he had encouraged him to take up riding and cross-country running. They had beagled and shot pheasants and become good friends. It was an added security net for Albert to have Louis for advice and comradeship on board. A crucial change had occurred since Osborne. Albert was no longer a young boy straight from the nursery; he was on the cusp of adulthood after four years' hard graft in the Navy's academies, putting him on a slightly more level footing with Louis.

It was an important rite of passage for Albert; his first voyage at sea and his first time completely cut off from his family, and indeed his country. But while Louis had good sea legs, Albert fared less well. 'The cadets were ill, so didn't do any instructions,' a young midshipman called Frank de Winton noted in his diary at the start of the voyage as the *Cumberland* entered the Bay of Biscay. But by day four, although massive waves were still buffeting the ship, naval instruction for the cadets started. They quickly picked up a few basic survival tactics alongside the rudiments of seamanship. 'Most of us learned that it was wise to eat even though one might have to throw it up before long. We learned, too, that if this became necessary, it must be done on the lee side,' said de Winton. It was only when the ship reached Tenerife that the sea as well as the cadets' nerves and stomachs were calm.

During the voyage the cadets had to demonstrate to the senior officers that they could put their seafaring theory into practice. If they performed badly, they would not qualify for the dirk and patches of a midshipman. For the officers, it was less stressful. Indeed, at times they appeared to lead a leisurely existence. Louis played tennis, hockey and rugger and swam at every port where the opportunity arose. He also found time to attend a series of 'at homes', fancy-dress balls, dances and picnics, often hosted by titled expatriate Lady Bountifuls eager to entertain young naval officers.

His relationship with Albert was still not unlike that of a teacher and a favourite pupil. Albert called Louis 'Dr Greig', while Louis called the Prince by his first name. As their friendship deepened over the years, Louis would call him 'Bertie' when they were alone but always 'Sir' in front of anyone else. The Prince then called him 'Greig', only much later on did he use his Christian name. Louis was thirty-three years old while the Prince was a coltish eighteen-year-old, and he told his brother Robert that the boy needed reassurance and steadying. The boy was slight, young for his age and far from self-confident.

A photograph of Albert on the *Cumberland* shows him looking more like a runaway chimney sweep's boy than a prince of the realm. His face is covered in grime from the coal dust after a morning spent hauling bags of coal to the engine room. A cloth cap is pulled over his ears and hair. The dark soot around his face makes his eyes seem exaggeratedly wide and bright. His clothes are pitch black. It was clear that he was given no special favours. It is probably a more realistic image of life on the *Cumberland* than the better-known portrait of him, all scrubbed and polished, earnestly standing to attention in his smart dark naval uniform.

For a period of more than five and a half years, between 1908 and early 1914, Louis supervised the medical care and training of hundreds of naval cadets. He was what his fellow officers referred to as a classic 'sea daddy' – a charismatic, guiding role model to whom cadets instinctively turned for advice and whose example they followed. As ever, formidable athleticism and colourful language made him stand out. His official records indicate his special flair for dealing with young people.

But Louis was no saintly mentor and certainly no goody-goody; he attracted a bad press on his first tour of duty on the *Cumberland*, eighteen months before Albert joined the ship. It was not his medical skills but a cheeky exchange with foreign women that thrust him into the limelight. A *Daily Mirror* journalist had heard about his saucy behaviour at a Greek dance in Alexandria, and poked fun at his insouciant gallantry with an article headlined 'A Way They Have in the Navy':

An amusing story of a Naval officer comes from one of the ports in the Mediterranean. The local people laid themselves out to entertain their British visitors and the ball was a very swell affair. One officer, not unknown as a Rugby footballer, was introduced to a foreign lady with an unpronounceable name. He was quite unabashed however and said with an engaging smile 'I'm very sorry. I really can't pronounce it. I shall have to call you Dolly.' And Dolly she was for the rest of the evening.

During his early voyages on the *Cumberland*, Louis seized every opportunity to escape ashore. He was always game for a night on the town – drinking, dancing or an occasional flutter in the local casino. His partner-in-crime was often Freddie Dalrymple-Hamilton, an easy-going Scottish naval officer, already a friend of Elizabeth Bowes-Lyon, whom he had met for the first time just six months prior to this voyage when he had been to stay at her family's Scottish home, Glamis Castle, in August 1911. 'My first visit. Very pleased to see Lady Rose again. Made the acquaintance of her younger sister Elizabeth for the first time who is a little angel!!!'[6] He was always ready for some fun in a rather Bertie Woosterish way. 'August 19: Fancy Dress – Elizabeth in an early Georgian kind of rig. We danced reels in the middle of which my bags fell off and I had to make a quick exit!!' It is extremely unlikely that either of them would even have mentioned Elizabeth Bowes-Lyon to each other at that stage, although Dalrymple-Hamilton was later to have a crush on her.

In Monte Carlo in 1912 he and Louis dined at the Café de Paris and afterwards 'lost about £7' on the gambling tables. (In 1999 that would be equivalent to about £280.) The next day, they hosted 'an enormous tea party of 16 young women' followed by dancing and then a gala dinner given by the captain of the *Leonardo da Vinci*, an Italian dreadnought. In Genoa, the two sailors sought out the late-night clubs and bars, downing a series of 'Sunday cocktails & such like poison' before joining a crowd of some three hundred students also out on the razzle. According to Dalrymple-Hamilton, Louis was the life and soul of the party: 'The students seemed very pleased to see us and we made speeches to them and were loudly cheered as a result. Greig insisted on sitting on his coat in the middle of the street because he said they made him giddy dancing round him. He was the hero of the occasion & kept the students at it for about ½ an hour!'[7]

Louis's energy appeared boundless; when ashore he would play a game of rugger or hockey in the morning followed by three sets of tennis in the afternoon, and then have a night out. Even if it was just a simple singsong, he was game. 'A very merry evening we had. I performed Farmer Giles . . . of course. Louis Greig also sang.'[8]

Louis was at the peak of his physical fitness, and Dalrymple-Hamilton found it exhausting to keep pace. 'Wasn't feeling particularly strong in the morning. Bathed up the club and visited a couple of shops with Greig. We played hockey against a team from the cruiser present in harbour in the afternoon & I am glad to say defeated them 3 goals to nil. A very good and fast game and rather tiring especially after 3 sets of tennis that Greig insisted I played with him.'[9]

While Louis's early days in the Navy were tremendous fun, he wanted substantially more from life than a dizzy round of parties and sport. He questioned the merit of his effortless pleasure-seeking lifestyle; a vein of Scottish puritanism made him feel guilty, even though there were downsides. He cracked a rib and had a front tooth knocked out during a particularly rough game of rugger against HMS *Implacable*. Needless to say, there was more than the occasional hangover as generous naval proportions of drink were readily available. 'Dined on board *Tereraine* & got well up the pole,' he recorded reproachfully in his diary, summarising his year as 'better physically but worse morally – the former thanks to Muller [exercises], the latter to opportunity'.

What gave his life a sense of purpose were his medical duties and the physical education of his cadets. Louis held two surgeries; one for officers and the other for the rest of the ship's company. The sicknesses and ailments ranged from suicidal inclinations to syphilis. He tried to keep a light touch: when treating a Cadet Arbuthnot for German measles, he pondered what he called the 'vexed question as to nationality of the measles! Rash like German. Tempre like measles.' Yet it was a serious matter which could put the whole ship into quarantine. Often there was no room for any banter, such as on the day when a sailor called Martin was found to be 'v seedy, breathless and altogether looks bad'. Two days later Martin was dead. Ten days later Louis dealt with a suicide. 'Ghastly news. WHG shot himself 2.30am. Poor old chap. Cherchez la femme. On looking back I remember he told me he would do it unless things came off.' A ship's doctor's work was always unpredictable.

Louis had been very conscious, since the death of his father, when he was nineteen, that his was the only surviving generation of men in the family. He had never been able to show his father his successes. David Greig had died before he played for Scotland or had even finished his degree. This left him with a sense of wanting to prove himself even more strongly than if his father had been around to give him the approbation he sought. Albert was in a similar position, but for very different reasons. He, too, desperately wanted to make his father feel proud of him, but he had so far largely failed. At home he had been semi-crippled with his knock-knees; at school he had come bottom of the class, and he was always stuttering and hesitant. On board *Cumberland* he was finally succeeding, passing the necessary tests to become a midshipman. Louis always maintained that Albert had the potential to succeed. He admired his grit and determination to persevere in the face of failure. 'He is a first-class chap, always trying, but what he needs more than anything is a leg-up, some encouragement,' Louis told his brother Robert. In some ways Albert was the ugly duckling, famously if unfairly compared to the elegant cock pheasant that was his brother. Louis felt that this was not right and always hoped that a swan would one day be a better comparison; a young cygnet desperate to emerge and take flight. It was a huge boost for Albert to have someone like Louis believing in him. Many years later, Martin Charteris, former private secretary to Princess Elizabeth, as well as when she became Queen, compared Louis's contribution to the role of a psychiatrist. 'He listened, he encouraged, he helped. He allowed Albert to help himself. He was the doctor who thought that he could set him right after a childhood with its own peculiarities. Louis was the right man in the right place to help him reach his potential.'[10] But there was an added dimension to his role with the Prince. Old-fashioned as it sounds today, with so much cynicism shown towards the royal family, Louis was a dedicated monarchist. To have the chance to help the son of the King was something of which he felt proud, patriotic and privileged.

While Louis worked and played hard, he always sensed that greater opportunities lay ahead. During a violent storm in the Bay of Biscay, when he lay in his bunk, his head spinning from seasickness, he tried to force out dark thoughts, reflected in the verse he copied into his journal:

> When your heart is feeling heavy
> And your brain is rather sad
> Don't think about your sorrows
> But of the time you've had.

He also copied out verse from Dante Gabriel Rossetti:

> Look in my face! My name is might-have-been;
> I am also called, No more, Too late, Farewell.

Inevitably there was a sense of standing still, trapped on board ship with a group of naval cadets while the 'real world' was passing him by. But what Louis's diary entries indicate is that what he most hated was wasted opportunities: 'Every year I live I am more convinced that the waste of life lies in the love we have not given, the powers we have not used, the selfish prudence which will work nothing, & which shirking pain, misses happiness as well. No one ever yet was the poorer in the long run for having once in a lifetime let out all the length of the reins.' But his natural optimism drove away such dark and serious thoughts, which fundamentally ran against the grain of his character.

For Albert the voyage to the West Indies was a marvellous opportunity to escape from the claustrophobic shadow of his family. It was essentially his first adult step. It was difficult for Louis and Albert not to enjoy themselves in the Caribbean in 1913, with the delights of palm-fringed beaches, breadfruit, mangoes, coconuts, a warm sea and a tropical climate. They cemented their friendship, spending time together, on and off ship. There was plenty of time for leisure ashore, and the Prince had a more relaxed time than most other cadets, as it was far more difficult to treat him like the others now that his father was King. He was singled out for invitations by ex-patriate grandees, and Louis was often his escort. Local dignitaries wanted to shake the King-Emperor's son's hand, and he needed some protection from over-zealous sycophants.

Albert quickly discovered the perils and pleasures of attention from strangers and made use of a fellow cadet, who looked physically very similar to himself. This look-alike acted as a perfect decoy to detract curious onlookers, entering into a pact of secrecy with Albert, often standing in for him at minor public functions where he did not need to make a speech. Sometimes there was no escape. In Bridgetown, Barbados, where he planted a commemorative tree, he was approached by autograph hunters. 'I write awfully badly,' he said, 'and I have heaps of names. Do you want them all?' In Kingston, Jamaica, he became a victim of the 'touching craze'. Any part of his clothing or body was fair game.[11] More than eighty-five years later, Albert's great-grandson, Prince William, would face similar difficulties when he travelled to Canada for one of his first royal tours abroad.

When the *Cumberland* berthed on 10 February at St Lucia, the second-largest of the Windward Islands, lying between St Vincent and Martinique, Louis went ashore with Albert. 'After lunch we did navigation in the hospital till 3.0. Then I changed and played tennis at the police court with Mr Cooper and Dr Greig,' Albert recorded in his diary.[12] Louis coached him at tennis but he was not yet good enough to be in the ship's team alongside Louis when the *Cumberland* played St Lucia three days later.

Louis was not always eager to escort Albert on trips ashore. A thirty-three-year-old man has ideas other than chaperoning a teenage novice around while on shore leave, especially a prince, where if anything goes wrong it will become very quickly and publicly known. The buck often stopped with Louis. On 26 March he wrote somewhat grumpily that he 'had to take HRH to a Regatta, a fierce affair'. It was a rare complaint, but the job always had an element of nannying. There were to be no high jinks in bars and casinos as on Louis's previous trips on the *Cumberland*, and no getting 'up the pole'.

Throughout their cruise, even though they were thousands of miles away from any European capital, politics was never far from their minds. Albert learned that his great-uncle, the King of Greece, had been assassinated, and the ship's ensign was hung at half-mast. King George V wrote from Windsor with the sad news, clearly shocked. 'Dear old uncle Willy the King of Greece has been assassinated at Salonica, by a Greek. It is too horrible. He was out for a walk as usual in the street, when this brute came up behind him & shot him through the heart.'[13] Yet even with such calamitous events, it was hard for a teenager, so far from home, to focus on the wider implications of a regicide. The year 1913 heralded rapid change, politically and culturally, but Albert, cocooned in royal houses or isolated in the Navy, was not really in a position to notice. It was the year in which Thomas Mann's *Death in Venice* was published and Stravinsky's *The Rite of Spring* was first performed. The cinema was becoming mass entertainment for millions of people, with Charlie Chaplin making thirty-five short films in 1913. All this heralded new departures. The build-up to a calamitous war was slowly emerging, although evident to few people, as war and bloodshed, unfortunately, were an annual feature of the first decade of the new century. Un-remittingly, the ratchet, which would eventually unleash the most horrendous carnage, was being tightened.

Their days ashore on various islands would, in retrospect, seem a pre-war period of Arcadian innocence. On St Lucia, Louis hired eight horses in Soufrière, the hamlet next to the Gros Piton and the Petit Piton, the two old volcanic forest-clad plugs rising a sheer 2,500 feet out of the seabed, creating one of the most dramatic sea panoramas in the whole of the Caribbean. Louis, Albert and seven others rode for ten miles along the shore where they could see soufrières: vents in the volcano that exude hydrogen sulphide, steam and other gases, and deposit sulphur and other compounds. They had a memorable time spotting the colourful St Lucia parrot, the *Amazona versicolor*, before calling at Laffittes, stopping for lunch at Malet Paret, and then riding back via more sulphur springs. The locals were fascinated by the idea of a king's son, and Louis noted their 'royal entry into Soufrière'. It was all a hoot for Albert, a revelation after all his years at his grandfather's and father's chilly, uptight courts, to be in the laid-back West Indies with its swimming, and tennis, being offered the odd rum cock-tail and surrounded by miles of white sandy beaches.

They left St Lucia and headed south to Trinidad, the most southerly of the Caribbean islands, lying just seven miles off the Venezuelan coast. Louis went ashore to watch the MCC play the West Indies, and played some tennis in the afternoons. It was a lotus-eater's life, with swimming in the sea, a formal dance at the house of a British resident, Sir Townsend Fenwick, and yet another dance the next night at Government House in Port of Spain. On Saturday, 1 March, Louis and Albert, along with the British Ambassador and the Captain, went sight-seeing, motoring more than fifty miles across the mountainous island to Manzanilla Bay on the east coast. On returning they again dined at Government House. And so this pattern of leisure carried on, as they sailed from Trinidad to Barbados for more of the usual round of 'at homes', tennis at the Savannah

Club and more dances. Louis escorted Albert to a pony gymkhana, at which the Prince won the Distance Handicap of four furlongs open to polo ponies, and was placed in the Polo Scurry of two furlongs. Albert also won the Farmyard Race, in which the mounted competitors had not only to cover the course, but also to imitate some bird or animal of the farmyard. He was allotted a donkey for imitation, and his braying earned him a prize.

Bermuda was the next stop. 'Scoop, self, HRH & De Salis played tennis & had strawberries & cream.' There Louis's tendency towards informality got him into trouble when, after taking some cadets to play football, he brought them to a thé dansant at Government House. The problem was that none of his cadets had brought any shoes other than their hobnailed boots. 'Awful frosty arrival,' recorded Louis.

The voyage was more enjoyable for Louis; the Prince was still among the lowest of the low in terms of rank, carrying out many menial tasks. While Louis had his own cabin and a surgery, the cadets lived in much less grand circumstances below deck, as Swinton recalled: 'One of the first things we had to do was to learn to string a hammock and how to lash up and stow a hammock, all of which had to be done smartly under the direction of a cadet Gunner Mr T Ahearn, a little man with a ginger beard and a high pitched voice.'

The routine was the same most days for Albert. Turnout at six o'clock, with time for just a hasty bowl of cocoa before physical drill conducted by Louis; bath and breakfast; divisions; working parties with the ratings or in the schoolroom with the instructor; and, then always last thing at night, slinging their own hammock.[14]

Leaving the Caribbean heat behind them, they steamed towards the chillier climate of North America. They entered the St Lawrence River on the way to Quebec, where they docked, and the cadets were taken to see Niagara Falls. Albert was closely followed by reporters, anxious for even a junior member of the royal family to give them a quote. The *Toronto*

News reported him as saying: 'I really do not mind being interviewed. But I can't bear these swarms of women with cameras.
I have not been bothered by any men but these women fluster
me. Are they suffragettes?' His comments point to his lack of
sophistication and social discomfort, but overall he got a good
press. The *Montreal Daily Star* described him as 'fair-haired,
red-cheeked, with a clear bright complexion, with just a slight
tan on his face, he looked as if he was just bubbling over with
health and lively spirits'. It was delighted to report that
'there was no "Your Royal Highness". It was just "boys" and
the prince was one of them' at a dinner for the cadets at the
Place Viger Hotel. It is interesting to compare Prince Charles's
embarrassment as a fourteen-year-old boy at Gordonstoun
when found in a pub and questioned by a freelance journalist,
having ordered a cherry brandy, apparently because he had
once had it out shooting. Albert was no less innocent when the
waitress came to take orders for drinks.

'"I'll have a glass of port wine" said one boy.

"Let's have a bottle of burgundy," suggested another.

"Ginger ale for me," the prince politely ordered and he
himself paid for the order.'

Albert was still a boy making the passage to adulthood. His
naïvety and lack of guile were transparent; he needed a
guiding hand from someone older and more experienced. The
trip to the West Indies and Canada certainly opened his eyes
to new worlds. At St George's Bay, Louis and the Prince were
entertained by a drunken businessman called Reid, 'a good
fellow, a dypsomaniac millionaire'.[15] No ginger ale was served
in his house; rather there was gin by the bottle until Reid
was decidedly pink in the face. They moved on to St John's, Newfoundland, where Albert recorded how he 'went ashore with
Dr. Greig . . . and afterwards we motored to see his [Reid's]
black fox farm and then went round the coast. We returned to
his house and had tea and then back to the ship.'[16] Louis saw
whales spouting, as well as white seals, and bought curios. He
noted that '2 amusing photos of PA & self were taken landing'.

It was a welcome change of climate and pace, with only one set-back when Albert was almost swept overboard in a squall.[17]

It was not until the middle of the summer that they finally returned to England, landing at Plymouth on 8 July 1913. All the cadets were given a week's leave before training continued again off the Nore. The tour formally ended with a visit by the King and Queen at Cowes on 3 August, when they were piped aboard as Albert and the rest of the crew stood to attention. Along with other officers, Louis was personally thanked for his part in keeping watch over Albert, who had met with all the requirements to become a midshipman. The Prince was immediately assigned to HMS *Collingwood*. The King hoped he would now prosper on his own. Meantime, Louis remained with the *Cumberland* for almost another year. But as the prospect of war intensified he asked to be transferred to the Royal Marines. He joined the Portsmouth battalion at Deal at a time when the threat of conflict from an increasingly aggressive Germany made it more and more likely that he was soon to become a war surgeon.

During the Agadir crisis, when Germany had provocatively sent a battleship to the Moroccan coast, Winston Churchill's initial instinct was to avoid any confrontation while the Germans goaded France into a fight over this one insignificant port on the Atlantic coast. Yet Churchill feared the worst, which was why, as Home Secretary, he advocated a preventative alliance between Britain, France and Russia to safeguard the independence of Belgium, Holland and Denmark without any hostilities. Herbert Henry Asquith, the Liberal Prime Minister, was impressed enough to send Churchill to the Admiralty in October 1911, where his principal task was to make sure that the British Navy kept the upper hand over the German fleet.

By 1914 Churchill was trying to ease the arms race and to reduce what he called 'the unwholesome concentration of fleets in home waters' by proposing that Germany and Britain should send their ships to Africa and the Far East. Still hoping to ease Anglo-German relations, Churchill suggested holding secret placatory talks with Admiral Tirpitz, Secretary of State for the German Navy, but this was vetoed by Henry Asquith, who feared 'a terrible splash in the European press'.

As a compromise, Churchill sent a British naval squadron to the Kiel regatta in the middle of June 1914. He later recorded a rather promising but eventually short-lived result from this diplomatic gesture. 'Officers and men strolled arm in arm through the hospitable town, or dined with all the goodwill in mess and wardroom. Together they stood bareheaded at the funeral of a German officer killed in flying an English seaplane.' But while the regatta was in progress, the Austrian Archduke Franz Ferdinand was assassinated at Sarajevo by a Bosnian of Serb nationality. Churchill did not see this as a prelude to any war involving Britain because he felt confident that no one would dare to challenge the might of the British Navy. After a Cabinet meeting to discuss the implications of a crisis enveloping Europe, Asquith wrote to George V, 'Happily there seems to be no reason why we should be anything more than spectators'.[18]

The belligerence of Austria and Germany quickly put such optimism to rest. At the beginning of August, after Europe had become embroiled in a hideous series of domino movements, each country dragging another into conflict, Churchill saw that war was inevitable for Britain. 'I cannot think the rupture with Germany can be long delayed,' he wrote to Lord Robert Cecil. His prophecy to his wife on that same day, unhappily, proved deadly accurate as he predicted 'it would be a wicked war'.

In very different ways Louis and Albert were to be tested in the ensuing conflict; their West Indian voyage would also seem in retrospect more a pleasure cruise than a preparation for men about to enter the most calamitous global war. Louis entered the hostilities as a surgeon serving with the Royal Marines, while Albert was a midshipman eager to prove himself on his first proper posting aboard HMS *Collingwood*, which prepared to confront the German High Fleet. Harry

Hamilton, the senior sub-lieutenant in charge of the gunroom for most of Albert's tour on the *Collingwood*, was kind and considerate but no replacement for Louis. Shyness and his stutter still plagued the eighteen-year-old, who was for security reasons known on board ship as Johnson. 'Johnson is very well, full of young life and gladness, but I can't get a word out of him, he treats me with great respect and seems to be in an awful funk of me! Thank goodness he is treated exactly the same as all the other minor snotties. It was quite a pretty sight seeing him polishing the brightwork this morning before divisions!'[19] Midshipmen like Albert were known as 'snotties' owing to their uniform having three buttons on the cuffs, allegedly to prevent anyone wiping their nose on them. He was a snotty very much on his own without a mentor to bolster him and keep his spirits high.

The next time Louis and Albert met, Britain was at war and the Prince would turn to him for help, more than he had ever done so before. Albert was about to find out how essential Louis was to his development as a young man.

Chapter Four

'The heroic marines decided to cut their way through the enemy's lines at all costs. After a warm tussle with the enemy, they succeeded in getting through. Greig remained behind at the railway station and nothing was afterwards seen of him.'

The *Scotsman*, October 1914

The events that swept Britain into war had been frighteningly swift following the assassination of Archduke Ferdinand in June 1914. His death had propelled Europe into crisis by unleashing a fatal chain of consequences which the British government, at first, refused to believe would lead to a global conflict. On 24 July, Asquith downplayed the political fallout between Austria, Germany, France, Russia and Serbia in a written summary of events he sent to the King. Even Churchill, the First Lord of the Admiralty and the man responsible for ensuring that Britain's Navy was prepared for war, appeared optimistic that conflict could be avoided. 'There is still hope,' he wrote to his wife, Clementine, on 31 July, 'although the clouds are blacker & blacker. Germany is realising, I think, how great are the forces against her & is trying tardily to restrain her idiot ally. We are working to soothe Russia.'[1] Unfortunately the belligerent Austrians would not accept Serbia's apology or assurances about punishing the Archduke's murderer.

When Germany invaded Luxembourg on 2 August, it was a clear sign that it also meant to invade neutral Belgium. Even if

Britain was wavering about being drawn into war to honour unwritten pledges to help France, its signed treaty with Belgium necessitated action. The Germans brazenly ignored every British ultimatum and were determined to march through Belgium, wanting first to defeat the French Army before turning eastwards towards Russia. And so, on 5 August, Britain declared war on Germany.

By 22 August, the German First and Second armies were grouped across the centre of Belgium. Opposing them were troops of three nations: the British Expeditionary Force between Mons and the French border, Belgians defending the fortress town of Namur, and the French left wing in the vicinity of Charleroi. A shocking blow to British morale at home and on the field was struck when the British Expeditionary Force was forced to retreat from Mons because it found itself with both flanks exposed after the French Army on its right withdrew and Namur was abandoned by the Belgians. Churchill's description of Lord Kitchener's face when he told him of the defeat was that it 'was distorted and discoloured as if it had been punched with a fist'.

This was when and why Churchill had decided to send the Marines along with two other naval brigades to Ostend, to distract the Germans and give the impression that a larger force was about to land. More than three thousand Marines, including the Portsmouth battalion, landed at Ostend, and the German High Command fell for Churchill's ploy as rumours quickly circulated of great numbers of troops amassing, which turned into a belief that eighty thousand Russians were there. But while it made perfect sense, in theory, to send over surplus sailors, who would otherwise not be fighting, the reality was they were untrained, often unwilling and utterly unprepared for the sort of combat expected of them.

In October 1914, Louis Greig was crouched inside a cold, muddy trench on the bleak Belgian coastline, watching a burst of shrapnel arch over the blazing city of Antwerp. It was one of the dreariest landscapes in western Europe: a depressing plain of sodden, unfenced fields, pasture and plough inter-mixed, overlying a water table that floods when any digging more than a few spadefuls deep takes place. The port had been turned into a raging inferno after constant German shelling, and the British and Belgian armies could now do little to prevent it from falling into the hands of the advancing German forces.

It was Louis's first taste of war, just five months after he had been transferred to the Marines. He had wanted more of a challenge in his professional life; the siege of Antwerp was a rude shock to all the sailors who found themselves fighting on land, stretching them to the extreme. Louis was hurtled without delay into a chaotic war. 'I had a lucky escape today. A shrapnel bullet passed through the fleshy part of my left shoulder, but there was no time to pause,' Louis recorded in his journal, a battered, black-covered exercise book he carried with him throughout the war. Dressed in the khaki field uniform of the Marines, with a Red Cross badge on his arm clearly visible, Louis treated the wounded where they fell or moved them to a makeshift first-aid post with the help of stretcher-bearers and St John's ambulancemen. He had a motorcycle with a sidecar, but more often relied on other people's cars to give him a lift or to help transport the wounded. 'Captain Coade was shot through the chest at the advance post & brought to me. As he was off his head a bit, I took him into Antwerp & left him in a British Red Cross hospital run by a Mrs O'Gorman, a very fine establishment with nurses and doctors from England.'

Louis had commandeered a pig farm and turned it into a temporary hospital where he and a Belgian doctor tended the wounded brought in from the trenches. The odour of pig manure hung in the air as he and his staff installed make-shift beds. The farmhouse had been abandoned, its owners either killed or among the stream of refugees fleeing the German guns. It was far from ideal in terms of hygiene or convenience, but it was better than being in a ditch or a trench.

Louis tried to arrange for Red Cross cars to come as close as possible to take the worst cases to a better-equipped hospital on the main road, but often the wounded had to be carried by stretcher across the muddy, uneven terrain, risking rifle fire. The majority of injuries treated were shrapnel wounds to the feet or legs, but he had to be ready for every sort of eventuality. 'Two cases have been operated on & tied. Another has gangrene commencing and a corporal has a rifle bullet which entered the left side of the chest, passed behind the heart & lodged in the skin in the right side,' he noted. Louis was exhilarated, but at the same time appalled. All those long and often tedious years studying anatomy and surgery at Glasgow University, found their purpose in the fields of Flanders.

Resources were scarce and he often had to tend to the injured without any anaesthetic, penicillin or proper bandages. He improvised with old cloth and argued forcefully for medical supplies to be brought from supply bases. Night and day, Louis lived with the agonised cries of shot sailors. On his way to and from Antwerp his car was bombarded by shells, and he had to twist and turn to dodge cavernous potholes and double-guess where the next shell might explode. 'I tried to find my battalion which had been sent out in the night to reinforce the Belgians. Only after some difficulty I found them in the trenches,' he wrote. The outlook was grim and depressing for the Portsmouth battalion: they were on the defensive in a foreign land under a constant hail of bullets from superior forces:

We saw the famous 42 centimetre shells at work and its effects were most terrifying; the ground for many yards round shook, and one felt the air concussion even at a considerable distance. As we got nearer, the shells began to get the range of the railway and the houses, and finally one of the 42s hit it fair and square, and literally there was nothing left. We moved back to our trenches unable to move for the fusillade that was poured on us. Our trenches had no head cover but were fairly deep and we managed to lie there with practically no casualties. There was one curious effect of a high explosive shell bursting in front. After the shell had detonated, one hears a curious musical sound like a large mosquito gradually coming nearer and nearer, not very rapidly. It gets louder and louder, and finally, with a vicious thud, hits the parapet of the trench in the front or rear wall, and one finds a fragment of shell of varying size which has caused this curious and not unpleasant noise in its passage through the air.[2]

The fight to save Belgium continued under the most difficult conditions. The Allied troops were unprepared, and lacked co-ordination and leadership. Yet it was strategically extremely important; Antwerp was Belgium's biggest port as well as one of Europe's most powerful fortresses. The Germans were employing only reserve troops in the area, but by 3 October, sixty thousand were closing in on the city. Churchill saw its defence as critical, not least in case Holland decided to join on the side of Germany, or insist on the fullest definition of neutrality, thereby isolating this besieged port from any help from the sea. 'No German advance to the sea-coast, upon Ostend, upon Dunkirk, upon Calais and Boulogne, seemed possible while Antwerp was unconquered,' Churchill wrote.[3] In a memo to the Prime Minister on 7 September, he under-lined its importance: 'It [Antwerp] preserves the life of the Belgian nation: it safeguards a strategic point which if captured, would be of the utmost menace.'[4] The situation became more grave when Belgium learnt that Germany was planning to besiege it by land. British intervention was needed to avoid immediate surrender.

When the Marines first landed in Belgium, they discovered to their consternation that Ostend had built no defences. The Belgians had been relying on their neutrality and were un-prepared for the invading German forces. 'We set about digging trenches and made barbed wire entanglements in a circle around the fortress town at a radius of about two miles,' recorded Louis. Their presence appeared to give some relief as the Germans initially withdrew their main forces about fifty miles. But, unfortunately, this was the calm before the storm that was to devastate the beleaguered city.

Antwerp may have been what really mattered at that stage to the Allies, but the defence of Belgium's second-largest city turned into one of Britain's least glorious ventures in the First World War. Winston Churchill, in particular, was blamed for its fall and the retreat of a British Expeditionary Force of 120,000. Churchill was lambasted for abusing his power as First Lord of the Admiralty to establish the Royal Naval Division, a new force from naval reserves. They were promptly nicknamed 'Churchill's private army'. With good reason, he feared that Britain did not have enough land troops, but unfortunately his new army, a chaotic, ill-equipped, makeshift collection of sailors, many of whom were reluctant to be fighting on land at all, was not the solution.

Among the 'raw recruits' was Asquith's third son, Arthur. 'Strictly between ourselves,' wrote the Prime Minister to Venetia Stanley, 'I can't tell you what I feel of the wicked folly of it all. The Marines, of course, are splendid troops & can go anywhere & do anything: but nothing can excuse Winston (who knew all the facts) from sending in the two other Naval Brigades.'[5] Also incensed were high-ranking officials from within the Admiralty, angry at what they perceived as Churchill's blatant empire-building at the expense of the country's defences. 'I really believe Churchill is not sane,' Captain Herbert Richmond, assistant director of operations, wrote in his diary. 'These men who are to be employed in soldiering know nothing about the business . . . The whole thing is so wicked that Churchill ought to be hanged before he is allowed to do such a thing.' One RND officer felt hijacked by Churchill's ambitions: 'We regarded Churchill almost as "Public-Enemy No 1" for the simple reason that we had spent our time and energies, at some financial expense to ourselves, in training for service at sea in the event of war. When war happened, we were turned into soldiers without any option although we retained naval terminology and many customs and practices. But the fact remains that we were a land force.'[6]

As the crisis deepened, Churchill volunteered to go to Antwerp in person. Plans had already been put in place for him to visit Dunkirk. Changes were made so that he could see the difficulties for himself and report back to Kitchener. Intense discussions took place about how long the Belgians would defend the city and when the British would launch a major relief operation. Churchill visited the paltry defences around the city on 4 October. He found the Belgian defenders 'weary and disheartened'. The ground was waterlogged after large parts of the terrain had been flooded to try to keep the Germans at bay. The sight of Churchill being driven around in a Rolls-Royce in his dark overcoat and box hat could not have been very uplifting for the dispirited troops on the ground. The feeling of antipathy was fairly mutual, as he was not pleased by what he saw. At one set of trenches he found the line very thinly held and asked where 'the bloody men were'. He was not mollified when told that everyone available at that point was in place.[7]

Louis and his fellow Marines, unhappily, had no choice about fighting alongside the other ill-trained, hapless battalions of Churchill's Royal Naval Division, many of whom were clearly there against their will, and who turned out to be more of a hindrance than a help. But there was no time for Louis to dwell on the foolhardy orders of Churchill as events on the ground overtook them.

The German Army swiftly advanced on Antwerp, ransacking dozens of towns and villages. 'The village of Orchies was a heart-breaking sight, having been torched, house by house, until there was nothing but bare walls standing, & no living inhabitants save a cat which we rescued,' wrote Louis.

The trenches were broad and shallow, and gave scant protection to the weary and inexperienced troops. It was one of the first instances of the landscape transmogrifying into a poisoned wasteland with dark, satanic scenes of mud and

mayhem which were to become all too familiar a sight in the
years ahead. Heavy shells burst in salvos of three and four,
with dense black smoke near or actually inside the ineffectual
shelters, in which the men crouched. Every prominent building
– château, tower or windmill – was constantly under fire.
Shrapnel exploded in the road, and in the distance thickets of
woods were specked with white puffs of smoke. It was a
dismal scenario, as fort after fort around Antwerp was
destroyed by monster howitzers, and line after line of trenches
was cleared by the barrage of field guns. Churchill despondently watched the city fall as 'the German infantry, weak in
numbers, raw in training, inferior in quality, worked and
waddled their way forward into the "second strongest fortress
in Europe"'. He was actually being more than a little xeno-
phobic here, as the German Army was reckoned even by its
enemies to be well trained. This was just one more reason why
he made such an error of judgement in pitting the Royal Naval
Brigades against it.[8] For the men on the ground it was a
disheartening process. Under the German shelling, trans-
porting the wounded became more dangerous for Louis and
his stretcher-bearers. 'We encountered some severe shrapnel
fire and had to take refuge behind a house. Setting off again
during a lull we ran straight into trouble again, this time heavy
shell-fire. We got in an open ditch after which a shell burst in
front burying us with earth. As things were really getting a bit
hot, we ran to a trench where some of my battalion were, and
there we had to remain for over an hour absolutely unable to
raise our heads on account of the shellfire.'

A hard-fought series of skirmishes took place as the German
military machine moved forward, until by 8 October the
Marines were waiting for the much-anticipated order to retreat
towards Antwerp. The battle conditions were treacherous, and
the prospects ahead far from rosy. Louis found himself in a
surreal landscape of corpses and empty streets. 'I proceeded
to the chateau where our base hospital and GHQ were. As I
went along everything looked very deserted & except for a

dead horse I saw no one. I found they had been shelling the main road into Antwerp.'

Passing a house where some more Marines were billeted, Louis found them in a state of shock because a shell had landed ten minutes earlier, killing three men. 'I found the chateau deserted. All that remained was a notice "Gone to Antwerp" & one freshly dug grave. The medical staff and our GHQ had retired further into Antwerp. We were on our own. There followed a horrible day of dodging shells & living in the streets & cellars waiting for orders from GHQ which never came.'

Rumours of total retreat buzzed around and were welcome as morale among the men was so low. Just when everyone thought that all they had to do was wait to go home, a messenger arrived from the trenches with orders for reinforcements to be sent immediately to cover the retreat of some Royal Naval Division stragglers. The Belgians were also in retreat, which left other troops vulnerable. With a heavy heart, the Marines started to head back towards the front, and after marching for an hour and a half, they found part of Churchill's 'barmy army', not huddled and afraid as they had been told, but asleep and unwilling to be disturbed. Louis was furious at their lethargy. 'By dint of hard swearing we dug them out after firing a few shots in the air to make the Deutschers think we were going to remain there.' On their way back, they witnessed an almost apocalyptic view of Belgium. 'We passed along streets absolutely deserted except for dead bodies here and there. Traces of damage to the city were visible everywhere and in three different places large fires were raging, one of which was a petrol store. I found they had been shelling the main street into Antwerp. I passed a house where Beith's Battalion (the 4th battalion of our RM Brigade) were sheltering and found they had lost 3 men at one go of shrapnel about 10 minutes previous to my arrival & the men were in a very nervous condition.'

The situation was even worse for the Belgians as hundreds of refugees from the countryside traipsed along the main roads in a pitiful trail, leaving their ruined homes behind. Antwerp was paralysed and its citizens could only wait and listen to the booming guns getting closer and louder. The famous spires, museums and churches, the broad warehouses along the River Scheldt, and the grand hotels, gave a false impression of calm, serenity and prosperity.

In the chaotic warzone outside the city, matters were made worse for the Marines when a group of men from the Royal Navy Division split into two groups by mistake. One half had lost the other. They had stopped to get water, but when one group had come back, the rest had moved on. A major concern had been how to cross the River Scheldt to avoid being trapped by the advancing German Army. 'It looked like us being caught like rats in a trap, but we busied ourselves and eventually got under way with "Winston's funny army", and found a bridge of boats whereby we crossed the Scheldt,' wrote Louis.

The chain of command within the British troops was breaking down, as was their luck. The Marines were nervous and jittery, their mission seeming unfocused and hopeless. 'After waiting for an hour we found the man in charge of the battalion in front and he said that he "<u>thought</u>" that he had lost track of the battalion in front. So there we were a lost force with no orders and not knowing where to go.'9

Spirits sank further when three men were blown up in one single shell blast. Louis was kept hugely busy tending the wounded. He zigzagged across a flat, muddy and shell-scarred no-man's-land back to his erstwhile headquarters to try to find out where the base hospital had been moved, but nobody knew.

I started off in a car with two St John ambulancemen and two stretchers, but we got bogged down and had to abandon the car and proceed on foot. We encountered severe shrapnel fire & had to take refuge behind a house. We set off again in a lull, but ran again into heavy shell fire. We dived into an open ditch & a shell bursting in front covered me with earth. Thinking that things were getting a bit hot, we ran to another trench where some of my battalion were, & we remained there for over an hour unable to raise our heads on account of the shell fire. The Germans seem to have got the range pretty accurately. We were getting it all round us. Fortunately, most burst in front or just behind & we had few casualties. One shell hit a house fair & square & burst the whole place up. We then retreated back to our trenches. The blast had killed my friend, the Belgian doctor, & his staff. Our Brigade retired about 2 miles to the rear & took up a new position in trenches.

The Royal Naval Division recruits were becoming the bane of the Marines' lives. They had gone on ahead, but instead of keeping on the road towards the town of St Nicholas, which had been their orders, they took a false turning and were marching in the wrong direction. A Marine motorcyclist was sent to try to bring them back, but by the time he caught up they had decided to head for Holland. Just a few hours later, they changed their minds and fell into line with the Marines once more. They were hungry, helpless and a handicap to any military operation. Louis was at his wits' end as supplies and medical help were running out. 'I found I was the only doctor with the force and except for a few first aid men from the St John ambulance brigade with a splint or two, we had absolutely nothing in the way of dressing or drugs as I had lost my NCO and field valise the night before.' The situation became 'tragi-comic', according to Louis, when 'one of the usual actors' – a RND soldier – shot himself and a friend and had to be carried by stretcher.

It was a ten-mile march to St Nicholas, and Louis managed to get a lift in a dilapidated old car to try to commandeer an ambulance to ferry the wounded. On arrival, there was more bad news. A mild panic set in when the Burgomeister told them that the Germans were returning in the other direction, having been routed by other Allied troops. If true, it would be disastrous. Louis knew there was no option but to keep on moving. 'Our force by this time – except for the 600 Marines –

was as much use as a sick headache due to fatigue and lack of ammunition and training, so there was nothing for it but to alter course and to try to find the main body of our forces in order to avoid the Germans.'

It was at this stage that they stumbled upon the last refugee train on its way to Ostend. The Marines and men of the Royal Naval Division scattered themselves among the civilians on board the train, and, at last, felt they, too, were on their way home. 'We found the refugee train at a village called Steykern and after getting rid of the household goods of some refugees we managed to get standing room,' wrote Louis. But luck was not on their side. The journey was interrupted by gunfire from Uhlans taking pot shots. All they could do was to keep their heads down and try to shunt past. But heavy German fire frightened the driver into bringing the train to a halt. It was a terrifying moment, as Louis knew it meant a final stand-off. It was early evening when the firing started, just as daylight was fading into evening gloom, making it even more difficult to defend their position. No one quite knew from where the Germans were firing. Some Marines got off the train and stormed a house from where gunfire seemed to be emanating. Others took up defensive positions on the train to return fire while refugee mothers and children huddled on the floor in terror. Family Bibles, bottles of wine, toys, overcoats, blankets, bulging saucepans and battered suitcases were crammed into every available corner on the train by desperate Belgians on the run in their own country. Children were made to lie under the seats, as adults shielded them from possible bullets. Entire families prayed and pleaded for help. During a lull in the fighting Louis tended to some refugees and soldiers caught in the gunfire. The sound of bullets hitting the steel doors, ricocheting around the carriage, jolted him, each time. Every hit came as a shock, seemingly louder, and from any number of directions as the Germans surrounded the train. He counted seven dead Germans at the crossing, where the train had halted, and he treated a mixture of English, Germans and

Belgians. The worst cases he tended were a shattered right elbow, which required a tourniquet to prevent further bleeding, and a woman and child both badly wounded in the head. Nearby, a German soldier had taken a bullet to the stomach.

The train was a critical communication and supply line for the Allies because Antwerp was in danger of falling into enemy hands, and if that occurred Germany would effectively control Belgium. The sixty-wagon steam train, more than half a mile in length, had been snaking its way along the track towards Ostend, packed with Belgian refugees – mainly women, children and some babies – eager to escape the advancing German Army. But when more than 1,200 Marines and members of the Royal Naval Division had clambered on board to join the exodus, it became a higher-priority target for the enemy.

Louis treated more of the wounded, during an apparent lull, when the fighting appeared to be finished. 'I was called to go and see the wounded & as I passed along I saw some half dozen dead Germans at a level crossing where we had stopped,' he recalled. The Marines thought that only a few random shots were being fired, but this proved not to be the case. 'More heavy rifle fire commenced against the train, chiefly at the front portion.' The gunfire came from a house near the rail track. The Marines rushed it from the train. At that stage, in a rather unclear sequence of events, they were surrounded by more German troops.

In retrospect, it still looked as if it was no accident that the train had halted. According to a later account given by an officer from the Royal Naval Division, the train driver had fled, holding a crucial engine valve. In the engine room, the stoker lay huddled on the floor with a baby beside him, paralysed with fear. The Marines also discovered that the track had been sabotaged. 'As we left a few shots were fired at us by some snipers but subsequent events made it appear as if this was some sort of signal. After we had gone some miles the train stopped with a jerk. We later discovered the line had been broken. A violent fusillade took place from the station buildings and there were a good many casualties,' Louis wrote. Even if the Marines had maintained control of the train, it would still have been going nowhere. It was more difficult to defend a train full of unarmed, terrified refugees. Surrender or retreat was inevitable as they were outmanned and outgunned.

The exact sequence of events is not clear, but Louis was startled when hundreds of men from the Royal Naval Division suddenly appeared to be surrendering. Cries of *'Nous sommes prisonniers'* followed from the Belgians, accompanied by more yells of surrender from the Royal Naval Division. When Louis asked why they were giving themselves up, he was told that it was the only option, owing to exhaustion. Louis had been fully focused on patching up wounded rather than the next tactical move, so he was more surprised than most other people by the sudden capitulation. The apathy and inefficiency of the RND were all factors in the defeat. He had heard cries of 'Marines this way' and saw many of them running along the railway line in the direction of Ghent. Those who hesitated found themselves German prisoners of war. Louis was convinced it could all have been avoided.

I felt sure that all the trucks had surrendered to an advance patrol of about 25 Uhlans, 12 of whom had been killed (I counted them afterwards) & the rest had decamped after signalling for reinforcements & I told the fellows so. This was borne out by the fact that for about half an hour after the Marines had gone there was absolute silence during which time I feel they could all have got away. But then up rushed a force of German infantry and took them all prisoner. If I had known for one moment that I should not be returned (as is a doctor's right under the Geneva Convention), I am not at all sure that I would not have decamped with the Marines who all got away, but I stopped with the wounded until they got into better condition. In all they bagged about 900 men and 5 officers of the Royal Naval Division and about 200 Marines and myself.

Louis's family in Scotland did not know if he was dead or alive in the autumn of 1914. Just two months after war had been declared, a letter from the Admiralty arrived at Robert Greig's home, Capelrig, Newton Mearns in Renfrewshire, with the news that Louis was missing, somewhere in Belgium. The Greig family prepared themselves for the worst, although they tried hard not to lose hope. For several days there was no news. Connie, Louis's elder sister, wrote from home in London to try to comfort their mother, who was habitually dressed in ankle-length black dresses following her husband's death in 1900. Jessie Greig was fading fast, simply through old age. 'We are so concerned about Louis and just pray to God that he is all right somewhere. We must not lose hope. It is a worrying time for us all.'

His disappearance was covered by several newspapers because of his celebrity as a sportsman. 'Famous Rugby Player Missing' was the headline in the *Scotsman*, which gave a few more details of his last sighting. Little more news trickled through until one officer from the Royal Naval Division, who had managed to escape, published a report of his journey on the last train from Antwerp on which Louis was thought to have travelled. The Greigs read and cut out the article with its fast action description.

We reached a station in the North of Flanders and caught the last refugee train to Ostend at 6.30 on Friday night. It stopped and started at ten minute intervals before all hell broke loose. A shot rang out, followed by a very hell of fire. We were surrounded by Germans, who were blazing away from all quarters, and incidentally playing a machine gun on us while overhead was an airplane throwing a searchlight upon us.

The trucks were chock-a-block full of women and children and babies and our party which was composed of 650 officers and men. In the pitch dark women and children yelled as the firing started. I looked over the other side of the engine to see that no one was about and found a German trying to get aboard, but my revolver did all that was necessary.

As the Germans had started firing indiscriminately on the women and children on the train, a decision was taken to surrender. Swords were unbuckled and revolver and ammunition laid on the ground but no Germans arrived to take the British soldiers prisoner. I waited until I saw a party of about 150 coming along. I couldn't see who they were so I hailed them and discovered they were a crowd of 139 Marines. They told me they refused to surrender and were going to cut their way through. For eight hours the Marines and the remainder of the RNVR marched at a cracking pace until they reached Salzette at 4.30am on Saturday morning and caught the train to Ostend and from there back home.

A few days later *The Times* published confirmation that Louis had been on the train. It told how 'the heroic marines decided to cut their way through the enemy's lines at all costs. After a warm tussle with the enemy, they succeeded in getting through. Greig remained behind at the railway station and nothing was afterwards seen of him.' The paper praised the 'doctor's humanity' for refusing to abandon his medical duties as he treated the wounded from both sides, even though it cost him the chance to escape. A week later, the Greigs learned that he had been taken prisoner. This was a huge relief to Jessie, who had not known if her son was dead or alive. But even news of his capture was no reason to rejoice. The *Penny Pictorial* reported how British troops had been shot without question after being arrested without warning. It quoted orders given by a lieutenant commanding the 7th Company of the 112th Bavarian Infantry Regiment: 'From today no more prisoners will be taken. All prisoners will be put to death.' Even if the reports were black propaganda put about by the German government, they made disturbing reading. An extract from a German officer's diary revealed the hate-fuelled intensity of the conflict: 'They got no mercy. The sight of the trenches and the fury – not to say brutality of our men in beating to death the wounded English affected me so much that for the rest of the day I was fit for nothing.' But the Greigs, as ever, tried to remain optimistic, because, at least, Louis was still alive.

The Greigs were not the only people upset by his capture. Louis had been wooing a childhood family friend called Phyllis Scrimgeour before he had left for France, and she was utterly distraught at his disappearance. Aged thirty, she was a strikingly handsome woman with auburn hair and sea-blue eyes. The Scrimgeours had shared summer holidays with the Greigs when the two families rented houses near each other on Orkney. Louis admired her fearless sense of adventure; she had skied across Lapland in Lapp costume. She was particularly proud of her skills as a driver, at a time when few women were allowed behind the wheel. She was a regular action girl who shone at tennis, rowing, cycling, swimming and sailing. And in early 1913 this energetic, irrepressibly jolly and forthright woman had fallen in love with Louis. She had always looked up to the older, more sophisticated one-time sports hero, and she was thrilled when he appeared as interested in her as she was in him.

Phyllis was attractive with her hair bundled up in a wide chignon. 'She was fiercely competitive and hated to lose but even when she did, the clouds soon moved away and she was all smiles and sunshine again,' remembered a contemporary.[10] Others remembered her as a formidable, big-hearted girl who always knew what she wanted, and who was prepared to bulldoze her way forward to get it. In her long, flowing skirts, brightly-coloured blouses and a wide selection of felt hats, often with a feather, Louis thought she was full of character and charm. Like Louis, she came from a large family and, also, like the Greigs, they were inveterate inventors of nicknames. Phyllis became Phig while her siblings were Beg (Beryl), Egg (Elsie), Cag (Carron), Mog (Marjorie), Dunk (Humphrey) and Stunk (Stuart). Only her other brother Michael escaped a diminution of his name. Phyllis was a powerful character who did not suffer fools, and even in her early thirties there was a hint of an emerging Lady Bracknell. Her voice could be discerned in a crowd, not only owing to its volume but also its clarity and sometimes shrieking resonance. 'LOO-EE,' she would call, and there was never any doubt as to his hearing her or Phyllis being ignored. She was exactly the sort of larger-than-life figure that he had been waiting for. He had found someone who would hold her own in his company, and who had a tremendous sense of fun. They were both from over-bearing families and shared a strong urge to create their own. Phyllis had the advantage of being a minor heiress. Her parents, Walter and Minnie Scrimgeour of Hemsby Hall in Norfolk, had promised her a modest dowry. The Scrimgeours were a very old family who, in 1093, fought for King Malcolm of Scotland near Monymusk on the River Don. When the King's standard-bearer fell, Hugh Carron picked up the standard and stormed towards the enemy. Afterwards, the King announced, in recognition of his bravery, that he would be known as Carron the Scurmisher. This later became Scrimgeour, the family name of the Earl of Dundee, which spells Scrimgeour with a 'y' rather than an 'i'. The present Earl remains the hereditary standard-bearer of Scotland.

The romance was welcomed by the other Greigs and Scrimgeours, as Louis's sister Constance had married a Scrimgeour, Phyllis's first cousin John. Louis and Phyllis were not engaged, but there was more than an understanding between them, and a great deal of hope on Phyllis's part. When Louis went missing, Phyllis was devastated as she waited for news at her parents' house. She raged against the Germans when out walking or in letters to Louis's brothers and sisters.

As Phyllis waited in Suffolk, pining for news of Louis, she learned that her brother Michael had been killed at the front. One of his close friends, Lieutenant Gordon V. Carey, wrote from No. 4 General Hospital, Versailles, describing Michael's last moments:

> He was standing out in the open; perfectly calmly, under a perfect hail of shrapnel, keeping his men together – but when I had to go back to the dressing station shortly afterwards I was told that he had been shot just as he reached the support trench and I gathered

that his death was instantaneous. We all loved him, and the other officers in my Company had often thought how miserable we should be, if anything happened to him. He was always so calm, and imperturbable when other people were fussed, and his quaint way of putting things was the chief asset in keeping us all in good spirits. And now within 12 hours they are all gone.

Phyllis knew it could so easily have been Louis. During a week of fighting at Antwerp, seven officers and fifty other ranks of the Royal Naval Division were killed. The number of wounded was 158, and 936 were captured and sent to prisoner-of-war camps.

It was of little comfort to the Greigs or the Scrimgeours, as they counted the devastating cost of war, that Churchill was pilloried for his part in the fall of Antwerp. H. A. Gwynne, the editor of the *Morning Post*, led the attack in a prominent article entitled 'The Antwerp Blunder': 'The attempt to relieve Antwerp by a small force of Marines and Naval Volunteers was a costly blunder, for which Mr. W. Churchill must be held responsible.'

It was the early days of the war and no one could have foreseen that the losses would be insignificant in terms of sheer numbers, and that later up to sixty thousand men would die in a single day. Churchill robustly defended his reputation, arguing that the delay in Antwerp's fall had been strategically beneficial for the Allied armies. But others saw it as simply a vainglorious exercise which had wasted men and morale. At the Admiralty, Captain Richmond had been furious that the Marine Brigade had been sent at all. In his diary he wrote on 4 October: 'The siege of Antwerp looks ugly. I hope it may hold out. The 1st Lord is sending his army there; I don't mind his tuppenny untrained rabble going, but I do strongly object to 2,000 invaluable marines being sent to be locked up in the fortress & become prisoners of war.'[11]

Unfortunately, that was to be Louis's fate. Phyllis had no

idea if he was wounded. Was he being well treated? Was he in danger? Not knowing even if he was alive was very difficult to bear. She was a robust, fiercely loyal and stalwart woman who could only pray that the man she hoped to marry would come home safely.

Chapter Five

'I must satisfy the authorities at the nearest field
hospital that I was a doctor, otherwise I should be
shot.'

Louis Greig's war journal, 1914

Louis looked up from bandaging a German soldier to find
five others pointing fixed bayonets at him. They barked
at him to put his hands up, surrender the revolver from
his holster and move away from their wounded comrade. In
the darkness in the shell-pocked waste ground around the
level crossing at Morbreach, just a few miles from Bruges,
Louis gingerly stepped away from the injured corporal and
tried to explain to his trigger-happy captors that he was a
doctor. They were incredulous that a British Marine should
have stayed behind to tend a German when most of his own
battalion had already retreated. 'I was asked how were they to
know I was a doctor. I mentioned my Red Cross [badge] but
was told that it was insufficient proof. The fact that I had been
aiding one of their men seemed to make little difference. I was
informed I must satisfy the authorities at the nearest field
hospital that I was a doctor, otherwise I should be shot.'[1]

Louis was accused of masquerading as a doctor with false
documentation which, in their eyes, was tantamount to being
a spy. To avoid a firing squad, he had to convince two stony-
faced German doctors of his medical qualifications by
answering questions on human anatomy. Only then was he
ordered to carry on treating soldiers and civilians wounded

in the battle. But this time he had to do so with a rifle pointed at his head. The Germans were far from grateful for his care: they were sullen, scared and fractious.

It was a long night with more than 150 men from both sides having been shot and needing treatment. There were very few medical staff. One of the worst injured was a British sailor with a shattered right elbow and in urgent need of a tourniquet. Another Marine had a bullet through the small of his back, and his intestines were protruding from his abdomen. 'I was told afterwards that he had 13 perforations which needed stitching,' noted Louis in his diary. A young woman and a child lay unconscious, with bullet wounds to their heads and chests. Others could not walk due to leg injuries. Corpses were scattered along the rail track, some hanging limply over the side of trucks, where they had been shot. A German aeroplane buzzed overhead throwing a spotlight on to the train, blinding the terrified refugees still huddled in the wagons. Those prisoners who were able to walk were marched off to a nearby village hall, where they were locked up. No one knew what the Germans intended to do with them. Meanwhile Louis remained at the battle scene, forced to carry on treating the wounded. 'I got the injured onto stretchers by about 1am, and we got to a temporary shelter by about 2am. Then, they wanted me to start dressing wounds, but I flatly refused as I was done to a turn, and they had two or three doctors already there.' Louis could be obstinate at the best of times, but he was livid with his captors and insisted he be allowed a rest. He was physically exhausted after working throughout the night in the adrenalin-charged atmosphere of war. There had been precious little sleep during the previous few days and the numbing sickness of defeat and capture left him drained. He saw that no one was remotely grateful for his efforts to save the lives of German troops, which had cost him his freedom. It was past three o'clock in the morning when Louis was locked in a dark, airless room with eighty other British prisoners. 'There was standing room only and the atmosphere was impossibly hot and fuggy, but eventually I got to the fireplace and sat with my head up the chimney. I was so tired that I slept in that position until 8am,' he recorded.

The next day they were marched to a village called Exaarde where they were kept for three days inside a church: there were 1,200 prisoners; 200 Marines, 600 sailors from the Royal Naval Division, 400 Belgians and four Royal Naval Division officers. Their impotence struck home when a sailor named Hanson was executed. Hanson thought he had seen some more Marines approaching and courageously called out, 'Don't come here' while other British men were being rounded up. 'They are Germans!' he cried out. A guard clubbed him with a rifle butt and Hanson reacted by grabbing the gun and wrestling over it, both men rolling on the ground. Other German guards panicked and ran in among the Allied prisoners, indiscriminately bayonetting three to death and wounding half a dozen others. The next morning, the senior British officer was told that he must break the news to Hanson that he had been sentenced to death. 'The poor devil did this after writing various letters for him (as Hanson's right wrist was damaged from a blow in the scuffle the night before). The senior officer was allowed to stay with him until 9.30am. At 10am, Hanson was shot. Comment is useless,' wrote Louis.

Captivity was particularly difficult for Louis to come to terms with. He knew he could have escaped by abandoning the wounded German soldier he had been treating. It had never occurred to him that he would be a prisoner of war as, under the Geneva Convention, doctors were supposed to be exchanged in a humanitarian gesture that benefited both sides. But Louis's captors refused to recognise any such rules of war. For the Germans to flout the Convention was bad enough, but to do so when he had risked his life treating one of their men was bitter indeed.

But Louis had little time to ponder his fate. Straight away he was sent on a long and uncomfortable train journey to Halle, in Saxony, where a disused steel and iron factory was to be his home for the next eight and a half months. Many German soldiers vented their hatred on the British troops as they were escorted through Belgium, France and then into Germany. 'We got the full brunt of the German "kultur" & Prussian politesse, being on several occasions spat at and on one never to be forgotten occasion spat on, with the curse *Dieu le punisse!*' At one railway station, an officer came up and huffily demanded 'What are you doing in Belgium?' Louis defiantly shouted back: 'Will you tell me what the devil you are precisely doing here?' The German responded by spitting.

But not all the Germans they met were hostile. One German corporal had worked as a clerk in London and wanted to marry his fiancée from Hampstead. Louis did not share his views on Germans being able to return so easily to London. 'I hope that never again are we to be troubled by these sausage-eating, beer-guzzling barbarians,' he wrote.

Louis travelled in a third-class railway carriage with wooden seats, while the ordinary soldiers were crammed into sealed cattle wagons. 'The whole country is simply pockmarked with shellfire,' he noted. Food on their journey consisted of pig fat in hot water. 'Our hunger was great at the start, but our enthusiasm for the seat of Lucullus quickly cooled,' Louis observed, as they were hurtled to an unknown destination in Germany. Trains travelling in the opposite direction had 'To Paris' and 'Express for London' chalked on the side. Whenever the train stopped, more insults were heaped on them: 'Englische Schweinhund' – cartoon cliché of an insult as it now seems – was the most familiar jibe. It was a depressing journey to an even grimmer destination. As Louis crossed over the border into Germany, he thought, 'My first journey into Germany. Please God, my last.'

The factory at Halle had been condemned as unfit for human use by the municipal authorities before the war, and earmarked for demolition. All the machinery had been taken out of the workshops and two circles of barbed wire were coiled round the outer walls. The courtyard in the middle was a morass of mud in the winter ('we all wore clogs as nothing else was any good') and in dry weather it was a dust-bowl. Each prisoner was given two blankets and slept on a straw palliasse on the often wet and muddy cobbled floor.

More than three thousand prisoners were locked behind its enormous wooden gates and high grey stone walls. By the end of the war it had earned the reputation as one of the worst German PoW camps,[2] run on petty, narrow, vindictive lines with prisoners constantly harassed. They would be strip-searched outside in the courtyard in freezing conditions in the winter months and sentenced to solitary confinement for petty offences, many of which were made up. The word of a German was always believed before that of any other nationality. Justice was, as a consequence, inevitably rough. When Louis was at Halle, the authorities let the Red Cross know that he was alive. Slowly letters started to come in from his family and from Phyllis. Food from their Red Cross parcels was often confiscated or stolen, and smoking was banned, although they were allowed to receive tobacco. The worst hardship for Louis was the boredom and the frustrating knowledge that he should not be behind bars in the first place.

Louis was determined to remain fit and healthy despite the dreadful conditions. 'My Muller exercises are a source of great interest to the sentries, who are not very sure whether it is not their duty to stick a bayonet into me, on the off chance of my being dangerous to the Vaterland, or for a lack of respect to their military uniforms.'

His diet consisted mainly of boiled pork with sauerkraut, Kriegsbrot, coffee and watery soup, although several times horse meat was on the menu. 'On one occasion, we undoubtedly had dog. The French officers for days after used to bark loudly when the portion was given out.' Sausage, butter and jam could be bought at the canteen, but these items were often on the '*verboten*' list for English prisoners, who were constantly picked on. Louis bribed a German boy working in the canteen, who spoke a little English, to keep himself well fed.

One of Louis's priorities was to maintain a high standard of hygiene. He mocked the Russian prisoners for refusing to take their clothes off and have a proper wash by the pump. 'They would only gargle and spit, but were not too concerned about their outer cleanliness,' he noted. Furious arguments took place between the two nations about whether a window in their crowded dormitories should be open or closed at night. It descended into farce with a Russian closing it, a Brit opening it, and so on, like a Punch and Judy show. In the end Louis took the window off its hinges to settle the argument. The Russians were a bizarre sight, many of them with long beards and ancient, ill-fitting uniforms. Unkempt, surly and seemingly uncaring about the outcome of the war, they were a lethargic lot who tried to keep to themselves. However, for the first few weeks prisoners of different nationalities were allocated sleeping huts, which only added to the tension.

Louis found that the camp had become a tourist show. The local German residents, whose houses overlooked the old factory, took advantage of their prime view. 'They evidently give "Prison teas" in the afternoon as there are crowds of people at the windows with opera glasses regarding the wonderful collection of prisoners taken by the noble German Army. Truth to tell, it consists, as far as I can see, of many half-witted Russians, French territorials, wounded Englishmen and some priests and doctors.'[3]

Terrier-like in his persistence, Louis never stopped fighting for his right, as a doctor, to be exchanged. He quickly discovered he was negotiating with an insane bureaucracy. It reached a farcical stage when he was informed he was officially *not* a prisoner of war, but only being held for his own safety because the local inhabitants were so hostile to the 'Englanders'. A few days later his status was changed; he *was* a prisoner of war after all, he was told. To clarify matters absolutely, a notice in the camp declared that doctors were prisoners of war, while another notice, next to the first one, made it abundantly clear that doctors were *not* prisoners of war. Louis was driven almost mad by the possibility of negotiating his exchange on any logical or legal basis. All he could do to prevent himself falling into utter despair was to hope that someone in the German High Command would see that an exchange of doctors would also help their country.

As a major – his given rank when he transferred to the Marines – Louis was paid fifty marks a month, which was increased to a hundred marks when it was decided he was not a prisoner of war, but merely a guest of the Kaiser. Such pay and privileges were meaningless as the extra money never came through, and anyway German currency became worthless after the prison introduced its own camp currency. Ordinary soldiers and sailors were paid thirty marks a month, but then meanly charged a mark a day for their food. This did not, however, halt the frequent searches of prisoners, with their clothes and mattresses being shaken to find foreign currency to bolster the Kaiser's war kitty. Louis was particularly proud of successfully hiding five sovereigns behind the badges on his cap and arms for the entire duration of his captivity.

The tedium was mainly alleviated by petty confrontations with the guards. In February, Louis had a lucky escape when one bone-headed German sentry threatened to kill him with a fixed bayonet. 'I reported him and was told 1) I had left a gate open. This I denied. 2) If I had shut the gate I had done so violently. This I disproved. 3) I had laughed at one of the sentries. I gave up protesting after that. The man went to the front shortly afterwards. I hope he died quickly.' It was a long, depressing internment for a man who was naturally hyperactive. He found chess with the Russians frustrating because they wanted games to go on for days and he was too impatient. The local newspapers were not much better as a diversion. They pumped out a constant diet of black propaganda, which made assessing the war difficult. At times, the reporting was so outrageously twisted that it became farcical.

One article asked whether it was insulting to dogs to refer to the enemy as English dogs. Another suggested that the phrase 'May God Punish England' was the normal daily greeting in many parts of Germany. One coal merchant had even had the catch-phrase stamped on his briquettes.

The Germans were always trying to take advantage of any prisoner who was well connected. One ludicrous ploy by the German authorities was a telegram sent from Berlin asking for any Englishman who had influence in his own country to give his name. No one deigned to reply. It was enquiries such as this that made it unwise for Louis to write to Albert from Germany. It would have drawn too much attention. He had read insulting articles in the local papers about the British royal family and told few people of his friendship with the Prince. Also, at this stage Louis was still more famous for having been captain of the Scottish rugby team than for any royal connections.

But his mind often turned to the progress of Albert aboard the *Collingwood*. The Prince's war had been far less eventful. In late June 1914, Albert had been on board his ship when the assassination of Archduke Ferdinand lit the fuse that started the war. But as far as the royal family was concerned this was simply another blow against reigning dynasties, rather than as an event of real political significance. Albert did not even consider it worth mentioning in his diary. 'After lunch at 2.30, 50 girls arrived from the Rodine [sic] School,' he wrote. 'We showed them around the ship and danced before tea.'[4] Shortly afterwards Albert left with the battle squadron for Scapa Flow in the Orkney Islands off the extreme northern tip of Scotland. The role of the *Collingwood* was to guard the northern entry to the North Sea. But because the German High Fleet was stationed five hundred miles to the south on the Baltic and North Sea coast of Germany, Albert saw almost no fighting. Three weeks after war was declared he was likely to see even less action after suffering violent stomach pains. It was the start of a serious illness that would scupper most of his war service. While Louis was trying to talk his way out of Germany, Albert was either in bed or trying to persuade the naval authorities that he was fit enough to fight. Louis knew nothing of his troubles as he had almost no opportunity of getting in touch. But he often wondered how his young friend was coping.

Escape also crossed his mind, but he felt that his best bet was still to try to be exchanged, particularly after a French doctor, Second Lieutenant Hubert de Larmandie, had managed to negotiate his freedom. In March 1915, de Larmandie wrote to Louis's sister, Anna, from Paris, following his release, to suggest a plan to outwit the German authorities, who were still preventing British prisoners from receiving food parcels.

His [Louis's] health and spirits are excellent and tho' life there is not exactly joyous, one succeeds in conquering the monotony of the long daytime. Louis indulges in sport as much as he can, that is to say, his Muller exercises, which keep him fit. He plays cards, reads, etc. When I left him the English were not allowed any longer to receive parcels of tuck, so he and I made this arrangement. When you have a parcel kindly address it to Madame Marion in Le Havre and my grandmother will send it to the address of a French comrade who is still in Halle. Since January 1st he was forbidden to smoke, under pain of imprisonment. We have undergone bodily searches executed by the Civil Police in order to take from us our money and our letters, but one develops a strange ingenuity, when one has had six months of prison life and the Germans have found nothing.

Louis was greatly cheered by letters from his family. On Boxing Day, 1914, his mother sent him a card addressed in a shaky hand, simply to Staff Surgeon Greig, Prisoners' Camp at Halle, Germany. It brought only sketchy news of his brothers and sisters, but any card from home was hugely uplifting. 'We hope you are well, and we often think and speak of you, and wonder how you are getting on. It must be difficult for you to think it is Christmas at all in your present surroundings. A [Anna] and I dined at Capelrig [with her eldest son Robert].

J [her son-in-law John] and C [Connie] are at Hemsby for
Xmas. They hope to see Arthur when there. K [Kenneth] still
in Singapore when we last heard. All good wishes from everybody here. Your loving Mother.'

It was the last time he would ever hear from his mother. She
had grown weaker in recent months and old age was taking its
toll. The strain of having a son behind enemy lines only made
matters worse. She died while he was still a prisoner in her
house in Lynedoch Crescent surrounded by family. When he
heard the news, it made him even more angry with the
Germans for holding him illegally and so preventing him
from saying his final farewell to his mother. He stepped up
his efforts to get out of Halle. He sent more letters in French
and English to the Camp Commandant to be passed on to
Berlin. After writing to Robert, who had broken the news of
his mother's death, he replied to a letter of condolence from his
sister-in-law Meg on a scrappy sheet of quadrille paper. 'I can
say nothing of our great loss. To me she was simply "The
Woman" although I always pulled her leg & I can hardly face
up to getting home without her there.' The letter was read, like
all correspondence by the Germans and marked with a purple
censor's mark: *Geprüft* (approved).

While Louis was at Halle, Robert still worked in Scotland,
being too old to enlist. His younger brother Arthur had joined
the Gordon Highlanders and Kenneth was in the Navy aboard
a ship in Singapore. Louis thought a great deal about his family
and also about Phyllis, exchanging as many affectionate letters
as he could in these difficult circumstances.

Louis's letters home were upbeat, but could not give
much detail of his prison conditions owing to strict censorship.
He asked for copies of the *Spectator* and food, but often the
jam or chocolate was confiscated by his captors. 'No parcels
except one from a blessed unknown donor from McVitie have
turned up,' he wrote to his sister Anna on 3 January. He
received little real news of the war's progress, only snippets
from the local papers, for instance that Italy had declared

war on Austria and that the *Lusitania* had been sunk. 'The German newspapers said that while seeing the necessity, she and other cultured nations regretted it.' The news was seldom good. 'On May 26th we heard of the sinking of the *Majestic* and *Triumph* by a German submarine – seriously alarming if true.'

A better diversion than the news outside were various escape attempts. Louis was fascinated by the whole idea.

Another hole in the roof of a sleeping chamber was discovered and an attempt to escape had certainly been *en train*. Much fuss and interrogation. A Belgian was discovered to be in possession of an old German overcoat which had been issued to us during disinfection. He had used this to close a hole in his palliasse (bed). This seemed blasphemy to the German mind, that the imperial uniform should be so misused & a bit of Teutonic eloquence from the commandant was the result, at the end of which, the Belgian said: 'Je ne comprends pas.' 'What!' said the major, 'You have been eight months in this country & not learned German. You must learn it, especially as you are now part of Germany.' *Nous verrons*.

Louis never gave up hope of being exchanged, and bombarded the German authorities with letters, always arguing that he was being held illegally. His persistence paid off more than eight months after his arrest. In June 1915, he was transferred to a camp at Augusbad, in Mecklenburg-Strelitz, near Berlin, where they buttered him up for a few days with sweetmeats and sweet talk before allowing him to return to Britain in exchange for a German doctor.

Augusbad had a far more relaxed regime:

The commandant was very nice and civil but very German. He ended up by saying that I must write to the papers when I got home, saying how well the prisoners were treated in Germany. I said that 8 days in Augusbad was not equal to eight and a half months of Halle. He asked me if I thought it would take long for the ill feeling between Germany and Britain to subside. I answered

that it would last his lifetime and mine and if I had any children it
would last theirs, too.

Louis was then escorted to Berlin where he got into a fero-
cious argument with German soldiers who blamed Britain for
starting the war. They showed him bullets which held what
they claimed were 'dum-dums' that caused unnecessarily
horrible injuries. Louis laughed and bet them a hundred marks
that they were, in fact, the victims of their own country's
propaganda, and were holding an ordinary bullet. As they
angrily denounced his remarks and barked at him for his
country's barbaric aggression, his train departed and he was
on his way to freedom. He was sent in a third-class apartment
with 'damned uncomfortable wooden seats', together with
some other doctors also being exchanged. They were taken via
Cologne and Aix-la-Chapelle to Brussels, where they stayed
for a few days in a crowded hospital dormitory. They were
asked if they had enjoyed their stay in Germany. Louis bit his
tongue, thinking that this was not the time to cause offence.
Under armed guard they were taken to Antwerp before their
final leap to freedom at a Dutch station called Rosendal, where
they were given 'a glorious reception with cigarettes and a
most welcome cup of tea'. They were finally delivered home
on 2 July by boat to Tilbury Docks, where tugs came out to
greet their vessel, horns honking and with bunting displayed
all along the wharf.

Louis's ordeal brought home how much he cared about his
family, whom he had missed terribly. The death of his mother
while he was away reinforced this more than anything. Letters
from his family had been a lifeline during the long months in
prison. He was now also certain that he wanted to have his
own family, and that Phyllis was the woman for him. At
the age of thirty-four, he was ready to settle down and restart
his life. Louis dropped a line to Prince Albert to let him
know that he was back in one piece. He wanted to know how

his young friend was prospering. But there was little time to spare. He had just twelve days' leave, two of which were spent travelling to and from Scotland to see his family. But all these plans were then altered when Louis was suddenly summoned to Buckingham Palace for an audience with the King.

Chapter Six

'It's so nice having a real friend as a messmate and
he is very cheery.'
                    Prince Albert writing to Queen Mary
                                    about Louis Greig

On 5 July 1915, the Court Circular in *The Times* announced that King George V had just two official
visitors at Buckingham Palace. The first was Field
Marshal the Earl Kitchener of Khartoum, the Secretary of State
for War, and the other was Staff Surgeon L. L. Greig, RN. The
King had been anxiously awaiting news of the Scottish
surgeon ever since his capture in October.

Louis was greatly excited to be free after almost nine months
behind barbed wire on a diet of pork fat and black bread. It was
somewhat surreal to be walking across the gravel courtyard at
Buckingham Palace to the Privy Purse door to call on the King.
Protocol and formality at the palace had obviously not diminished with the outbreak of war as he was escorted up the
red-carpeted stairs, past impeccably turned-out footmen in
their brass-buttoned red tail-coats, to see the monarch.

Louis gave a colourful account of his experience as a prisoner of war, but was also keen to use his private audience to
recount the hardship and courage of the British servicemen
still held captive. The fate of prisoners of war was a growing
concern for every nation caught up in the conflict; by the end
of the war hundreds of thousands of soldiers would have been
taken prisoner. Some were tortured, others shot; some died of

disease; most suffered deprivation of food, clothing and shelter. Even at this early stage in the war, Louis felt he had a duty to speak up on behalf of those who remained in captivity.

After they had talked of his time in Halle, and discussed the general course of the war, the King steered the conversation round to Prince Albert, whose health had deteriorated to an alarming extent while Louis had been away. George V had asked to see Louis because he remembered his impressive care of Albert during the influenza epidemic. When Britain had declared war against Germany at 11 p.m. on the night of 4 August, 1914 (midnight German time), King George had written in his private journal of his fears for the safety of his eighteen-year-old son. 'Please God that it will soon be over & that he will protect dear Bertie's life.' He could not have fore-seen that the greatest threat to Albert's wellbeing would turn out not to be the 'Hun' but his health. The King recounted his son's catalogue of gastric ailments, which had virtually left Albert a war invalid. He wanted Louis's advice and guidance.

Albert had tried to lead a normal life as a midshipman on the *Collingwood*, rather than being singled out for special privileges as the King's son. When George V came on board for an inspection, Albert passed him 'with the click of heels and salute that everyone in the line had given. No word was spoken.'[1] But no matter how hard he tried to fit in and prosper, his naval career was severely stalled by his incapacitating stomach pains. He lost several pounds and was confined to bed. Depression and anxiety attacks caused his self-confidence to plummet.

The first symptoms had occurred on 23 August 1914, which Albert noted in his diary. 'After lunch I kept the afternoon watch, I then went to the sick bay with a violent pain in the stomach and I could hardly breathe. They put hot foment-ations on it, which eased it . . . Morphia was injected into my arm. I was put to bed in the Commander's cabin at 8.0 and I slept the whole night.'[2] Vomiting, diarrhoea and violent pains left him debilitated, listless and feeling very sorry for himself.

It was far more than a physical complaint; his entire psychological wellbeing was affected. Albert realised that his naval career was in jeopardy.[3]

Diagnosed with appendicitis, he was transferred to the hospital ship *Rohilla* at Wick. After being seen, at the insistence of the King, by Sir James Reid, the eminent physician who had been Queen Victoria's favourite doctor, it was decided that he should be taken ashore as soon as possible. However, his evacuation was disrupted when the *Rohilla* was recalled to the fleet at Scapa Flow to move other sick sailors. There was a heightened sense of anticipation as intelligence reports suggested that the German High Seas Fleet was about to launch an attack on the British fleet. The Navy wanted as many of its infirm moved to safety as quickly as possible. Albert stayed on board until 29 August, when he was swung by crane with forty-five other patients in cots onto tugs, and from there to the quay at Aberdeen, where he was driven to the Northern Nursing Home. While he was in hospital, the British fleet achieved its first formal naval victory, sinking three German cruisers and two destroyers in the Battle of Heligoland Bight – Albert felt deeply despondent to have missed his first chance to participate in the war.

Naturally he hoped that an operation on his appendix would end his troubles. 'I am afraid you must have been rather frightened when you heard I was ill. I am much better now and feel quite happy,' he wrote to his father. 'Sir James Reid arrived yesterday and examined me. The pain had practically gone away, although it hurt a good deal last Sunday.'[4] While he was convalescing for a month in Aberdeen, Louis had been in Belgium with the Marines preparing for the siege of Antwerp, and was completely unaware of Albert's problems. If appendicitis had been the only complaint, his illness would have been just a minor inconvenience. But his health problems were far more serious and this was just the start of three years of almost constant sick leave.

Albert's situation was made worse by comparisons with his

more glamorous elder brother, the much-fêted Prince of
Wales. In November 1914, while Albert was convalescing at
Sandringham, Prince Edward was attached to the staff of Field
Marshal Sir John French, the commander-in-chief of the British
Expeditionary Force in France. The elder brother had joined
the 1st Battalion Grenadier Guards and been detailed to the
King's Company; five feet seven inches tall, he self-mockingly
described himself as a 'pygmy among giants'. Although
Edward was never in the trenches, he was at least in the battle
zone. He was prevented from taking on an active role at the
front by Lord Kitchener, who told him: 'If I were sure you
would be killed, I do not know if I should be right to restrain
you. But I cannot take the chance of them ever taking you
prisoner, which always exists, until we have settled a line.'[5]

Albert felt humiliated to be lying around at home while
almost all his contemporaries were at war, but there remained
little choice. To his dismay, his sickness and pain did not
improve. The only gunshots he fired at this time were at a
rutting stag that went berserk on the estate at Sandringham,
attacking his sister Princess Mary and the keeper, Bland, when
they were out riding. The future looked dismal as Sir Frederick
Treves, the King's Surgeon, told the King that Albert should
never go back to sea, and extended his period of compulsory
convalescence. When Albert objected, it was agreed that he
could rejoin his ship, but only after serving ashore for several
weeks. And so, in November 1914, Albert joined the War Staff
at the Admiralty in London. 'It is a good thing as now nobody
will be able to say I am doing nothing,' he wrote to his
mother on 29 November 1914.[6] Winston Churchill showed
him around the Admiralty's War Room, and gave him the task
of charting the movements of ships from both sides. But it
was not enough to keep a restless nineteen-year-old content.
'Nothing to do as usual' is a typical entry in his diary.[7]

It was to be more than six months following his emergency
removal from the *Collingwood* on a stretcher before Albert

returned to his ship on 12 February 1915. But even then, his good health was short-lived; in May the sickness returned, and Albert was out of action once more. 'I have been very fit on the whole since I returned to here, but just lately the infernal indigestion has come on again,' he wrote.[8] The authorities became increasingly concerned, and the Fleet Surgeon called in Sir Watson Cheyne, a professor of clinical surgery at King's College, London, for a second opinion. Albert's health faltered again, and by July, when the King saw Louis in Buckingham Palace, it was becoming a crisis for the royal family. Two days after their meeting at Buckingham Palace – and after consulting other doctors – the King reluctantly gave orders, while on a visit to the Grand Fleet at Scapa Flow on 7 and 9 July 1915, that Albert should again be moved to a hospital ship for further observation. It was the second time that he was forced to leave the *Collingwood* for a hospital ship – the *Drina*, this time – and it was very disheartening.

It is difficult to overestimate Albert's sense of failure. He dreaded being sent home and finding himself in civilian clothes while his contemporaries risked their lives. Men not in the services were often deemed cowards, and white feathers were sent to them through the post. His fears can be understood from a letter that his brother, the Prince of Wales, wrote to the Queen on 6 December 1918, arguing that Albert should stay as long as possible in France after the Armistice: 'Bertie can be of far more use in this way than sitting in England where he has spent most of the war, not that this was his fault!! But by remaining with the armies till peace is signed he will entirely erase any of the very unfair questions some nasty people asked last year as to what he was doing, you will remember.'[9]

Louis was unable to see Albert after his talk with the King at Buckingham Palace because he had been immediately assigned to HMS *Attentive*, the parent ship of the 6th Flotilla of destroyers. Straight back into the firing line, he took part in a number of raids up and down the Belgian coast. He also made several excursions to the front with the Marines, visiting Nieuport, Ypres and the British lines near Dixmude. Part of his mission was to organise medical facilities for the Royal Marine Artillery Howitzer Brigade. 'I continue to visit the gun positions twice a week to see any sick,' he recorded. It was exactly the sort of excitement and action that Albert wanted. Louis survived a German raid on the *Attentive* in early September when 'a bomb exploded on contact, pierced the upper deck and landed in the dispensary on the next deck where the medical stores of the Flotilla are kept. The bomb had the character of a shrapnel shell. It is about the size of a golf ball and has holes punched in it to give it an expanding effect'. Louis was uninjured, but two men were wounded and died shortly afterwards.

Albert was not well served by the senior doctors from the palace or the Navy, who procrastinated about what action to take to solve his health problems. In the *Rohilla*, they came to the inconclusive, unhelpful prognosis that Albert had a 'weakening of the muscular wall of the stomach and a consequent catarrhal condition'[10] for which rest, a more sensible diet and nightly enemas were prescribed. Albert was in despair as nothing seemed to improve very much; he desperately wanted to be fit and fighting. While convalescing, he made Captain James Ley, the captain of the *Collingwood*, promise not to leave for battle without him. But despite gaining such assurances, the Prince's future did not look good as he suffered yet another relapse. The royal family was by now extremely sensitive to his semi-invalid status while so many thousands of men his age were losing their lives in battle. Albert's psychological wellbeing was not helped by his family's belief that he was somehow failing by not taking part in the fighting.

Lord Stamfordham sent a robust letter of Roman sentiment to Captain Ley, indicating that Albert must be allowed to risk his health and, if necessary, his life, rather than miss an opportunity to take part in a sea battle: 'From what you report, HRH has evidently improved considerably; there is no reason to expect any early naval engagement, but even were the unexpected to happen and the Fleet were ordered to sea the day after you receive this letter, the King would prefer to run the risk of the Prince's health suffering than that he should endure the bitter and lasting disappointment of not being in his ship in the battle line.'[11]

It is difficult to see in whose interest such an order was made. To force a sick cadet to sea would have been merely a hindrance to the rest of the crew and a mere illusion of any real contribution to the war effort by Albert.

Confrontation with the German fleet was delayed, but Albert's sickness persisted. By October 1915 – more than eleven months after he had first fallen ill – he was still unfit and without a proper diagnosis. The frustrating thing was that some days he felt fine, only to feel ill without warning a few days later. He suffered another relapse after his father was injured falling under his horse while inspecting troops in Hesdigneul. Nervous tension evidently aggravated Albert's condition. He was forced to take yet another three months' sick leave, during which time he was again attached to the Admiralty for 'light duties'. Albert's prospects only seemed to get worse. 'They don't think I shall be able to go to sea again till April,' he wrote despondently to Bryan Godfrey-Faussett, one of his father's oldest friends and longest-serving courtiers. 'What an awful thought, another 3 months to come before that. I am longing and have been longing for centuries to get back to my ship.'[12] Albert undertook a few untaxing royal engagements in March 1916, including opening the House of Commons rifle range, fearing it was as close as he would ever get to firing a weapon during the war. Louis wrote from Belgium, trying to raise his spirits. It was evident from Albert's reply that he was doing extremely little except resting, and that he was bored and dispirited. 'I am still leading the quiet life with a Serbian Prince thrown in last week. Pretty stiff with him, as he can't talk English.'[13]

To cheer him up, Louis sent over a piece of Zeppelin, a large dirigible airship, as a war souvenir, but knowing Louis's puckish sense of humour too well Albert suddenly panicked, fearing that it might be a fake. 'Please don't tell me it's all a joke as I have given it to the King for his room of war relics at Windsor,' he wrote.

Albert confided in his former doctor his fears concerning his never-ending health problems, confident that Louis was someone he could turn to. He had few friends of his own age, but instead wrote to old buffers like Bryan Godfrey-Faussett, in attendance on his father at York Cottage. Louis was the nearest thing he had to a best friend. It often seemed that Albert was looking for someone to be able to commit to, to trust and to lean on, and that he sought, in effect, a comforting father figure, just as his choice of women, as Sarah Bradford, his biographer, perceptively pointed out, usually favoured mother substitutes. At times, his letters to Louis during his convalescence were self-pitying and hinted at despair about the medical advice he was receiving. 'Percy [a friend] has not been passed as fit, and I don't expect he will go back for some time yet, as he was sent down to Plymouth for examination, and he has got into the hands of Rolleston [Consultant Physician to the Navy who became a royal doctor in 1923] a man who examined me and I did not think he knew the least what was wrong with me. So very likely it will be the same with him.'[14]

Albert often repeated to Louis his desire to get back to sea. 'Bertrand Dawson [the senior palace doctor] returns here this week so I hope to get back at the end of the month worse luck,' he wrote.[15]

Meanwhile, as Albert's career was sinking fast, Louis's life took a positive turn when he asked Phyllis to marry him shortly after his return from Germany. He had first met his bride in London at a party hosted by the Duguid family, friends from Glasgow, one of whom had married a Scrimgeour. The Greigs had been taken up by the more cosmopolitan Scrimgeours, who regularly invited them to their grand and elegant house in Park Lane. 'The Scrimgeours rather polished up the hearty Greigs; they took to them in a big way. They liked their humour and their energy,' remembered Nancy Maclay, Louis's niece.* Louis was thirty-five years old and wanted to get on with starting a family of his own. Their love, loyalty and affection for each other combined with a shared unswerving optimism to provide the basis for a long and happy marriage. Phyllis knew she had found her perfect soul mate when she touchingly wrote to her fiancé: 'It was rotten having to leave Swan Bister [summer house in Orkney]. I did enjoy myself, unjustifiably sometimes! Anyway Louis, you are the only man with whom I can be absolutely natural & friendly & I can't help feeling raised several pegs in my own estimation by the fact that you think me worthwhile caring for.'

They married on Wednesday, 16 February 1916, at St Mary's Church, Hemsby, Norfolk, with a reception afterwards at the home of the bride's parents. The best man was Louis's brother, Arthur, dressed in the uniform of a second lieutenant in the 3rd Battalion Gordon Highlanders. The bride's sister, Elsie Scrimgeour, and her niece, Esther Scrimgeour, were bridesmaids. Another niece, Pamela Scrimgeour, was train-bearer. Phyllis wore a white faille trimmed with lace and silver tissue, a court train of silver brocaded tissue fastened at the shoulders with orange blossom and an old lace veil (which had been worn by her mother at her wedding) with a wreath of orange blossom.

Prince Albert was unable to attend but read about it in the newspapers from his sickbed. He missed a glorious country wedding. The bride carried a bouquet of white lilacs, which was a gift from the bridegroom. The bridesmaids wore pale grey taffeta trimmed with white lace and mauve sashes with hats to match. The train-bearer was in a white muslin frock

---

* Born in 1908, the daughter of Louis's brother Robert Greig, she married Lord Maclay.

with mauve ribbons and a cap of Dutch lace, and she carried a basket of lilies of the valley. After the service eighty guests returned to Hemsby Hall, where Louis gave Phyllis a platinum pendant set with diamonds and pearls and the bridesmaids received naval cross brooches set with pearls, rubies and sapphires. The local paper's incredulous reporter noted that 134 presents were given which were 'very valuable'. The new Mrs Greig was described in the wedding report as 'an expert motorist, golfer and skier who once spent a whole winter in Lapland in Lapp costume. She had been a scoutmaster.'

Early in Louis's courtship, Albert had been introduced to Phyllis, and he was delighted for his friend, writing to congratulate him on his marriage on 28 February 1916 from his sickbed in Buckingham Palace. 'I saw it in the illustrated papers yesterday. How are you and how is life with you? With me it is pretty mouldy as I have been on sick leave for a very long time ever since July. I am nearly all right now and hope to return to the Fleet in April. If you are in London do come and look me up here one evening, as I should love to see you.'

At this stage Albert was making the running in the friendship. Bored, lonely and in need of companionship, he turned to Louis. He inscribed a flamboyant capital A in black ink on the front left corner of the envelope to signal the personal content of his letter. It was addressed to Hemsby Hall, forwarded to HMS *Attentive* and then on to Brown's Hotel in Dover Street, London, reflecting the lack of settlement in the first days of the Greigs' marriage. Albert was anxious to send a wedding present, and on 9 March 1916, Henry Hansell, his erstwhile tutor, wrote on Albert's behalf to arrange this. 'Prince Albert has been trying hard to get hold of you today! Mallowes, the Steward of the Bath Club, has just telephoned your movements. The Prince of Wales and Prince Albert have directed me to carry out a scheme for a little wedding present. Will you please telegraph to me the date of your marriage? and also will you let me know where to send it on Monday? I shall also send you a wee affair on my own account. In frantic haste.'[16] A silver cigarette case, with Albert's signature and the wedding date engraved on the lid, duly arrived.

In May 1916 Albert was finally allowed back on board *Collingwood* after making yet another emotional appeal to his doctors. He was almost demented with boredom. It would soon be two years since his health had started to fail him. 'What I find the awful part is that one never sees a female of any sort, which is just part of one's life here, so now one gets mouldy and fed up with everybody. Both my younger brothers are home now, which livens things up a bit, though they become a nuisance at times.'[17] Three weeks later, Albert was back in the sick bay, with the usual symptoms, only this time they were triggered by him eating too many 'soused mackerel'. When what he referred to as the 'Great Day' came, the chance to experience battle, Albert, seemingly miraculously, was able to put his illness behind him and leapt into action.

On Wednesday, 31 May 1916, the *Collingwood* was ordered to take up battle stations against the German fleet, and by 5.37 p.m., according to Albert's diary, they opened fire on some light cruisers. It was the start of the Battle of Jutland. One cruiser was sunk after two salvos, and then a second one went down. Another battle cruiser was hit when it emerged into sight through mist and smoke. As darkness descended, the sea fell quiet and the crew went to Night Defence Stations. Albert felt elated that finally he could say that he had taken part in the war.

His friend Lieutenant Tait described Albert's amazing (albeit temporary) recovery in a letter to the Prince of Wales: 'Huge excitement, Out at Last. Full speed ahead. Sound of "Action" – you can imagine the scene! Out of his bunk leaps Johnson [Albert's *nom de guerre*]. Ill? Never felt better! Strong enough to go to his turret and fight a prolonged action? Of course he was, why ever not?'[18]

For the first time the Prince of Wales was even a little envious of his brother. 'I'm glad old Bertie was in the fight, as

it will buck him up,' he wrote to Godfrey-Faussett, thanking
him for sending him a copy of Albert's Jutland letter. 'It seems
to have cured him of the slight return of his old complaint
which was a d——d bore as I really hoped he was cured once
and for all!!'[19]

Albert sent Louis a gung-ho description of what it felt like
to be engaged in a sea battle: 'I was back here a month just
before the Jutland show and we were properly in it, though we
were not hit or damaged. We fairly strafed the Bosche ships
and flames etc leaped up off them after each of our salvos got
home. It was a fine night and I thoroughly enjoyed every
moment of it. I don't know why, but one feels quite different
in a show like that and doesn't care a damn about what
happens as long as one sees one's shells hitting the enemy.'[20]

The twenty-year-old was exhilarated and also sent the King
an excited account of his first taste of war. 'My impressions
were very different to what I expected. I saw visions of the
masts going over the side and funnels hurtling through the
air etc. In reality none of these things happened and we are
still quite as sound as before. No one would know to look at
the ship that we had been in action. It was certainly a great experience to have been through and it shows that we are at war
and that the Germans can fight if they like.'[21]

The family were delighted by his exuberance and what
they hoped was a permanent recovery. 'Bertie is very proud
of being in action but is sorry that his ship was not hit
(although he was straddled by several salvoes) as she has
nothing to show she has been in the fight,' wrote the King to
his uncle the Duke of Connaught.[22] His experience at Jutland
reinjected a sense of confidence and purpose into Albert, as
he told Godfrey-Faussett's wife: 'I am quite all right and feel
very different now that I have seen a German ship filled with
Germans and have seen it fired at with our guns. It was a
great experience to have gone through and one not easily
forgotten. How and why we were not hit beats me, as we were
fired at a good part of the time . . . It was a great nuisance

getting ill again but the action put me all right at once.'[23]

Notwithstanding Albert's jubilation at Jutland, the Germans cheekily claimed victory because they had lost fewer ships than the British (eleven of 62,000 tons compared to fourteen of 111,000 tons). But what really counted was that they had retreated while the British Navy still controlled the seas. It was a potentially decisive moment in the war. The Kaiser had always hoped for a battle to break the British naval blockade on the German North Sea ports; the British had always hoped to destroy the German fleet, leaving only the submarines as their naval adversary.

While the battle was a great boost to morale at home, there were some fearful statistics to digest. The British lost more than 6,000 sailors; 1,017 on the *Indefatigable*, 1,266 on the *Queen Mary* and more than 2,000 on the *Invincible*. The German losses were 2,551. In a moment of bravado, the Kaiser declared that 'the spell of Trafalgar is over'. It was a hollow claim, however, as the German Navy did not venture out again for the rest of the war. But it was equally frustrating for the British naval commanders not to have destroyed the German fleet, and Admiral Jellicoe recognised this and told Beatty: 'I missed one of the greatest opportunities a man ever had.'

Three days after the battle, any celebrations were crushed by the death of Lord Kitchener when his cruiser *Hampshire* struck a mine and, in fifteen minutes, sank to the bottom of the sea, taking down the entire ship's company of eight hundred officers and men. Just a few hours before it sank, the *Hampshire* had passed by the ships of the fleet, the *Collingwood* – with Albert on board – among them, and the men had been able to see the tall, grey figure on the bridge of his ship in field uniform, his greatcoat buttoned around him. 'His loss to the Nation is so very great & we could ill spare him now, but this will make us redouble our efforts to win the war,' wrote the King to Albert.[24]

Albert's elation after his first taste of war was soon deflated. By August 1916 he was ill yet again. It was back to the same depressing procession of doctors – Sir Frederick Treves, Bertrand Dawson and Dr Stanley Hewett. They were now all of the opinion that a duodenal ulcer was causing the problem, but no one would recommend an operation. It was considered too risky, and so while they wavered Albert's career and health remained in limbo.

Not until May 1917 was Albert allowed to report back for sea duties. The King had agreed to transfer him to HMS *Malaya* as an acting lieutenant on the 27,500-ton battleship. The King again wanted Louis close to his son, and just a month later he was ordered to join the ship as the second surgeon. Albert was delighted. 'It's so nice having a real friend as a messmate and he is very cheery,' he wrote to the Queen.[25]

The two friends were able to spend time together as, more and more, Albert relied on Louis for emotional as well as medical support. His illness had taken a heavy toll on his life and the knock-on effect was to exacerbate his stammer, dent his confidence and make him doubt his ability and worth. Cut off from his naval contemporaries, he found he had remarkably few friends. As a royal prince it was never easy for him to make friends as there was a suspicion that some people were more interested in his royal status than his personality. Albert was highly strung and easily dejected by criticism, including his own. It was not easy for him to see his war record so far as anything but a failure. He was acutely aware of his inability to live up to his father's expectations. Louis was a calming influence whose opinion mattered to Albert, as well as to his father. He was a useful bridge between father and son.

On board the *Malaya*, Louis took over care of his health, recording in his diary on 16 June that he was tending 'PA's pain. Gave him NaSO4'. The stomach cramps and nausea came in waves. For several days he would be unable to move and would then feel a great deal better. When he felt all right he and Louis went ashore in Orkney. They spent some time at Scapa Flow, and on fine days they visited Swan Bister, the

Greigs' holiday home, for afternoons of tennis and swimming. Albert even felt well enough to order a suit from the local tailor. The Orkneys were a place of particularly fond memories for Louis. He had spent his childhood summers there learning to fish and shoot; he had wooed Phyllis and their friendship had turned into romance. Swan Bister was a modest farmhouse overlooking rough hill pastures dotted with sheep. It was a place at the very tip of the British Isles where time seemed to stand still, where the hustle and bustle of a noisy mess-room aboard a clanking coal-fuelled ship seemed light-years away. It was the perfect place for quiet recuperation.

The King made a visit to the fleet, and Louis was summoned to give him an update on Albert's condition. His medical and personal care of the Prince was by now considered essential, and it did not go unappreciated. On Sunday, 24 June, when the King boarded the *Malaya*, Louis gratefully recorded: 'He was good enough to tell me how glad he was I was here.' Louis may not have realised it, but he was slowly being swept into the heart of the royal family. The King insisted that he spend time with him and his son, and on Wednesday 27 June Louis had both lunch and dinner with the King. It was an extraordinary singling out of a junior surgeon, but as far as the King was concerned Albert's health had become a matter of urgency and he needed Louis to play a central role in helping to solve his son's deepening crisis. Moreover, he enjoyed Louis's company; he was never short of conversation, expounding robust views and regaling him with colourful tales of his time in Germany.

Just two months after joining the *Malaya*, Albert yet again suffered a relapse and had to be transferred to South Queensferry Hospital. 'Personally I feel I am not fit for service at sea, even when I recover from this little attack,' he wrote to his father in despair.[26] By now Louis was in permanent attendance. It was more than three years since Albert's problems had started, but the palace doctors were the more senior medical advisers, and they were calling the shots. 'I am too distressed to hear that you are again suffering from yr old trouble, it is really too [un] lucky and just when you were so fit and we hoped that it had been cured,' his father replied on 6 August 1917. 'I have heard . . . you are comfortable, are being well looked after & that Greig is with you.'[27]

It was clear to courtiers such as Clive Wigram, the King's assistant private secretary, who was one of Louis's closest friends, that Dr Greig was crucial to the Prince's wellbeing. 'Louis was able to give him a sense of perspective, as well as practical medical advice. He was one of the few people in whom Albert felt able to confide; to no one else could he tell the full details of his problem. The other advantage was that he had known him well at every stage of his life in the Navy.'[28]

After eight years' training or serving in the Navy, Albert would only be able to record twenty-two months spent at sea, and six of those were on a leisurely training voyage island-hopping in the West Indies. He felt he had let himself down as well as his father, who had such high hopes for his naval career. On 10 August Albert informed his father he was abandoning ship to return home with Louis and, also, Tait:

> I spent two nights at the Caledonian Hotel [in Edinburgh] with Greig. It has been practically decided that I am to leave here on Sunday night, arriving in London on Monday morning. Both Tait and Greig are coming down as well. I am making an appointment with Hewitt to come and see me at 10am. Dr Rolleston is sending a full report of my case to him tonight . . . I may tell you that Captain Boyle, Dr Rolleston and Greig are all three of the opinion that I cannot stand the sea life, at any rate for some time to come. May I bring both Greig and Tait down to Windsor with me so that we can talk over matters as they are? Captain Boyle thinks this is a good thing to do, and has given them leave. Personally I feel that I am not fit for service at sea, even when I recover from this little attack.[29]

Three days later, on Monday 13 August 1917, Louis and Albert arrived in London by the night sleeper at 7.30 a.m., and went straight to Buckingham Palace, where Louis briefed Hewitt, Rolleston and Cheyne over breakfast. In the afternoon, Albert rested and Louis slipped away for lunch with his sister Anna, and also to see Phyllis, before returning at teatime to Buckingham Palace to escort Albert to Windsor by train. 'Dined at Windsor with TM [Their Majesties],' he wrote in his diary.

Louis was by now a constant go-between for the King and his son and the other medical advisers. He was one of the only people who had the confidence of all parties. Louis was in favour of one course of action: an operation to remove the ulcer. It would be swift and the impact would be dramatic. It was clear to him that this was the only way to clear up Albert's problems for good; the disadvantage was that it carried a risk. But Louis's advice was not the only counsel sought. There was still the string of older palace doctors who were more cautious and nervous of implementing any measures that carried even the slightest risk. Rest rather than risk might as well have been their slogan. It was frustrating for Louis, the can-do surgeon who had been used to making snap decisions about far worse ailments and living with the consequences. As a naval surgeon at war, as well as in his work as a GP in Glasgow, he had amputated arms, cut open abdomens, pulled out teeth and delivered babies. In Belgium and France gaping wounds had to be sewn up. In his view, an ulcer of such severity which had failed to react to rest, needed surgery. It was not that he was more courageous or adventurous than other surgeons. It was simply that his experience as a war surgeon meant that little fazed him. He believed in making a diagnosis and sticking to it, even in the face of powerful opposition from the palace. Louis always argued that supreme confidence in a doctor and swift action was crucial to the patient's recovery. If the patient felt secure, their whole psychology was poised for recovery. Louis was frustrated that Albert was surrounded by so many other medical advisers, though he greatly respected most of them. He did not have the clout to insist on an operation, so he could only have his say and wait. And for a time Albert felt that waiting was the right decision, particularly in August 1917, after he had had a reprieve from his illness for a few days. It was hardly surprising that he agreed with the palace doctors. They had emphasised the risk of any operation. Nevertheless, Albert kept Louis constantly updated, even if he was away for just a few days.

> Well, the operation is not going to take place after all. Treves etc came down today and after a consultation it was now decided not to do it. Rolleston & Watson Cheyne wanted it done, it appears. They thought it risky and serious and the result uncertain as to whether it would be a permanent cure. I have no wish to take any unnecessary risk, and especially as I am feeling so well now. I am remaining here for the present with a special diet, of course, as before and under observation . . . I must thank you for all you did for me while I was on the ship, and I hope we shall be shipmates again some day.[30]

By late August the palace doctors had decided to send Albert on a short break to the country for some more rest. It was further procrastination, with the doctors banking on his temporary recovery taking effect. They were too cautious to make a firm long-term decision. Louis was asked to accompany him to Wales to stay with Sir Harry Verney, Queen Mary's private secretary. Albert was rather excited about his trip with Louis, and by getting away from London and the dreaded doctors. 'I am asking him what forms of exercise there are nearby. I do hope there will be golf, don't you,' he wrote to Louis.[31]

By 5 September, plans for the Welsh break were in place. 'Riding, fishing & tennis are the form of exercise to be had. That ought to suit us well I should think . . . I am not taking any uniform at all. Only a smoking jacket for dinner and any old clothes for the day, I told Verney what we wanted was a wild life and nothing formal about it. He has got a small motor, which is something. I hope these arrangements will suit you.

I think it is better to go as soon as possible don't you? I am getting fed up here.'[32]

Albert was feeling better – temporarily again, as it turned out – and was as excited as a boy scout going to summer camp. 'I am taking lunch for us in the train. What do you want to drink? As you know, I can't get anything like whisky from here,' he confided to Louis,[33] revealing his excitement at spending a few days on their own. All alcohol was still banned by George V from royal households. Their normal naval schedule was put on hold as Louis's medical duties for the King took priority and excused him from returning to the *Malaya*.

Louis had been married for about eighteen months and had recently bought a house at Godstone in Surrey. His absences cannot have been easy for Phyllis, who, at times, felt she was sharing her husband not only with the Navy but also Albert, as the Prince took up more of Louis's time. He was increasingly on call to the royal family, and often having to rush down to Sandringham, Windsor or Buckingham Palace at the last minute. Phyllis had always known that naval wives had to endure long absences from their husbands, but it was even more frustrating to have him in England and not to be able to see as much of him as she would have liked.

In Wales Louis had a long and serious talk with his patient, and a turning point was reached in their approach to his illness. Louis persuaded Albert that an operation on his ulcer was needed to clear up his problem once and for all. They plotted to bring this about by persuading the King that it was the only practicable solution left. Anything was better than the continuing uncertainty and bouts of depression that were wrecking his life. Louis urged Albert to tell his father that he wanted an operation, so that he could stop his Yo-Yoing schedule; one minute well, the next in bed. On 22 September Albert tried to pave the way for a frank exchange with his father by enclosing a letter from Louis forcefully presenting the medical reasons for an operation. Louis's advice was more

difficult to ignore once it was down in black and white. Albert
sent a plaintive covering letter to prepare the ground:

> Since I last wrote I have been leading a quiet life with riding and
> tennis most days. All the same I haven't really been well. I have
> had a certain amount of pain and sickness. After the latter I feel
> perfectly well for about 3 days when it comes on again.
>
> I have had long talks with Greig on this subject and I am
> enclosing a letter from him which I asked him to write. From it you
> will see I cannot lead a normal life without getting pain. My food
> has to be very plain and everything in the minced form. My
> stomach works very well between the attacks and the pains I get
> are due to the food leaving the stomach having to be forced
> through a small hole which is really an obstruction.
>
> I am perfectly convinced in my mind that an operation would
> put me right. I hope you don't mind me writing to you like this,
> but I think you ought to know what my feelings are on the subject.[34]

Albert was at the end of his tether and desperate for any
remedy. At the same time he was nervous of offending his
father by following a course of action with which the latter
disagreed. He felt secure with Louis's kind, practical and
supportive presence, as he intimated in a letter home:

> May Greig sleep at the Palace when I return there next Wednesday
> as then he will be at hand? No doubt you would talk to him some
> time about me. There is really nothing seriously wrong with me,
> but it does depress me so not being able to eat anything especially
> as I feel so fit. Will you please keep all this to yourself, and I hope
> you won't worry about it all. I don't think I can get any better
> without an operation and I should like to get it over and done with.
> I know exactly where the pain is situated and everything shows it
> it [sic] is the best thing for me. Would you please show this and
> Greig's letter to Mama as well. I am afraid this letter is not a very
> cheery one but I wanted to tell you everything about myself. Best
> love to you my dearest papa.
>
> Ever your devoted son Albert.[35]

King George's reply on 24 September was immediate and
sympathetic. He had talked to Dawson, the éminence grise

of the palace medical establishment, who appeared, at last, to have come round to the idea of an operation. His reasons were that the condition was persisting. He conveniently appeared to forget that it had been persisting for almost three years.

> I am sorry that you continue to have a sickness every four days which certainly shows that things are not as they should be. I will have a talk with Greig as soon as you return on Wednesday and then we shall see what is best to be done. Bertrand Dawson made it quite clear to me that if you continued to be sick while leading the quietest of lives with the simplest of food it would show that an operation is probably necessary. I quite understand how depressed the whole thing must make you. I have shown your and Greig's letter to Mama and shall not mention it to anyone else. Of course Greig can have a room at BP when he comes on Wednesday.[36]

But having gone to the edge of the precipice, the palace doctors then retreated, and by 24 October the physicians were again dithering. 'Saw Bertrand Dawson & arranged for 1 weeks trial of all diet,' noted Louis, who was more and more frustrated by the slow pace of the cautious medical grandees. It is important to remember that Louis was really a very junior surgeon, and had to bow to their senior rank. 'My darling Phee,' he wrote to Phyllis, 'Dawson wishes me to remain a week at least to see how the result of the full diet works.'[37] Louis privately predicted to Phyllis that the diet would not work, and he was right.

While his son was suffering, the King, of course, had the larger-scale worries of the war claiming hundreds of thousands of lives. George V wanted clear, firm advice, and turned to Louis, just as he had done in 1915 on his return from Germany. Louis's response was blunt and heartfelt: 'If he was my son or brother, I would operate.' At this point the King at last gave the go-ahead. On 27 November it was finally agreed that Albert would have the operation. His visit to Sandringham to celebrate Queen Alexandra's birthday was cancelled so that he could be in London on Thursday, 29 November at 10 a.m.

Sir Hugh Rigby led the operation but included in the medical team were Sir Frederick Treves, Bertrand Dawson, Stanley Hewett and also Louis. Surgeon to successive sovereigns, Rigby would later remove one of George V's ribs to treat a general septicaemia of the blood when an abscess behind the diaphragm needed to be drained. Sir Frederick Treves had removed Edward VII's appendix fifteen years previously so deftly that his patient was able to sit up and smoke a cigar the next morning. Bertrand Dawson was considered the leading medical statesman of his day. (He was made a baron in 1920 and a viscount in 1936 for his services to medicine.) It was a sign of the seriousness of the operation, as well as the status of the patient, that such a prestigious team of physicians was assembled. Sulphonamides or antibiotics were not available at this time, which was partly why there had been so much procrastination.

The pressure was intense on Louis, who felt that it was his decision alone which had finally brought them all to the operating table. Every day for five days the Court Circular published a medical bulletin detailing the Prince's progress. On 4 December, it stated: 'HRH Prince Albert is better this morning. The temperature is normal, and the cough is diminishing.' Albert could start to get his life back at long last.

The King was overjoyed and told friends that he valued, in particular, the plain-spoken advice from Louis, who was immediately rewarded with an MVO, making him a Member of the Royal Victorian Order. It is one of the few honours which is solely in the personal gift of the sovereign. The other doctors were also decorated by the King with different grades of honour from the Royal Victorian Order.

Although delighted that her son was returned to health, Queen Mary hinted in her diaries that the experts in charge had failed him prior to the operation. 'It was very successful & they found the cause of all the trouble he has been having since

1915,' she noted on 29 November 1917.[38] It was hard not to conclude that a faulty diagnosis of 'the cause of all the trouble' had kept him in poor health. John Wheeler-Bennett, George VI's official biographer, also suggested that the appendix operation on 9 September 1914 might have been a waste of time.

Albert felt greatly indebted to Louis and later told his equerry James Stuart that Louis was responsible for 'saving his life'.[39] Inevitably, Louis and Albert were brought even closer. There was little in the Prince's life they had not analysed together in their lengthy conversations about ways to restore him to health, including his fear of upsetting or disappointing his father, and his reluctance to force the issue over the operation. Albert let all his barriers down with Louis. He relaxed and confided in him the most intimate and uncomfortable aspects of not only his physical symptoms, but how they had sapped him mentally and psychologically. Louis made Albert believe that he could regain control of his own life. In the first official biography of Albert, the historian Taylor Darbyshire gave Louis the credit for the decision to operate, noting that it 'was on his [Louis's] strong advice that the King finally consented to the operation on his duodenal ulcer'. This view of Louis as the man who guided the King during Albert's health crisis was endorsed by Queen Mary. She took Darbyshire's book from the Privy Purse Library at Buckingham Palace and, after autographing the title page, presented it to Louis. She, too, turned to him for advice on her health, enjoying his good-humoured banter as much as his medical expertise. Louis had landed firmly in the royal fold and enjoyed his unofficial courtier's role. For the next seven years, he and Albert were to be virtually inseparable.

The King and Queen immediately invited him to stay at York Cottage for Christmas. It was ostensibly to help Albert through his convalescence, but the King simply wanted his new adviser to hand, even though he held no official position other than as Albert's friend and medical minder. Even the other doctors were impressed by their younger colleague and his clear-cut opinions. Frederick Treves told him: 'Young man, your foot is on the ladder of success.'

But Louis retorted with hearty emphasis: 'If there is one thing I want to give up, it is doctoring.' He had only become a surgeon as a means of joining the Navy when he had been too old to enlist as a cadet. He did not want to be a doctor for the rest of his life.

Louis was far from being 'born to serve' in the traditional way in which some aristocratic families pass down the same royal household positions from generation to generation. But he was about to join the inner circle of favoured courtiers. George V had singled him out, and Louis was flattered. His whole life was about to be altered forever by his entry into full-time royal service. The King was determined to make sure that Louis's friendship and influence over Albert were permanent.

Chapter Seven

> 'Greig is going there as well: very lucky for me
> having a man like that don't you think. He is a
> perfect topper.'
>
> Albert, writing to his tutor, Henry Hansell

Louis found himself face to face with the most badly behaved member of the royal household on 22 December
1916, his first morning at York Cottage, the King's
modest house on the Sandringham estate. Charlotte had the
most appalling table manners, but as far as George V was concerned she could do no wrong. Even when Louis found her
rudely snatching the toast from his plate, no one seemed to
notice, let alone mind. But then Charlotte had always got her
own way, and she was an accepted member of the King's
personal entourage. He was besotted with his pet parrot, 'the
most privileged member of his household'.[1] The bird, a gift
from Princess Victoria, would come in to breakfast on his
finger and wander over the table, foraging for whatever
morsels she could secure. If Charlotte forgot herself and made
a mess on the table, the King would surreptitiously slide a
silver mustard pot over the soiled area so that the Queen
would not notice. 'The parrot repeated her performance today
and it is most embarrassing,' complained Louis.[2]

Charlotte was the King's most constant companion, and
even on his deathbed in 1936, she was at hand in the next
room, afterwards travelling up to London with the funeral

party.[3] After breakfast in York Cottage, Louis went up to his bedroom to write to Phyllis of his unorthodox introduction to Charlotte. 'That damned parrot is still weird & makes straight for me every morning, at breakfast even when I come in quite quietly & never speak to it at all.'[4]

Dodging the parrot turned out to be the least of the changes that the royal family brought to Louis's life. He was coming to terms with the fact that his naval career was about to be brought to a premature end. While in Wales with the Verneys, he and Albert had talked late into the night about why Albert would be better off leaving the Navy, to join the ranks of the Air Force. It was clear to Louis that if the King agreed to the plan, he would join Albert and learn to fly. Albert had already alerted Hansell, his former tutor, on 6 November 1917 to this possible shift in career:

> I am now finishing off my sick leave by being x-rayed. I was photographed today and the results seem to be very favourable – more so than ever before. A statement will be published almost at once, and then I shall start hunting for a job. I am trying for an aerodrome if possible as then Greig will be able to go there as well. Dawson is very strong on that point and just as well. I am all for it. I have known Greig for a long time and we get on very well together. Charles Cust is all in favour of it and he is always a good person to have on one's side. What I want is a useful and permanent job which will keep me busy for at least a year till I am fit for sea again . . . I am longing to go to work again, now that my insides seem to have made up its mind to behave decently for a change. All the same it's a great blow.[5]

Albert was still very much under his father's influence, and relied upon court favourites such as Captain Sir Charles Cust to talk to the King on difficult matters. Cust's relationship with George V dated back to when they were young naval officers in the Mediterranean. Old-fashioned, outspoken and with rather a heavy, salty sense of humour, Cust was one of the few people to risk the King's wrath by complaining about Charlotte's table manners, or lack of them. In an age when almost no one dared contradict the sovereign, he was considered a useful safety valve – particularly for a rather cautious younger son. Cust once brazenly told the King at Balmoral: 'You haven't in the whole of this house got a book that's worth reading. Your so-called library is nothing but beautifully bound piffle.'[6] His tirade resulted in the speedy purchase of a complete set of new books.

But this time Albert need not have worried, as the King immediately embraced his suggestion about the change in his career. A bulletin released by Buckingham Palace declared that 'it would not be possible for His Royal Highness to resume duty at sea'. Shortly afterwards the Palace announced that 'Acting Lieutenant Prince Albert had been appointed to Cranwell air station for executive duties'.

Albert excitedly scribbled a note to Hansell: 'My own suggestion for once came off and papa jumped at the idea. Greig is going there as well: very lucky for me having a man like that don't you think. He is a perfect topper.'[7]

This was just the latest dramatic change in Louis's life; in June he became a father when Phyllis gave birth to a beautiful healthy girl they named Bridget. Louis adored the new addition, and was torn between the long hours his work with Albert took up and his desire to spend more time with his wife and infant, whom he nicknamed Biddles. Louis's royal duties, just as much as his naval ones, took him away from home. He had been looking forward to his first Christmas with his family, but had to break the news to Phyllis that he would not be at home. The invitation to Sandringham was for him alone, as was so often the case with courtiers. The court was a very male-oriented world, and only the very senior members with grace-and-favour houses on the Sandringham estate could bring their wives. Louis's visit was seen in the same light as an Army or indeed Navy special attachment; even though he was at the royal family's home he was on duty, and he was told there would be no opportunity to spend time with his wife.

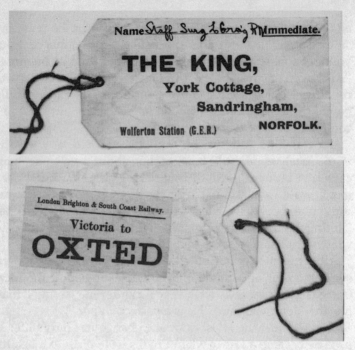

Name Staff Surg L Greig R N Immediate.

THE KING,

York Cottage,

Sandringham,

Wolferton Station (G.E.R.)   NORFOLK.

London Brighton & South Coast Railway.

Victoria to

OXTED

While it was exciting for Louis to stay at Sandringham, it meant Christmas alone for Phyllis with their new baby. However, she knew that it was better to have Louis in flat, safe Norfolk, rather than at sea facing the German Navy, or back in the trenches with the Marines. But it was still a disappointment, and Louis tried to soften the news of his absence with a breezy self-mocking letter about receiving his MVO from the King: 'Following on my apologies, the worst occurred & I am now a full-blown MVO, being Staff-Surgeon Louis Greig MVO & it's an 'orrible outrage. I feel to have got an MVO in a big war like this is approaching the limit . . . I'm here for a month, old duck, & how I'm going to stand it, I can't think.'[8]

He also posted a Christmas present: 'If you get a very inferior pair of old silver tongs, don't chuck 'em away. I sent them. My love, old darling, to you, & the beloved Bridget whom I'm beginning to adore. Buckets of love to you, Phee darling. Ever your affectionate husband Louis.'

Phyllis understood that it was an invitation Louis could not turn down. She was glad for him that he had been taken up by the King. Every day they wrote to each other, each anxious for the other's news. Louis wanted to know how his baby daughter was doing, while Phyllis wanted the inside scoop on life with the King.

Louis was very much the favourite guest over Christmas, and was overwhelmed by gifts. The royal family were immensely grateful for Albert's restoration to health. The other doctors involved were also generous with their praise. 'I had a very nice letter from Bertrand Dawson thanking me for all my great help! Also Ridley gave me a charming speech of thanks when we parted, in the same vein. Most amusing if they only knew my ignorance,' he confided to Phyllis. What had impressed the King and the other doctors was the supreme confidence and cast-iron certainty of Louis's judgement, which luckily had proved to be right. They enjoyed his refreshingly open, direct and occasionally outré conversation. Louis was a good raconteur and liked to spin yarns about his time behind enemy lines that amused the King. The older royals, in particular, liked him. Princess Victoria, the King's sister, for instance, gave him an elegant silver ashtray for cigars. After lunch on Christmas Day at York Cottage, Louis slipped off to his bedroom to write home of his astonishment at other lavish gifts:

My darling Phee,
   I don't think I wished you a merry Xmas at all & now it's too late, but old sweetness, I can wish you very many happy New Years, & may we, as you say, have them together. Mum's letter [his mother-in-law] & fiver simply overwhelmed me, & I couldn't half thank her enough.
   I have never seen anything like the presents these people chuck about. On Xmas eve, we all assembled in the billiard room after tea to receive presents. A really marvellous sight. The K & Q gave

me their signed photographs in most beautiful antique gilt frames about 1 foot & half high. HM also gave me a most priceless cigarette case with monograms on it. PA gave me a pair of gold sleeve links & I'm getting Raemakers [book of war cartoons] from Princess Mary & the other boys. Mrs Wig [wife of Clive Wigram, assistant private secretary] got a lovely enamel & pearl brooch from the Queen – most beautiful – also huge books on wild animal life. Princess Mary got an ermine muff & stole. PH [Prince Henry] got pearl studs. In addition they each get a piece of silver like a salver or toast rack etc for their future households. I expect you all had a nailing Xmas together & I am sweating at what I am missing. I should hate to live among complete families if you were away so perhaps I suffer less here. PA remains better & cheerful. I hope you got my stinking tongs, old duck. They aren't much in themselves but they carry a devil of a lot of love & affection to you dear & also to Biddles.

All sorts of love to you Phee darling.

Your ever loving husband Loopot.

My dear, I nearly omitted to grovel for the handkerchiefs. They're lovely & oh so badly needed. Thank you *mille fois*.

Christmas was an important focal point for the royal family ever since Edward VII had established it as a time for magnificent feasting and presents. It was by tradition a grand and luxurious affair which Prince Edward described as 'Dickens in a Cartier setting'.[9] Before the war seven bullocks were slaughtered to provide joints of meat for everyone on the Sandringham estate. The main setting for the festivities was in the ballroom, where a twenty-seven-foot-high Christmas tree, aglitter with candles and decorations, created a magnificent display. But George V preferred a quieter, more toned-down celebration in snug York Cottage, and the war meant that it was more subdued than usual. It was difficult for Louis not to be acutely aware of his very privileged and safe situation when every day he read in *The Times* a new list of names of men who had been killed in action.

The war overshadowed everything, which made Louis's time at Sandringham particularly unusual. During Christmas week, the King announced a peerage for Admiral Sir John Jellicoe for his courageous role at the Battle of Jutland in command of the Grand Fleet. It was partly a sop, as Jellicoe was pushed aside to be succeeded by Sir Rosslyn Wemyss as First Sea Lord. The talk in every household was incessantly of the war – even in the remote flatlands of Norfolk, where life seemed so distant from the massacres and mayhem in the front line. An inevitable topic of conversation on Boxing Day – it was the subject of most sermons in the country that week – was the Kaiser's blasphemous and megalomaniacal Christmas boast to his troops that 'God is the unconditional and avowed ally of the German people'. Almost every page in the newspapers was devoted to the war. On Christmas Eve *The Times* wearily recorded that it was the 143rd day of the fourth year of war. Yet despite the awful pain and anxiety for so many families with sons wounded, killed, missing or still fighting, life at home continued with a surprising degree of normality. *Peter Pan* played to packed houses in London's New Theatre and *A Kiss for Cinderella* was staged at the Queen's Theatre. The papers were filled with advertisements for domestic servants, and pets and presents were still bought. Ordinary life did not come to a halt, even though times were hard and rationing had been imposed. Sir Arthur Yapp, Director of Food Economy, warned that an excess of Christmas feasting would have a 'very direct effect on military activities'. His fear was that if every family exceeded their ration by two or three ounces every day during Christmas week, the 'demands upon our tonnage would be sufficient to delay the transport for some thousands of American troops to the Western Front'. Such restraint was not always shown by the politicians and senior officials. Lord Bertie, the British Ambassador to France, was scandalised that a British minister travelling with five companions and three servants drank between them twenty-seven bottles of wine, thirty-nine glasses of liqueur and nineteen bottles of beer – all at the expense of the taxpayer.[10]

Christmas fare at Sandringham was not lavish, as George

V's contribution to the war effort was to give up alcohol in his households. His self-denial was announced in the Court Circular in April 1915, but instead of gaining respect, he was gently mocked. Yet according to Louis he was 'very honest about his teetotalism – it bored him to tears but he and *malheureusement* we stick to it.'[11] Not everyone adjusted so smoothly. Lord Rosebery was reported to have got such hiccoughs after drinking a glass of ginger beer that he could not continue talking to the Queen. Meanwhile, on 27 December, Louis and the rest of the royal family could not have failed to read in a prominent report in *The Times* of the paper's special correspondents enjoying restaurants within shell range of the front line with a rather more wide-ranging menu than Sandringham could boast:

> *Oysters*
> *Hors d'oeuvre (half a dozen sorts)*
> *A good vegetable soup*
> *Filleted plaice, beautifully fried to a deep golden brown*
> *Roast chicken, veal and vegetables*
> *A kind of chocolate custard sweet*
> *Coffee*

Louis felt mildly guilty about his situation, singled out by the King to look after one patient in a royal house while hundreds of his contemporaries were risking their lives at war. 'Splendid about UK's DSO. Poor old girl, your damned husband can't get anything like that & I'm sorry for your sake, but expect to get cursed for saying it,' he wrote to Phyllis.[12] In fact, Louis had been given the Croix de Guerre by the Belgian King for his brave attempt to rescue wounded Belgian soldiers near Antwerp in 1914.

Louis was very fond of his royal charge, but hinted in a letter to his brother Robert about the remoteness of the royal family from most people's lives. '*Tout va bien* & the monarchy still stands, tho' whether it'll last *après* the guerre, I don't know. The little man [Albert] is really A1 and a wonderfully hard-working Englishman & I'm very fond of him.'[13]

Louis had entered a rarefied world where senior courtiers either enjoyed a private income or were given sufficient perks by the King to make their lives more comfortable than their bank balance would allow. Louis's means were modest. 'Cashed a cheque for a fiver, old duck,' he wrote to Phyllis from York Cottage, 'spent £2 for my dress coat; so money flies. I wish time did as fast . . . also I had to pay 15/- for a miniature MVO, which one has to wear on one's dress coat at dinner, every night. (damned waste of money.)'

The King was not unsympathetic, and just after Christmas Louis wrote to Phyllis, telling her that the King had offered him a house on his Norfolk estate: 'The King has a rather nice house near here, beautifully got up inside with oak panels & unfurnished. He said he wouldn't charge much rent! I said possibly after the war I'd deal with him. It is rather exposed & perhaps a little big, but it would be nice in many ways, tho' at present not to be thought of.'

The logistics of equipping himself for a royal house party in the middle of the war were not easy. 'I have sent for my gun as I shall be wanted to shoot the first part of the visit, so I am informed. God knows where the cartridges are coming from,' he complained to Phyllis.

These minor worries aside, Louis greatly enjoyed himself. He felt quite at home and did not find life at York Cottage the least bit intimidating. But then Louis never did lack confidence when it came to people. 'It might have been a curate and his wife in their new home,' Cosmo Lang had once remarked of the King and Queen on a visit he paid them before he became Archbishop of Canterbury.[14] It was certainly a far cry from the pomp of Buckingham Palace courts and lévées, which usually took place in the grandest of ballrooms with the King in the full dress uniform of an Admiral of the Fleet or Field Marshal, and the Queen weighed down by rock-like necklaces and bracelets, her train carried by two pages of honour in scarlet uniform, while the Lord Steward and Lord Chamberlain, holding their white staves, walked backwards before them. The voice of Lord Cromer, the Lord Chamberlain, would drone ceaselessly on and on as the ladies were endlessly and pointlessly presented. Fortunately for Louis, these rituals were suspended during the war. At Windsor life was almost as starchy, with female members of the household expected to carry gloves at mealtimes and on every official occasion.

It was all far more relaxed at York Cottage, where the King really felt he was at home. In her memoirs, Lady Cynthia Colville, a lady-in-waiting to Queen Mary, captured the semi-formal style of life at York Cottage when she stayed with the King and Queen.

> We swept through the main gate and past the 'big house' – not the most attractive type of domestic architecture, but still an impressive reproduction of Elizabethan design, surrounded by a pleasant garden. The front door was open and with lights behind, one could discern Queen Alexandra's household standing in respectful formation to greet their sovereign's arrival and passage to his insignificant dwelling. As about forty people were crowded into York Cottage I was lucky to have a reasonably roomy, though dark, bed-sitting room, and a somewhat dreary outlook into the small courtyard perhaps made concentration on the business in hand freer from distraction of scenery and country life.

The main house on the estate was still lived in by Queen Alexandra and her unmarried daughter, Princess Victoria, while George V, his wife and five of his children continued to squeeze into the more modest house in the grounds. Louis was taken to visit the old Queen and her spinster daughter. 'They are charming – and never tire of my German yarns,' he boasted to Phyllis.

What was intimidating for Louis was the standard of shooting. The King was a phenomenally good shot, firing as many as 30,000 cartridges a year from his twelve-bores made by Purdey. The shoots were often on the grandest scale. 'Seven guns in four days at Sandringham killed 10,000 head. The king one day fired 1,700 cartridges and killed 1,000 pheasants. Can this terrific slaughter possibly last much longer?' asked

Lord Lincolnshire.[15] Louis was initially not in any of the big days' drives. 'I haven't shot yet as, of course, the guns are all complete. I hope I won't, honestly, as it's a bit overpowering with loaders, keepers, boys, dogs to each gun,' he wrote. But some days Louis shot with just the King and Albert; Prince Henry, Albert's seventeen-year-old brother, sometimes tagged along, 'Just off for a quiet shoot with HM & PA & Prince Henry. I hope if I hit anything it's not HM,' Louis joked to Phyllis. A formal game card was filled in after their day out and presented to each gun as a record of the bag. 'HM is a wonderful shot & keeps pulling them down with marvellous shots (hammer guns!). The birds (partridges) are driven and come screaming over,' he told Phyllis.

Louis's direct manner was not always a success, as he tried
to explain to his brother Robert:

> I feel a line might amuse you because the whole show is too
> damned funny for words. Here I am, with my homely habits &
> Elizabethan language, plumped down & living right among it.
> It's a small house and there is only the King, Queen, Princess
> Mary, PA, an equerry and 2 ladies-in-waiting & myself. We have
> every meal together and never get away. Can you figure to your-
> self me picking the last bit of omelette & finding HM hadn't got
> any. Things looked fierce till a very welcome (to me) nobleman
> arrived bearing a second effort from the royal cookhouse. As a
> matter of fact they are all most simple & friendly and awfully
> easy. The equerry & I take alternate nights at dinner sitting next
> to the Queen & Princess Mary & conversation is fairly good. HM
> is damned funny; he uses refreshing language at meals & I nearly
> get sick with laughing at his remarks. By Jove they do hate the
> Huns & I don't mind what they say about them.

He enjoyed reporting back to his relations on how the royal
family lived their day-to-day lives in the privacy of their home:

> Very much *en famille* here & as simple as anything. Teetotalism &
> Rations – the former HM simply cusses at, but sticks to nobly, &
> the latter are most carefully gone into by the Queen who runs the
> house entirely. The only thing is one simply never gets away from
> the family as we have all our meals together which is fierce, as they
> say, when HM is a bit 'morningy'. So far he is in wonderful form
> as the weather is perfect & the shooting good. They are most fright-
> fully anti-German & their language is unrestrained & refreshing
> to a degree on the subject. They are dying to bombard their towns
> & make reprisals etc.

Queen Mary, who was fifty in 1917, had the reputation of
being chilly and formidable, but Louis found her surprisingly
warm and welcoming beneath her outer glacial demeanour.
She took him into her confidence about her minor ailments,
asking him not to tell the King when certain medicines were

prescribed. When her husband had forbidden her to take some particular pills she went to Louis to try to get them from him. According to one contemporary he got on well with her because 'he treated her like a human being and she adored him for that'. Once he saw what present-givers the royals were, he entered into the spirit by presenting her with a war trophy. 'I gave the Queen one of my Zeppelin rings for a napkin & she's simply all over it & is taking it up to London on Wednesday to have it engraved – a great success that was,' he wrote to Phyllis on New Year's Eve in 1917.

While Louis was intrigued by his glimpse into the private life of the royal family, he was aware of its limitations. 'Altogether life is most entertaining, tho' how long this is going to last and how long it will be entertaining, God alone knows,' he wrote to Robert. And it certainly was a world of its own, where even the time was different; all the clocks were half an hour fast at Sandringham in order to gain more time for winter shooting. This self-indulgent time-warping remained in operation until 1936, when King Edward VIII, during his brief reign, abolished it in an abrupt move to sweep in some much-needed modernity and change.

Louis continued to pass on his fly-on-the-wall view of court life to Phyllis. Relaxing was not easy, as Louis was effectively always on duty. 'I went for a long walk with Mr & Mrs Wig & enjoyed it very much, *talking to humans & not royals*,' he confided.[16] 'They are most wonderfully kind, however, I'm not sorry to shove off from here. Prince George has to go up to London so I jumped at the chance to take him & fade away on a few days' leave.'

Throughout his stay, the war hung heavily on everyone's mind. In January 1915, Zeppelin raiders had appeared over Sandringham and dropped bombs in the area. Queen Alexandra had shown a spirited sense of bellicosity with a request to Lord Fisher, the First Sea Lord, for arms to repel the attack: 'Please let me have a lot of rockets with spikes or hooks on to defend our Norfolk coast. I am sure you could invent something of the sort which would bring down a few of those rascals.'[17]

She was exposed to Zeppelin attacks throughout the war:

> We have been living through some gruesome moments here – just a fortnight ago we had those beastly Zepps over us. At 10 o'clock that Saturday evening they began. We were all sitting upstairs in Victoria's room when we suddenly were startled by that awful noise! Everybody rushed up and wanted us to go downstairs. I must confess I was not a bit afraid – but it was a most uncanny feeling – poor Victoria was quite white in the face and horror-struck . . . [the Zepps] came back about four o'clock in the night and dropped bombs all over the place![18]

It was difficult for those who had never experienced the front line of war to comprehend the horror, and Queen Alexandra was no exception. Although she was fervently anti-German, she could never fully comprehend the magnitude and degrading nature of the massacres. In one letter dated 8 July 1916, during the Battle of the Somme, she wrote: 'Thank God we are all doing so well in France just now.' By the end of that same month of July, the British had gained two and a half miles on a two-mile front and lost approximately 171,000 men. Yet she was not alone in feeling an excitement at the first news of this advance. Her biographer, Georgina Battiscombe, believed that the Queen's lack of comprehension about the war was 'shared by the majority of her fellow-countrymen' owing partly to censorship and the reticence of soldiers on their return to talk about what they had seen or experienced.

Louis's main task at Sandringham was to keep an eye on Albert. 'The boy is very well at present & my job is a sinecure for the moment. I go out with the guns & stand with each in turn,' he told Phyllis. A few days later he shot alongside the King. 'Just come back from another fine shoot, about 400 pheasants & about 400 woodcock with some hares & partridges. I think I must have used some of HM's cartridge but I don't know. I enjoyed it very much.'

*

With Albert needing less attention, Louis was called upon to give medical advice to the rest of his family. But Louis and the Prince did find time to talk about their future in the Air Force. They were both nervous about the business of learning to fly. He liked Albert and admired his pluck at dealing with his problems with great determination and little complaint. He felt that the Prince was a young man with a great deal of unfulfilled potential.

But it was not just Albert who sought his attention, as he told Phyllis: 'The Queen has a slight sore throat & I had to have a look at it & gave her the iodine muck to gargle with. The Queen's cold is still there & she's using your nose douche today. I nearly died laughing trying to teach her how to use it. It all went down one of her splendiferous dresses, but perseverance was her motto & so it seemed to work in the end.'

He also learnt that diplomacy as much as medical expertise was needed. 'HM's hand is better but he is not going to shoot. It swells up behind & I feel sure it was simply a mosquito bite, but he is one of those people who swear they have good blood & never swell up, so he says it's a strain. As the treatment is the same I let him have his strain – to gain peace of mind & lose more self-respect.'

Money remained a concern for Louis – even when he was spending other people's. He simply did not like to appear as if he was taking anything for granted, as he explained to Phyllis when he tried to hatch a plan to get back to see her for a few days. 'I am most unsettled tonight at the idea of not coming up, but I find HM has to pay my ticket in addition to the special & I don't like to ask on that account, a first class return fare without uniform rate is perhaps a bit too steep to ask.'

But eventually he did get away to see Phyllis and Bridget. His departure was immediately felt. Sir Bryan Godfrey-Faussett complained in his diary about feeling low after Louis left. Albert missed him too, and on the day of his departure plaintively wrote: 'It is very sad that you have gone. We will miss you very much.'[19] Three days later he wrote: 'Many thanks for your letter which crossed mine in the post. I'm still very fit and put on another 1lb in weight in the week which makes me 9st 12lb. I'm not overdoing it a bit. There is no need to worry about that as I know what I can do.' He added as a postscript on 23 January, 'Just received your letter. So glad you will be in town on the 2nd.'

The relationship between Louis and Albert essentially moved from being defined by its doctor and patient roles to being that of a prince and his courtier during that Christmas at Sandringham. Louis did not yet have an official role, but it was being suggested that he become a full-time equerry, which would give him a small stipend on top of his Air Force salary. The King personally requested that he take the job of looking after his second son. The benefits he brought in terms of building his confidence as well as safeguarding his health were enormous. 'He was an encourager and everyone at Albert's age needs that.'[20] More than anyone else, Louis was able to make the Prince feel valued. For too long Albert had felt a failure, and now for the first time in his life he believed that his future looked bright.

At this time, after much hesitation, George V bowed to public pressure to delete any German trace from his name by erasing Saxe-Coburg-Gotha in favour of the solidly British name of Windsor. Louis followed suit. He had Leisler as a middle name because his father had been extremely fond of his Hamburg business partner. In such a climate of anti-German rancour Louis felt it was necessary to excise his middle name. In the official records after 1917 he became Louis Greig instead of L. L. Greig. On Boxing Day he boasted to Phyllis he had been writing to his bank. 'My new signature is permanent now, so it is no use trying to forge my old one,' he quipped.

George V had initially been impervious to most criticism of his German family or ancestry, as he appeared to think such historical links were above mere national boundaries and

Prince Albert as a
15-year-old naval
cadet at Osborne
in 1910 when he
first met Louis.

Louis, aged 30, in
his naval surgeon's
uniform on the Isle
of Wight in 1910.

Leader of the pack: Louis as captain of the Scottish rugby team, *seated in the centre*, before the match against Ireland, in Dublin, in 1908.

Louis and his siblings in Glasgow in 1890, *top row; from left*: Jack, George, Robert, Herbert; *second row*: Anna, Ethel, Constance, and Marjorie, and *bottom row*: Arthur, Louis and Kenneth.

The scruffy schoolboy: Louis aged ten.

Below: School days: Louis as a young rugby player at Merchiston Castle School, Edinburgh.

On parade: Louis in ceremonial naval uniform.

Louis's wife: The indomitable Phyllis Scrimgeour.

Love match: The engagement
announcement of Louis and Phyllis
in 1916.

Right: Cambridge days: Phyllis and
Prince Albert on the tennis court at
Southacre during Albert's under-
graduate days.

Below: Three in a row: Prince Henry, Prince Albert and Louis at Cambridge
when the King asked Louis to look after his sons.

Above: Learning curves: Prince Albert with Louis and Phyllis two steps behind him at a degree ceremony at Cambridge in 1920.

Right: Doctor in charge: Louis as a surgeon with the Royal Marines in 1914 just before he was captured by the Germans.

Below: Rivals in romance: Prince Albert, standing in front of the car, with Louis, *second on his left*, and James Stuart, *far right*.

Taking the biscuit: The Duchess of York, Sir Alexander Grant, Louis and Prince Albert visiting a McVitie & Price factory in 1923.

At ease : Louis and Prince Albert relaxing at RAF Cranwell in 1918 while learning to fly.

Top: At play: Louis and Albert in a wheelbarrow race at Cranwell in 1918.

Above: Keeping fit: Albert and Louis exercising during the last months of the war.

An inseparable pair: Louis and Albert in 1919.

Double trouble:
Louis and Albert
playing in the
Wimbledon doubles
in 1926.

Set and match:
Louis and Albert at
Wimbledon.

disputes. He had even rather naïvely tried to explain to Asquith that his cousin Prince Albert of Schleswig-Holstein was 'not really fighting on the side of the Germans', but had only been 'put in charge of a camp of English prisoners', near Berlin. 'A nice distinction,' the Prime Minister observed satirically to Venetia Stanley.[21] Not everyone was so understanding. Lloyd George commented to his secretary after being summoned to the palace in January 1915: 'I wonder what my little German friend has got to say to me.'[22] The royal family were, for a long time, short-sighted about the effect of their German links, as they saw themselves as inalienably British in spite of their lineage. George V was furious when H. G. Wells spoke of 'an alien and uninspiring court' and retorted: 'I may be uninspiring but I'll be damned if I'm an alien.' One historian called it 'a momentary loss of nerve' when the royal family ditched their German name to become the House of Windsor. It was, as it turned out, a masterly tactical move which met with a surge of patriotism all over Britain. (But the Kaiser still made a good joke, letting it be known that he would be delighted to attend a performance of that well-known drama, the Merry Wives of Saxe-Coburg-Gotha.) The anglicisation had a ripple effect down the social pecking order. His Serene Highness Prince Louis of Battenberg relinquished his German style and title, assumed the surname Mountbatten, and became the Marquess of Milford Haven.

The war was particularly complex for the royal family, because of their widespread and tangled relationships all across Europe. Queen Alexandra, for example, had relations fighting on both sides. One nephew, the son of her sister Thyra, Duchess of Cumberland, was with the German Army, while another nephew, Prince Maurice of Battenberg, was killed fighting on the British side at Mons. His death made the forced resignation of his uncle, Prince Louis of Battenberg, from his position of First Sea Lord seem even more bitterly unfair when, in the very early stages of the war, Battenberg was routed from office on a tidal wave of national hatred against Germany. No one doubted he was an able sailor; it was simply made plain he had to go. 'He is of a noble character and has sacrificed himself to the country he has served so well and which has now treated him so abominably,' wrote Queen Alexandra bitterly.[23] Thirty years later, Battenberg's son, the future Lord Mountbatten, found his identical German antecedents were no obstacle to his becoming Viceroy of India. Some felt that it was his father's disgraceful dismissal which made him so ambitious. The young Mountbatten wrote to his mother from Osborne, where he was a cadet, complaining of the teasing he was subjected to owing to his father's resignation. 'What d'you think the latest rumour that has got in here from outside is? That papa has turned out to be a German spy and has been discreetly marched off to the Tower, where he is guarded by Beefeaters . . . I got a rotten time of it for about three days.'[24]

Name changes notwithstanding, Christmas at Sandringham had been a huge success. For the first time Louis and Albert were on an equal footing as they prepared to learn to fly. Louis was sad in some ways to leave the Navy, but with the King as his backer it was hard not to go with the royal flow. He had spent more than eleven years in the Senior Service, and as he had decided he did not want to be a doctor all his life, he felt a career change would be of benefit. He was daunted by the idea of learning to fly so late in life. Most pilots were in their twenties and he was nearly forty. More worrying was the large number of fatalities at Cranwell, where they were to be stationed. Louis saw that his royal patronage was likely to lead him in diverse directions and provide the chance to meet a great many more interesting people than if he was stuck on board in a ship's sick bay. It was a time to embrace a wider, larger and grander world; if nothing else, it was going to be an adventure.

Chapter Eight

'I am glad to hear you agree with my proposal to stay
with the Greigs.'

Prince Albert, writing to the King

The birth of the flying age essentially spanned Louis's
adult life. He was a medical student when the Wright
Brothers inaugurated the era of flight by taking off
from Kitty Hawk, North Carolina 1903. While Louis was super-
vising Albert as a naval cadet at Osborne, the French pilot
Louis Blériot flew the Channel in just forty minutes on 25 July
1909, denting a great deal of British pride. H. G. Wells had
brilliantly captured the public's imagination for air warfare
with his serialisation of *The War in the Air* in *Pall Mall* magazine. His fiction alerted thousands of readers to the actual
possibility of international conflict in the skies with this newly
born medium of armed flying machines. The most striking
scene was a description of an attack on New York by a fleet of
German airships, a dramatic reminder of the end of protective
isolation through water for any island. The obvious implications for the British Isles were that 'the little island in the
silver seas was at the end of its immunity, [and] that nowhere
in the world any more was there a place left where a
Smallways [Wells's fictional aviator hero] might lift his head
proudly and vote for war and a spirited foreign policy, and go
secure from such horrible things'.

It was on New Year's Day, 1918, that Louis and Albert learned they were officially to start their flying careers aboard HMS *Daedalus*. It was not a ship, but a barren stretch of land at Cranwell in Lincolnshire, just twelve miles north-east of Grantham, where pilots and aerial gunlayers were trained. 'I proceed to Cranwell & await PA to whom I am "attached" – whatever that means. It really is in loco parentis & as a sort of equerry & I may get a small screw,' Louis wrote to his brother, Robert, about his change in career on 15 January. Louis was still concerned about his finances, and he enquired about the small portfolio of shares that Robert managed for him – 'What about those damned Coalites? Are some British C or simply Coaldix because one's gone up like hell?' He weighed up what his visit to Sandringham would cost in tips for the staff. 'I can't see my way to getting out of their house for under a tenner, but I'll try & slip away,' he wrote to Phyllis.

As an equerry, Louis's job was to look after Albert and make sure that he remained safe and healthy. In early 1918 the Prince appeared physically fit, but he was understandably nervous and hesitant about flying. His self-confidence was not helped by his father's ambivalent attitude towards the RAF. George V was a naval man to the core; the Air Force, after all, was where he had dispatched Albert as a last resort after he was declared unfit for duty at sea. One of George V's Secretaries of State for Air, Samuel Hoare, recorded his being 'strongly prejudiced against flying, the Air Ministry and the Air Force'.[1] It was hardly a basis on which to build great confidence for Albert, who must have felt buffeted around like a ship in a storm, trying to find a port that would welcome him.

The idea for an armed flying service had started in 1911 when a subcommittee of the Committee of Imperial Defence recommended the creation of the Royal Flying Corps with a naval wing, a military wing and a central flying school for the training of pilots. The competitive natures of the two services led to the separate formation of the Royal Naval Air Service and the Army's Royal Flying Corps. It was not until 1918 that a single flying force was created by the Air Force (Constitution)

Act of 1917. The amalgamation took place on 1 April 1918, when Louis and Albert were at Cranwell – with the unified air service to be thereafter known as the Royal Air Force.

However, Louis and Albert's excitement was at first diminished by squabbling in the embryonic RAF, right at the very top. Lord Rothermere had been appointed the first Secretary of State for Air, and Major-General Sir Hugh Trenchard, the father of the Royal Air Force, became the first Chief of the Air Staff. Unfortunately, these two titans clashed and Trenchard resigned, causing considerable anxiety to the men in the new air force. Shortly afterwards, Rothermere was forced to resign. Trenchard was then subsequently brought back to take command of the Independent Air Force (IAF), simply because of his popularity. His task was to implement the policy of bombing Germany.[2] Louis and Albert were minor players in the game, but the knock-on effect from the discontent was felt right down the line. 'Everything as you can imagine is very unsettled here,' Albert complained to the King.[3]

Cranwell offered little by way of comfort for its staff and trainees. Most buildings were made of corrugated iron, painted black, a bleak contrast to the more palatial architecture of Osborne. What was also different was the people; the Air Force was far less 'socially smart'. Albert wrote with typical British understatement to Queen Mary to note that they were 'very nice, though a curious mixture of people in every walk of life'. What he was saying was they were not from the narrow base of well-connected public school boys that had predominantly been the case in the Navy. Sarah Bradford has noted in her biography of George VI that had the Navy been run on the same lines in Nelson's times it was unlikely that he would have been able to enter thanks to its snobbish élitism. Prince Edward found the Grenadiers far more to his liking, where he was surrounded by kindred spirits, 'all my friends & the friends of friends at home'.

Louis urged Albert to put his best foot forward, which is what he did, sending cheery letters home. 'I had a very comfortable journey down here with Greig on Monday,' he reassured his father on 9 February 1918.[4] 'Our quarters are very comfortable, a bedroom and a sitting room. The life is very different to a ship . . . As I think I told you I am looking after the boys, of which there are 500 . . . and I am known as the Officer Commanding Boys. I shall have to punish them myself and grant their request for leave etc. The work is entirely new to me and I find it rather difficult to begin with but I shall get used to it.'[5]

Once again Louis found himself Albert's only close friend, and seeing that he was going to be somewhat isolated and lonely at the airbase, he invited him to move into a house that he and Phyllis had rented. It was a small Victorian, neo-Gothic house at South Rauceby, a village just a few miles from the base. Of course, this only made it more difficult for Albert to make friends with contemporaries in the RAF, but it was what he wanted. It was easier to stay with Louis and Phyllis, who provided all the creature comforts and companionship that he needed, living away from the base. Never able to make a move without his parents' approval, he wrote to the Queen to ask if he could live with Louis:

I did not get a chance the other day to ask you whether there was any objection to my staying with the Greigs in their house about 4 miles from here after the 1st of May. He asked me if I would and I said yes, and told him I would find out from you if it would be all right. They are very hard pressed here for accommodation for officers and shortly the Commander is going to take over this hut where I am now, as his own house. That means that I shall have to move out into some other hut. Of course, during the day I shall do my ordinary work here and sleep there only. If you and Papa approve of this suggestion I will tell Greig it is all right. I have already arranged with him that I will pay for my board and lodging, so that I needn't be treated as a guest. Mrs Greig has also asked me to stay with them. I hope you do not think this an odd request to make, but when Greig asked me I jumped at it as I know the delight of getting away from this place after work is over . . . Another officer was killed flying yesterday which was very sad.[6]

Albert's nervousness came across in his letter as he constantly justified his request, fearful of being turned down. He was very keen not to move into the standard Air Force accommodation. Apart from being less comfortable, he would also have been a constant centre of attention and subject to the usual teasing service banter and inevitable comparisons with his more glamorous elder brother, whom the press had taken to calling Prince Charming.

The King and Queen jumped at the suggestion. After all, they believed it was their idea in the first place that Louis be close to their son. 'I am glad to hear you agree with my proposal to stay with the Greigs in their house after May 1st. It was very kind of them to suggest it to me. The Germans have had all the luck again with the weather for their offensive. During this week three PFOs have been killed flying; one of them only this morning.'[7]

One great advantage of staying with Louis – the first time Albert had lived in a non-royal household – was a greater sense of independence from his family, and a loosening of the Palace reins. 'The Greigs have made me very comfortable in their house and it does make a difference being able to get out of the camp after work,' he reassured Queen Mary on 8 May 1918.[8] There was no standing on ceremony. Louis enlisted his lodger to help build a chicken run, dig potatoes, weed the garden and do other outside chores. It was a simple country life with just Louis, Phyllis and little Bridget. The Prince was more relaxed and happy than he had been for a long time and his confidence grew. 'I never trouble my head about myself now, as I feel a different person,' he told his mother.[9] Louis and Phyllis encouraged Albert to think of the South Rauceby cottage as if it was his own home. There was no need to impress or to be on his best behaviour. The house was run very informally, and that is what the Prince liked. Prince Henry, Albert's younger brother, then aged sixteen, sometimes came for the weekend and also enjoyed the Greigs' relaxed hospitality, which was so different from his own family life. 'I was so very comfortable and enjoyed myself thoroughly. I miss seeing the dogs and chickens running about the tennis court and our rides to Sleaford. I hope that Bridget's tooth is all right now. I missed Biddy very much last night . . . I again thank you for your kindness.'[10] It was a typical family weekend in the country with a delicious Sunday lunch of roast chicken, but such simple informality and normality was a novelty for Albert. It was noisy, casual and lively; the sort of life that the princes seldom saw. Much later Louis recalled this time in a BBC programme about Albert's early years which was never broadcast. 'He spent a great deal of his time gardening and motoring, but he was fairly busy with his duties at Cranwell most of the day and, of course, he was always good with the children. He was most understanding with my small daughter of five at the time, but nothing seemed to give him a greater pleasure than playing with her and bathing her.'[11]

In many ways Louis was a father figure as well as being a more sympathetic elder brother figure to Albert. He coached him at tennis and took him riding along the country lanes. But he was firm and did not hesitate to reprimand Albert if he behaved badly. When Albert flung his tennis racquet down in rage after losing a match point, Louis tore a strip off him in no uncertain terms. He had never lost his colourful command of language. He was also useful in keeping the King at bay. 'Greig was able to act as a buffer and interpreter between the prince and his father . . . not the least of Louis's qualities was his skill and good temper at games, which enabled him to act as an ever willing but never too obsequious partner to the shy young prince.'[12]

Albert saw a lot of Phyllis, who he soon discovered was deeply competitive and hated to lose at croquet or cards, which they often played in the evening. She taught the princes how to play Lou, perhaps the most dangerous of all gambling card games. With stakes at just a penny, it was easy to run up frighteningly large debts; the Greigs and the princes found it safer to play for matchsticks. Albert and Phyllis would gang up on Louis, teasing him about his restlessness and inability to sit still for more than a moment. 'You must have had a fine old time with 5 children, and I expect Louis was in good form. Do make him take a rest as he wants one!!!!' Albert complained to Phyllis, when they had other children to stay. Prince George, Albert's other younger brother, then aged fifteen, also became very fond of her. Both boys felt able to express themselves utterly freely about their relationship with their parents. 'I am sending you two combs as they would not sell one alone. I hope you'll not smash them at once. I am glad to be back from Aldershot as on the whole it was pretty awful – old "woolly face" [presumably George V] was rather annoyed about my not wanting to go,' he wrote to Phyllis.[13] They could talk to Louis in a free and irreverent way about the King and Queen, knowing that it would be understood in the context of a family's private conversation.

Louis was increasingly an anchor in Albert's life, and, if away for just a few days, Albert would send him a note. 'I would love to come and dine with you and your brother that Friday evening and go to a theatre and the dance at Princes [club] afterwards,' he wrote to Louis while at Sandringham for a weekend.[14] Louis taught Albert to drive a car in the narrow country roads around Cranwell. Motorcycles were then used by most officers to get around, but Albert – as always hemmed in by his parents – was not allowed to ride one. 'Only bounders ride motor bicycles,' pronounced the King.[15] When Wing Commander A.E.F. McCreary, Albert's second-in-command, asked him if he would like to ride a 'gharry', as motorbikes were called, the Prince replied, 'Oh you don't know my father. He doesn't even allow me a push bike.'[16] What they were allowed to do was to hunt with the Cranwell beagles, the Blankney and the Belvoir hunts. A favourite pastime was playing tennis at the Physical Training School at Cranwell.

It was a good diversion from the continuing teething problems in the newly combined air service. Staff from the Navy and Army defiantly wore their old uniforms and remained separately identified until the new RAF uniform of khaki, which preceded the later Air Force blue, was decided upon. In this far from unified community, Albert was understandably jittery about the actual business of flying. A constant roll-call of pilots killed was alarming.

Albert wrote on 1 March to Godfrey-Faussett, threatening to give up flying – 'an overrated job altogether'. But three days later he made his first flight in awful wet and windy conditions, flying for twenty-five minutes at a height of just a few hundred feet. 'It was a curious sensation,' he wrote to his mother the next day, 'and one which takes a lot of getting used to. I did enjoy it on the whole, but I don't think I should like flying as a pastime.'[17] Louis was impressed by Albert's constant and courageous drive to succeed. 'I well remember when we had four days' consistent bad weather and I as an old man was delighted there was no flying. On the fourth morning the prince came to my room while it was still blowing and raining and said to me: "If I don't go up in the air today I believe I shall not go up again." So, much against my will, I accompanied him down to Croydon where we went for a short flight and the result was that in his wisdom he was right because he was never hesitant again.'[18]

While Albert was fearful of flying, Louis found it even more difficult. He was almost forty years old, and was competing with pilots half his age. He was also apprehensive about the extraordinary skills needed to battle in the sky, as every day in the officers' mess they listened to tales of disaster and triumph. Lieutenant Norman Macmillan, a contemporary pilot from 45 Squadron RFC, later suggested that some sort of 3-D vision was necessary: 'We were continually on the alert against the enemy whom we had to fight. We had to look in front of us, above us, around us, behind us and below us. We had to develop an entirely new sense of sight, of vision, the enemy might be anywhere. On the ground the enemy was ahead, in the air he might be anywhere. We had to live within a sphere instead of a life that was horizontal on the ground.'[19]

In the officers' spartan mess, Louis and Albert sat around in front of a coal fire listening to anecdotes of terrified rookie pilots being unable to pinpoint the presence of enemy planes, and how patrol leaders had to make allowances when they were joined by novices. Some pilots, such as Gwilym Lewis, later recorded that it was a miracle that anyone survived a dogfight. 'It was an extraordinary thing that a fellow coming out couldn't see half the things that were going on. Their eyes didn't register into the far distance. We had to see things – just a twinkle of the sun on a bit of metal – that's all we would need to make us conscious that there was something in the sky way in the distance. We would get into dog fights and they hardly knew what was going on. They were shot down pretty freely.'[20]

Training was often on a bizarrely *ad hoc* basis. The average time taken to train a pilot during the war was eight months, two of which were spent in a Cadet Wing where drill and military instruction were given; two months in a school of aeronautics to be taught aviation and rigging; three months in a training squadron where the cadets learned to fly; and one month on a postgraduate course to learn to fight with the use of the machinegun in the air. In 1916 new qualification tests were drawn up to raise the standard of flying: the pilot had to have spent at least fifteen hours in the air solo. He must also have flown a Service-type plane, carried out a cross-country flight of sixty miles and made two landings in the dark, assisted by flares. But the pressures of war meant that these rules were often ignored, and in 1917 most pilots going to France only clocked up an average seventeen hours' flying. Many had less than ten hours' solo flying. The fast learners were sent to France first, and so often the most promising pilots were shot down because they could not fly well enough. The tremendous casualties of 1917 led to the establishment of a school for instructors, and by September the average flying hours of pilots going overseas had risen to forty-eight.[21]

The most significant change in Louis's relationship with

Albert was that they were novices in the RAF together, learning and relying on each other much more. Louis's friendship moved more into his private life as they planned trips to London for dinners or the theatre, mostly with Louis's friends. 'It would be good to have a really good evening and I feel like a shake-up, as things are very mouldy down here,' Albert wrote from York Cottage.[22] When he corresponded with his parents, Louis was almost the only friend he mentioned. They were an odd couple, in many ways opposites, but they enjoyed each other's company. Albert, now aged twenty-three, was far from sophisticated and welcomed an older guide initiating him into the wider world. For instance, Louis introduced him to a number of glamorous women outside his usual social circle. One such new friend was Madge Saunders, a South African former chorus girl who became well known for musical comedy, and also her saucy role in a film called *Tons of Love*, made in 1930. Born in Johannesburg on 25 August 1894, she was only a year older than Albert and clearly, judging from remarks he made to Louis, she had taken his fancy. She was a dark-haired, voluptuous woman with a full bosom and an even broader sense of humour. She was well aware of the powers of her attraction and had a reputation for never hesitating to get her man. Albert was not the wild, carefree man of the Jazz Age like his elder brother, and was struck by her open, easy, approachable manner. While Prince Edward had numerous affairs and was relaxed and guiltless about it, Albert was a slower and more cautious developer in that regard and, as with most things that he tried for the first time, he lacked confidence and flair. There was never any doubt that he was interested in women, but meeting them was the problem and Louis became a useful escort. Louis loved the glitz and glamour of the showbusiness world, befriending some of the best-known actresses from the stage. It was an entirely platonic and open pleasure, and indeed Phyllis was often with Louis at some of the parties. He simply liked the fizz and verve of their exuberant theatre world, and enjoyed introducing those who were part of it to his friends.

After meeting Madge Saunders through Louis, the Prince felt she needed to be handled discreetly, precisely because she was an actress. He was aware of other royal princes encountering beguiling young actresses, only to receive blackmail demands for the return of their billets-doux. Albert did not want to be caught in that way, and implied as much to Louis. 'Many thanks for your letter telling me about the arrangements for Friday,' he wrote. 'If you don't mind I would rather not write Madge Saunders as I don't know her address, and also it is rather risky from here, as she hasn't got another name. In these cases it is always better not to have any correspondence. If you could get it arranged it would be all right. It ought to be good fun though that Saturday and what Rigby [Sir Hugh Rigby, royal surgeon 1870–1944] finds when he comes to see us God only knows!!! I like your way of putting it!!'[23] It is not clear what Rigby was going to find out, but Albert was, at last, having some fun.

Saunders came to England in 1913 having been hired by the New Theatre to understudy the part of Etelka in *The Laughing Husband*. She toured all over Britain with different troupes, and in 1918, when Albert met her, she was playing the part of Elsie Gray in *Very Good Eddie*, and then later in the same year appeared in the Gaiety Theatre as Grace Douglas in *Going Up*. But what Albert did not know was that, while she was catching his eye, Madge had also set her cap at what she thought was a more realistic marriage bet. She was dating Leslie Henson, one of the most outstanding comic actors of the first half of the century. Henson was famous for his ability to contort his face into exaggerated elastic expressions. 'The result was frequently unforgettable, and in moments of anguish and ecstasy he had been variously described as resembling a mandarin about to sneeze or a moth that has eaten too much wool.'[24] She might even have been playing one admirer off against the other at the same time, but if so, Albert was in the dark. In 1919 she married Henson, and was never seen by the Prince again. The marriage lasted just a short time and is not even mentioned in Henson's autobiography.

Women were increasingly becoming part of Albert's life, and invariably he and Louis would talk about girls he knew and liked. There was very little he would not tell Louis, who was the only person the Prince saw almost every day of his life. Albert needed an older guide and mentor: he was clearly no fast mover, and lacked savoir-faire, sophistication and confidence. He also sometimes lacked judgement. The next woman in his life was even less suitable; she was married and simultaneously being pursued by another lover. Louis watched with little enthusiasm as Albert fell for Sheila Chisholm, a stunningly beautiful twenty-eight-year-old Australian, who had married the raffish Lord Loughborough, heir to the Earl of Rosslyn, in Cairo in 1915. She was a close friend of Freda Dudley Ward, the Prince of Wales's mistress, who described her as the most beautiful girl she had ever seen. As their clandestine friendship was observed by Edward, he nicknamed Albert and Sheila the 'Do's', perhaps due to an affectation of speech by one of them as to how they pronounced the word 'Do'.

But while Louis had managed to keep his friendship with Madge Saunders quiet, and, of course, it may have been merely an innocent crush, the dalliance with Lady Loughborough met with violent objections from the King. Albert complained to Edward that he was being forced to stop seeing her. Edward expressed his irritation at his father's interference in a long, whining letter to Freda: 'Christ! How I loathe & despise my bloody family as Bertie has written me 3 long sad letters in which he tells me he's been getting it in the neck about his friendship with poor little Sheilie.'[25] But it was not, according to the Prince of Wales, a physical affair. 'As there's really nothing entre S & B I can't see why they can't agree to be just great friends but as I've said before cut out the love stunt!!'

Although Edward believed their liaison to be simply

platonic, that was of no consequence to the King, to whom appearances mattered above all else. He ordered Albert to stop seeing Sheila, even threatening not to make him Duke of York unless he abandoned his friendship with her.[26] What Edward knew, but Albert apparently didn't, was that Lady Loughborough was at the same time carrying on an affair with a Russian émigré called Dmitri Obolensky. Edward knew that Lord Loughborough was aware of being cuckolded and was understandably furious.

While Louis was often able to act as a useful buffer and interpreter between the Prince and his parents, keeping the King sweet over the Prince's affairs of the heart was not easy. On the whole he stuck to basic professional matters or his health when talking to the King about Albert. But Louis would also occasionally broach more delicate subjects on his behalf. 'Greig told me that he stayed with you at Aldershot. I am so glad you had a talk with him about things in general here,' wrote Albert to Queen Mary from Cranwell on 20 June 1918. Louis was a constant guide and adviser on all aspects of his life. He always urged him on.

Albert needed a strong dollop of common sense to bring perspective to his life. Often the trivia of Palace protocol became ludicrously important. For instance, Albert tended to become over-anxious about issues of protocol or status. He was furious when the RAF senior staff failed to consult him in advance about a visit by his sister, Princess Mary. He felt slighted and left out, and used Louis to try to sort it out.

I know for a fact that he (our general) wants Mary to come down here for July 30th to give away the prizes for some Sports which are being arranged. He has not and I don't expect he will ask me if I think she would be able to. I just tell you this in case it comes as a surprise to you, but it shows the disposition. One of the officers gave it out at a meeting which was being held about the Sports that Mary was going to be asked. I suppose this was done by Briggs's orders. If you did think of letting her come down here about then I hope you would ask the Greigs to have her to stay with them as I know they would be only too pleased. Briggs, of course, wants Mary to stay with him!! He is a frightful trial for us all.'[27]

Louis was good at reducing the tension over such piffling matters with light, humorous quips. When the King grumbled at Albert for visiting a nightclub, Louis stepped in to point out that they were not going to an 'orgiastic coven' but visiting the most respectable of dining clubs which looked more like 'a gathering of geriatrics', and furthermore everyone would be in black tie. He was able to make the King stop and occasionally laugh; 'Louis had a knack of making tensions disappear so as to avoid confrontations and flare-ups,' remembered one courtier.[28] It may have been the flapper age but tweedy, squirearchical George V was not comfortable with it. Louis made sure that Albert had his fair share of fun.

In August 1918, Louis and Albert were transferred to Hastings on the Sussex coast to broaden their experience of air training; they also underwent a number of sessions of 'square-bashing'. Once again the King had intervened to make sure that Louis stayed at Albert's side. Clive Wigram wrote to Major-General Sir Godfrey Paine on 2 July 1918, on behalf of the King, to ensure Louis stayed near to the Prince. 'His Majesty quite approves of Prince Albert being transferred from Cranwell to Hastings, but hopes that you may be able to arrange that Greig goes with him at the same time.'[29] They had both found Cranwell a restless place with the rival groups from the Army and the Navy endlessly bickering, and so were glad to move. Albert had been dismayed to find that the training course, of which he had been in charge, was dismantled, and less experienced officers given seniority over him. It was a blow. 'I am rather depressed about the whole affair as you may imagine, as I was very keen on this job, and was doing my best to make it a success,' he complained to his father.[30]

Their friendship deepened through living and working

together to overcome the challenges of a flying career. While Louis wanted to be more involved in the war, he also saw the potential of a career in the Air Force, and he would continue to gain personal satisfaction by helping Albert. He enjoyed nurturing the younger man. He always felt that there was a huge amount of potential that had never been tapped to turn him into an outstanding professional. He was very fond of the Prince and did his best to 'put steel' into him as he steered him towards achieving personal success and professional satisfaction.

The sense of failure surrounding Albert's career had never quite disappeared, although Louis never thought of it in such harsh terms. There were signs that parts of his life were improving. He was out and about more and girls were starting to enter his life. Louis, on the other hand, was enjoying life with his wife and baby daughter and hoping to expand the family. But dominating both their lives was the war; they each felt they were missing out on the chance to take part in the final push to victory.

Chapter Nine

'We are staying *chez le roi* tonight & going on to
Bruges tomorrow to have a look at Zeebruge & so
towards Brussels where I think we may meet the
Head of the Firm [George V] who is coming out. I
hope to hand the young partner [Albert] onto him &
get home but at present I can only hope.'

Louis, writing home after the Armistice

By the autumn of 1918 the Allies were scenting victory
across the Channel, and Albert told his father he wanted
to reach France before the war was over. Permission
was then given for him and Louis to report to the headquarters
of the RAF at Autigny. It was a clear, crisp day as they sped off
in a Handley Page bomber on 23 October to catch a glimpse of
the closing stages of a war that had dragged on for four years
and cost more than nine million lives. 'A good but tiring
journey,' noted Albert, 'the flight I thoroughly enjoyed, though
he [the pilot] had to land at Marquise as one of the engines was
running badly. It was not too cold but he flew more or less all
the time under 1000 feet.'[1] They were able to witness the last
days of bombing and anti-aircraft activities, and were quickly
caught up in the excitement of a victorious army about to see
the collapse of the German war machine. 'The [British] officers
all seem in very good spirits and never look upon a raid as
more than an ordinary flight, which, of course, is only right,'
Albert told his father.[2] That month the German High
Command started to accept the inevitability of defeat and

offered an initial peace deal which was risible, as it would have left German troops still in Belgium and France. It would have been more of a pause than a retreat and certainly no surrender. David Lloyd George, Georges Clemenceau and President Woodrow Wilson demanded complete surrender and the evacuation of all territory occupied by Germany. But it took some time for the spirit of surrender to be accepted. In early October, *Vorwarts*, the main German Social Democratic paper, proposed a massive call-up of recruits who had not yet been called to serve, as a final effort to rout the Allies. It turned out to be mere bravado, as the war was by then effectively won; the Allies' advance was unstoppable. Louis and Albert made their contribution to the final push more as observers than participants, but they were glad to be there at the final act. A little-known German soldier called Adolf Hitler was one of the wounded, temporarily blinded by a British gun shell on 14 October near the Belgian village of Werwik and evacuated to a hospital north of Berlin.

The peace for which all Europe had longed finally came at eleven o'clock on the morning of 11 November 1918. 'The great day has come & we have won the war,' the King wrote to Albert.[3] 'At long last the killing is over and we can all get back to our normal lives and our homes,' wrote Louis. Four empires were divided into a multitude of republics, and the dire consequences of war condemned the world to its worst modern economic depression. Yet at that moment there was a sense of overwhelming jubilation that the massacres on a scale never before imagined had finally halted.

For the first time Louis acted as Albert's equerry on an official royal engagement abroad. The Prince represented George V when King Albert of the Belgians made his triumphant return to Brussels to celebrate its liberation on 22 November 1918. The Prince of Wales had been asked, but he was too busy working with the Canadian Corps. Second choice was the Duke of Connaught, the King's uncle, but he had returned to England and was reluctant to travel out again.

So Albert – the third choice, if not the last resort – represented his country on behalf of the sovereign. He learned to hide his sense of frustration and the undermining of his confidence by never being the King's first choice as they made their way towards Belgium. There was plenty to distract his attention as he witnessed the war-torn landscape. 'I motored to Paris with Greig on Thursday and went through Rheims and Château-Thierry. The former town is a terrible sight and the cathedral absolutely shelled to pieces . . . The whole way from here to Arras is a scene of the most awful desolation. It does make one wish one could have done the same in Germany.'[4]

Louis had not been in Belgium since his time as a prisoner of war in 1914, and he was elated as old memories of defeat and capture were superseded by the Allied victory. To see the defeated Belgians, once a routed and depressed nation, now take to the streets to dance and cheer was a joyous sight. Proudly wearing their new RAF uniforms, the two friends accompanied the Belgian royal family on horses along the victory parade, the English prince on the monarch's right hand. King Albert wore a field uniform and a battered trench helmet, his queen elegant in a faded dove-grey habit, carrying a bunch of orchids. The crowd lined the streets, surging forward and roaring in jubilation as they paraded through the city. They wound their way to the Place de la Nation, where they were received by the Burgomeister Max, the hero of Brussels, and Cardinal Mercier, the spiritual saviour of free Belgium. The King delivered his celebratory address in the Chamber of Deputies, which just a few weeks earlier had been used by the Germans as an officers' club and casino. Louis wrote to his brother Robert from the Palais de Bruxelles, where he and Albert were staying as guests of the Belgian King:

> We've been travelling everywhere & ended up in this solemn entry into here where we have to ride unknown horses thro' a yelling crowd waving flags & throwing flowers. We are staying *chez le roi* tonight & going on to Bruges tomorrow to have a look at Zeebrugge & so towards Brussels where I think we may meet the

Head of the Firm [George V] who is coming out. I hope to hand
the young partner [Albert] onto him & get home but at present I
can only hope. The Bosches have done but little damage beyond
insulting the people & pinching their money. It is funny to see
people like Burgomeister Max & Cardinal Mercier in the flesh, but
they are very much alive.

Louis was already looking beyond the war to a time when he
could spend more time with his family: 'I don't know what
may happen to the air force after this but if I can raise a small
retiring pension I think my name is "op it" if possible as I'm
going for a quiet life chez moi & will watch my half-witted
children grow up. It's wonderful that peace has come, almost
unbelievable.'[5]

But thoughts of home had to be delayed as in December
Louis was asked to accompany Albert on another trip to
France with George V, the Prince of Wales, and a large retinue
of the King's closest courtiers, including Sir Derek Keppel, Sir
Charles Cust, Colonel Clive Wigram, Lord Cromer, and Lord
Claud Hamilton. It was a grand affair with them divided into
three groups, each allotted their own château. Albert, Cromer
and Louis were billeted together at Romont before continuing
by train to Paris. They were greeted at the Bois de Boulogne
station by President Clemenceau and his Prime Minister
M. Pichon, and an impressive array of senior French Army
officers. Louis took his place in the procession of carriages
with the Prince of Wales and Albert as they paraded past
the Arc de Triomphe, down the Avenue des Champs Elysées,
through the Place de la Concorde and across the Seine to
the Quai d'Orsay, at which point the King alighted. The
inclement weather did not diminish the rapture and jubilation
of the crowds who waved flags and shouted 'Vive le roi,
vive l'Angleterre' and 'Vive le prince de Galles' until they
were hoarse. France had waited a long time to celebrate its
freedom.

Louis travelled with Albert and the King for several days as they toured the desolate battlefields, where they were moved by the apocalyptic evidence of damage and loss of life. Upturned ploughs, abandoned carts, empty houses and bullet-scarred walls were just some of the signs of chaos. Everywhere there were lines of troops marching. The battles were over but the largest gathering of armed men ever convened was sprawled across Europe, many of them soldiers disillusioned and disorientated after such slaughter and mayhem. The King and his party lunched in a house in a town called Avesnes that had been the headquarters of Field Marshal von Hindenburg and had been constantly used by the Germans as an army headquarters during the town's occupation. The mayor told them that when the German Emperor and the Crown Prince had visited their town all the inhabitants had been confined to their houses. The Germans had also forced the women in Avesnes to salute all their officers.

The King took Louis and Albert with him for a private moment of contemplation and prayer on the sodden field where crude wooden crosses stood in rows, each marking the body of a British soldier who had lost his life. The King knew this was simply a tiny sample of the millions who had laid down their lives on behalf of his empire and the rest of his allies. The royal party clambered across the windswept lowlands to observe the desolate gravescape. They stood in the cold in silence in their thick woollen, ankle-length greatcoats before the King took just Louis and Albert for an even more private moment of mourning at the grave of his cousin, Prince Maurice of Battenberg, who was killed fighting in the British Army at Mons. An army photographer caught the moment of private grief, showing the King, bowed and withdrawn, with Louis and Albert just a few steps behind.

At Christmas 1918 Albert and Louis found themselves attached to General Sir Hugh Salmond's staff at Spa in Belgium. There was a huge amount of clearing up to do. After the initial exhilaration of victory, there was also a sense of anti-climax and exhaustion. Although they had not physically fought in the final push to victory, they, too, just wanted to go home. Belgium was a bruised, battered and depressed country as it geared up to rebuild itself. Any chance for light relief, including the odd snowball fight, was very welcome, as Alec Cunningham-Reid, a fellow RAF observer, discovered:

> We were divided up into two messes, and as there had been a heavy fall of snow, one mess challenged another to a snow ball fight . . . Prince Albert, in a flanking movement and at a range of two feet, dislodged the hat of what appeared to be Lord Doune, the GOC's ADC, who retaliated, at even closer range, by neatly depositing a couple of the best down the Prince's back . . . Major Greig and Colonel Tyrrell, head of the RAF Medical Corps forgot themselves in the excitement of the battle and tackled each other low even though they were on the same side.'[6]

Louis found he had time on his hands and made a chillingly memorable visit with Albert to see Princess Victoria of Prussia, the ex-Kaiser's sister, at the Schaumburg Palace in Bonn. Princess Victoria's mother was the eldest daughter of Queen Victoria, who married the German Emperor Frederick III and whose son, the Princess's brother, became Kaiser Wilhelm II. Victoria had married Prince Adolph of Schaumburg-Lippe, and then later, to her family's dismay, a Russian waiter half her age, Alexander Zoubkoff, who deserted her, leaving her in debt and forced to sell all her possessions. But in 1918 she was a sad, unrepentant and confused figure. Like hundreds of other Germans she was bewildered at the hostility shown by the Allies towards her and her country. Albert was not sympathetic, as he indicated in a letter home.

> She seemed to have little idea of what our feelings are towards Germany. All the atrocities and treatment of prisoners seems to be a revelation to her, as everything like that had always been kept secret from them. Greig told her some of his experiences as a prisoner which I think gave her an idea of how things were then. She asked after you and the family, and hoped that we should be friends again shortly. I told her politely I did not think it was

possible for a great many years!!!! She told everybody there that her brother did not want the war or any Zeppelin raids or U boats, but that, of course, was only a ruse to become friendly with us.[7]

The Prince of Wales was equally unimpressed with his second cousin's lack of repentance, and expressed his disapproval of her, and indeed all Germans, in a letter to Freda Dudley Ward on 9 January 1919. 'I had a stroll in the centre of the town [Bonn] afterwards & had great fun making the Hun men civilians get off the pavement for us; it wasn't difficult as they've all got their tails properly between their legs . . . Gud! how I loathe them all the more now that I'm actually in Germany & it does one worlds of good to know how humiliating it must be for the Huns to see us!!'[8]

Louis and 'PA', as Albert is always referred to in Louis's diaries, fell into a routine, sharing a mess and spending most days together, often witnessing historic events, such as the meetings of the Armistice Commission. 'All the Huns headed by General von Wiklisfelt at one side of a long table & the allies headed by General Nugin at the other,' Louis observed as they sat through the drawn-out, bureaucratic proceedings in which 'notes are read in French, then German, then English'. Louis was constantly outraged by the extent of the war damage. 'Came home by Divant which is a typical outrage by the Huns. Tablets up all over the place: "Here were killed so many Divantois, shot by the Saxon hordes".' The royal party grabbed whatever light moments they could, including local point-to-point races, and hunting wild boar in Luxembourg.

A dramatic change to their routine was marked when they joined up with the Prince of Wales in early December. Outside England, Albert had been enjoying the chance to relax away from Buckingham Palace with all his family's protocol and formality. Edward was even more glad to escape and brought with him all the energy and fizz of the Jazz Age. 'We danced at the Palace Hotel full of whizzbangs [fast young women: "whizzbang" was trench slang for a mortar or small artillery round] with whom we danced & then I went on to a night club with Claud & some Canadian friends where we stayed till 4.00,' noted Edward.[9]

Even at this stage Albert was more of the traditionalist and appeaser, while Edward seemed incapable of avoiding confrontation with the King, the court and his own destiny. He whinged to Freda Dudley Ward about his aversion to the protocol expected of a prince: 'We had quite a cheery party for the last night & H.M was in wonderful form & his trip has done him worlds of good & he is quite human; it's getting away from Buckhouse & the real court life that does it! Oh!! that court life, beloved one, that's what's going to hasten the end of it if it isn't modified; people can't & won't stand it nowadays & how well do I understand it & abhor all that sort of rot.'[10]

At Lille, the headquarters of the 5th Army, Louis and Albert were swept up in a run of wild nights with Edward. 'My brother took me to supper with some RAF friends where we sang & danced & told dirty stories in their mess till 2.30 . . . this last week has been a sort of course for "how to get old quickly" & my brother & I needed a cheery evening badly.'[11]

But the partying stopped abruptly on 19 January 1919, when a telegram arrived from Buckingham Palace with the news that Prince John, Albert's youngest brother, had died in his sleep aged just thirteen. He had developed epilepsy at the age of four and had been living in seclusion at Wood Farm, Wolferton, in a remote corner of the Sandringham estate, for some time. Queen Mary later saw it as a release. 'I cannot say how grateful we feel to God for having taken him in such a peaceful way, he just slept quietly into his heavenly home, no pain, no struggle, just peace for the poor little troubled spirit.'[12] Yet to his brothers in France it was a terrible shock, and they presumed they would immediately return home. 'Great hopes of going home. All arrangements made,' noted Louis on Sunday, 19 January. But these plans were then abruptly abandoned. 'On the point of starting for England a wire came from

HM negating our coming. Much disgust,' Louis wrote. It was appalling to him, and to the two princes, that they should not be allowed to return to attend the funeral. It is difficult to know exactly why, but it seems likely that the King and Queen wanted the funeral to be very low-key. The little boy was hardly known to the public, having been mostly kept out of sight. The arrival of his brothers at the funeral would just make it more of an official occasion. It is unlikely that the King realised the pent-up anger and frustration the boys felt at being kept away. Louis recorded that he had a 'long walk with PoW'. It is, however, evident from the Prince of Wales's rambling letter to Freda Dudley Ward that he was furious at the King, but not just for the obvious reasons. Selfish and narcissistic, Edward appeared to be more upset about missing a few parties in Paris and a rendezvous with his mistress than the actual death of his brother.

I'm in a fever, beloved one, as I arrived here about 4.00pm to find a wire from H.M to say that my youngest brother had died & that I wasn't to go to Paris; I wired back to say that I was returning to England at once for a few days which I thought was a good move & should have arrived in London tomorrow, Tuesday evening . . . so of course I didn't finish this letter last night as I had great & wonderful hopes of seeing *TOI* tomorrow evening if the goddess of fortune had been kind to us.

I'm so miserable darling as I've got another wire from HM telling me not to return to England though not to go to Paris & just to carry on visiting DIVS!! Isn't it all too heartbreaking & of course my little brother's death plunges me into mourning; don't think me very cold-hearted, sweetheart, but I've told you all about that little brother, darling & how he was an epileptic & might have gone West any day!!

He's been practically shut up for the last 2 years anyhow, so no one has ever seen him except the family & then only once or twice a year & his death is the greatest relief imaginable & what we've always silently prayed for. But to be plunged into mourning for this is the limit just as the war is over which cuts parties etc. right out!! . . . No one would be more cut up if any of my other 3 brothers were to die than I should be, but this poor boy had become more of an animal than anything else & was only a brother in the flesh & nothing else!![13]

The death drew Albert and Edward closer to each other, while also exposing their fundamental differences.

'We've had some great talks the last 3 days & got to know each other well again & that's a good feeling, sweetheart; he's a d——d good boy really,' Edward told Freda.[14] Such compliments were short-lived. 'Queer boy, that, & I don't miss him a scrap, though I'm very fond of him!!!!' he wrote later while at sea on HMS *Renown* in August 1919.[15] The Prince of Wales cared only about himself, and Albert was to learn this the hard way. He might look up to his elder brother, but he could not rely upon him. George V recognised this, which was why he wanted Louis as a guide and mentor to Albert. Louis was amused by Edward but saw him as a shallow playboy – 'he was interested only in himself'.[16] Edward was a gadfly dilettante with no understanding of responsibility, while Albert was always anxious to try to do the right thing.

To Louis's relief, Clive Wigram wired approval for him to go home on leave on 30 January 1919. At last he thought he would be able to see Phyllis and Bridget. But the day he arrived back his plans were disrupted. He was summoned on 5 February to Buckingham Palace to see the King, who wished to discuss Albert's next career move now that the war was over.[17] The King also wanted to ensure that he would continue to look after Albert. His idea was for them to complete their training with the RAF to gain their pilot's licences.

They were sent to Waddon aerodrome near Croydon to be taught by a war pilot called Lieutenant Alec Coryton (later Air Chief Marshal Sir Alec Coryton), flying an Avro 504K. The dilemma facing the authorities was whether Albert and Edward, who had also signed up for the flying course, should be allowed to fly solo. They were understandably paranoid about the princes' safety, because flying was extremely precarious at that time. Engines were unreliable. There was no communication between ground and air, and the number of crashes involving pilots under instruction was alarmingly high. The two having survived the war, it would have been disastrous for the nation's morale to lose them in a peacetime accident.

Louis was responsible for the princes' safety and decided to refer the matter up, asking J. G. Hearn, the Director of Training, for advice. He sent a letter by return, marked confidential and urging caution. 'Spoke to Major Greig with reference to the position in regard to the Prince of Wales learning to fly at Croydon. Major Greig said that the King knew that the Prince of Wales was going up as a passenger and also receiving dual instruction and did not disapprove of this. Major Greig also said that the Prince of Wales had no intention of going beyond dual instruction until he had definitely received the King's permission to do so . . .'[18]

The Chief of the Air Staff, in a letter also marked confidential, on 8 May,[19] banned the Prince of Wales from flying solo under any circumstances. Albert, however, was still allowed to do so, with special permission, the clear implication being that he was more dispensable than the Prince of Wales, not being the immediate heir. But Albert's greater freedom in the skies lasted a short time. Permission to fly solo was the least of his problems, according to a medical report which had been drawn up by Lt-Col. James Birley, the RAF's Director of Medical Services. This report showed Albert to be psychologically unfit to fly.

The RAF had no choice but to ban Albert from making any solo flights except with the written permission of the Chief of the Air Staff, who would never allow it. An order, banning him from flying solo, was sent by Brigadier General T. I. Webb Bowen, the officer in charge of the RAF's South-Eastern area. It was another blow to Albert's career, and Louis was left to pick up the pieces. Albert was not good at hiding such setbacks; his stammer became more pronounced when he was under stress, and increasingly it was a source of worry and embarrassment. He had been looking for a speech therapist. Meanwhile, it was, inevitably, galling for him to see Louis and other pilots having unrestricted access to flying solo while he was too highly strung to be allowed to do so. It did not mean that his pilot training was over, just that he had to be accompanied. It also did not mean that he gave up his determination to obtain his pilot's wings. The whole saga was somewhat symbolic of his whole life.

Coryton found that teaching Albert to fly sometimes needed some delicate diplomacy, after his encouragement led to panic at the Palace that Albert might be about to fly solo:

> One day I must have corrected him [Albert] through the voice pipe and during that trip he got depressed and I said to him, 'If this was the training of war pilots, you'd be solo tomorrow!' That cheered him up and when he got back he must have told the Queen this, because when I was on weekend leave I suddenly got a telephone message that I had to report to Colonel Newall of Inland Area [later Air Chief Marshal Sir Cyril Newall] and I went there and Louis Greig, who was the Prince's ADC, he'd heard about this and told me what was happening and he said, 'I'll get on to Newall so that you aren't torn to pieces in the morning!'[21]

Nevertheless, Albert did persevere and gained his pilot's licence in July 1919. Coryton sensed the historical significance of helping the first royal prince to qualify to fly and salvaged the Avro's joystick, and many years later, at Louis's suggestion, presented it to the King. 'What a good idea of yours and I propose putting it at Windsor along with armour, battle axes, swords and pistols etc., used by my ancestors. It will give a modern touch,' George VI would later write to Louis.[22]

The official photograph of Prince Albert staring out in his RAF uniform shows a clean-cut, confident-looking young man, with not even a hint of the setbacks and heartache he had overcome to learn to fly or the efforts Louis had made to keep him on track. 'Louis was a bolstering figure, always there to listen and give him resolve. He was a strong force that the prince needed,' Clive Wigram told his son Neville.[23] Louis's contribution went far beyond that of a normal equerry as he reverted to his role as doctor as well as minder. His constant refrain was that Albert always had the necessary qualities to succeed if only he was given support and encouragement. Yet it was frustrating for Louis always to see Albert fail to reach his full potential. He was sure that it was simply a matter of time. While Louis encouraged, it was Alec Coryton who got Albert through his flying classes, for which he was given a thank-you gift – a silver cigarette case with the words 'in memoriam' engraved on it.

The RAF careers of Louis and Albert did not last long. On 1 December 1919, Albert received a memo from the Air Commodore, the Director of Training and Organisation, that abruptly ended his flying days. 'I am directed by the Chief of the Air Staff to inform you that it has been decided that it it not necessary or advisable for you to continue flying. Orders have therefore been given for the re-allotment of the pilot, mechanics and machine hitherto at your disposal.' In effect, he was grounded. The King again summoned Louis to Buckingham Palace and told him this would constitute another 180-degree turn in his career path. Not only had he left the Navy to follow Albert to the RAF, but now he was being asked to end his military career altogether to look after Albert and his brother Henry as undergraduates at Trinity College, Cambridge. Louis was not sad to leave the RAF, as flying was something that he never really liked. He was also glad to stay with the Prince, as he felt that his task of trying to bring out the best in Albert had not yet been completed. Albert had no academic bent and was destined not to get a degree at the end of his time at Trinity. The King wanted Albert to have just a taster of life at University, and insisted that Louis stay in charge of him. The Prince Consort had started the tradition that the sons of the sovereign should attend a university. King Edward VII, when Prince of Wales, was enrolled at three different ones.

And so it was no surprise when George V decided that Albert must pursue the same path, and the Prince was by now used to following his father's every wish. 'I am giving up a Service career now and go to Cambridge in October for a year, to learn everything that will be useful for the time to come,' Albert wrote to his old Dartmouth Term Officer in July 1919.[24]

The King wanted his sons to have a proper family home under Louis's watchful eye rather than to live in rooms in college. To this end Louis rented Southacre, a large Edwardian house with a spacious garden and tennis court set back from the main road. It was just big enough for Louis and Phyllis, Bridget and the two princes, although by this time Phyllis was expecting another child. Jean was born in May 1919 and Albert was made a godfather.

One small step towards greater independence for Albert was that Louis overrode the King's restrictive orders and allowed the two princes to ride a motorcycle – or 'snorter', as it was by then called. He could often be seen riding between the city centre and Southacre, just off the Trumpington Road, only about a mile from Trinity. It was a very untypical under-graduate life for Albert to be living with a forty-year-old married man and his children. In essence, he was always chap-eroned. The King kept in close touch by letter and telephone, Louis eventually getting quite used to his voice booming down the line, his unfamiliarity with the telephone making him forget that the whole point was that you did not have to shout to communicate.[25] On 29 April the King paid an informal visit to their new home.[26] '[He] went all over it, and I think found it very comfortable. I went to meet him outside the town & I don't think anyone here knew that he had been,' wrote Albert.

Louis was very conscious that the princes wanted and needed parental approval above all else, and he tried to achieve this by passing on positive reports to their father. It was also obvious to Louis that Albert would gain enormously if he was able to gain a degree rather than merely dipping into university life for a year. J.R.M. Butler, the Trinity don in charge of the boys' academic studies, wrote confidentially to Lord Stamfordham on 16 November 1919 to try to extend their time at Cambridge. 'I am venturing, at Greig's suggestion, to write to you about Prince Albert and Prince Henry and their time here. So far as Robertson, who is teaching them economics, and I can judge after these few weeks they seem unlikely to be fully achieving educationally from being here.'[27] Butler suggested they needed to spend at least another year to gain any proper benefit, but his plea was to fall on deaf ears at the palace. Louis's role was as protector, nanny and safe companion and friend, escorting Albert and Henry to lectures and other undergraduate activities. Yet tied to the Greig family home, they were never able to integrate into student life.

Henry was the least academic of the brothers and took up polo as well as the rather unkingly sport of hunting mice. 'Bertie told me that you had asked him what I did all day here and that you were surprised that I killed mice,' Prince Henry wrote to his mother in November 1919. In the conservatory, Henry set traps which caught about fifty mice – 'a splendid bag', according to Queen Mary.[28] Albert was a more attentive student at lectures on history and constitutional affairs. Louis patiently sat alongside them in the lecture halls and the three were like triplets, sometimes even dressed in almost identical clothes. At the Union Society they heard Winston Churchill oppose the motion that, 'this House considers the time is now ripe for a Labour government'. Louis was following closely the rise of Ramsay MacDonald at this time. Albert's cousin, Lord Louis Mountbatten, was an undergraduate at Christ's, and cocksure as only a nineteen-year-old can be. At the debate he spoke up to oppose the resolution, while Albert's stammer once again prevented any spontaneous speeches. It was an interesting but somewhat low-key time for Louis. There were occasions when he felt he was treading water, but on the whole he enjoyed his involvement in the royal family's private and public lives.

On only one rare occasion did Albert get into trouble, when

he was fined 6s 8d for smoking in academic dress. 'I was made to regard the cigarette which I was then smoking as one of the most expensive I have ever sampled,' he told the Union when he returned some years later. But such instances of normal student life were rare. J.R.M. Butler tried to persuade Lord Stamfordham that it would have been better for the princes to live in college in undergraduate rooms, where they could mix with their contemporaries – as Prince Charles was to do fifty years later. But the King was adamant that he wanted them to stay with Louis, and Stamfordham wrote a letter echoing his master's voice.[29] Unfortunately, Butler's warnings of unnecessary isolation from his contemporaries eventually proved apposite, as Albert made no lasting friends at Cambridge.

Albert enjoyed having a second family life. He grew very attached to Phyllis, or Phiggie, as he called her, and would wander into the woods and fields when at Sandringham for the weekend to find jay feathers to send to her, sometimes writing two or three times in a single day. Phyllis provided some welcome maternal affection, while Louis was always the father figure urging Albert on, pushing him to have fun, to test himself and to embrace the opportunities before him. And Albert did gain confidence. Even his stammer seemed to be more under control. 'I don't know if Greig told you that at the luncheon to the recipients of honorary degrees on Thursday Prince Albert for the first time discarded the written draft of his speech and spoke in his own words,' reported Butler to Lord Stamfordham.[30] The King was pleased with his progress at Cambridge and in June 1920 paid him the highest possible compliment by making him Duke of York, the title he had himself been given by Edward VII before becoming the Prince of Wales.

The most notable outward sign of success that Albert achieved was winning the RAF tennis championships, which Louis had persuaded him to enter as his doubles partner. It was the first time that he was seen by the public as a young man who could succeed. It dislodged the idea of him as a stay-at-home semi-invalid who had missed most of the fighting during the war. With great pride, Albert wrote home to the King about his triumphant partnership with Louis:

My Dearest Papa,
    Very many thanks for the telegram, which I received last night. We are both very pleased at having won the Air Force Cup for the Doubles. Our hardest match was the semi-finals as we lost the 1st set and after winning the 2nd set easily we only just won the 3rd, after our opponents were 4–1 in games.
    I was very surprised to get through the 3 rounds of the Singles into the Semi-Finals. The 1st round was a walk-over as my opponent scratched. The 2nd & 3rd rounds were all very long matches, & I lost the 1st set in each, but won the last 2 sets. Greig defeated me in the semi-final, which I knew he was sure to do. Greig scratched in the final of the singles as he had played 4 matches in the day and was very tired. As it was, in the doubles we nearly collapsed from fatigue. I don't think I have ever played so well in my life, and I did not lose my head at the critical moment which was very lucky.[31]

The King was convinced that Louis did precisely that: stop the Prince from losing his head during critical moments in his life. But the tennis game was more than a simple sporting victory. It marked an important moment in Albert's own sense of achievement and his friendship with Louis. He had been swept along by Louis's enthusiasm to enter the tournament, and Louis had coached him hard so that they would win. Louis gave up the chance to play in the final of the singles to ensure that he and Albert won the doubles. Such public successes were rare and extremely beneficial for Albert's self-esteem. And as their time at Cambridge drew to a close, Albert was excited to be moving to London to start his adult life afresh and begin his royal career.

It was a thought at the back of some prescient courtiers' minds that the young man whom Louis was trying so hard to encourage might one day become King. How exactly was not clear, but Albert was just one step away from inheriting the throne. Much to the despair of George V, Edward had never shown any enthusiasm for the responsibilities and burden of being sovereign. Clive Wigram, always a wise man at court, privately predicted that Albert would become king.[32] He saw Louis's role as potentially that of 'king maker', quietly moulding the hesitant Albert into a confident and self-assured man who could be King.

Chapter Ten

'Louis rose from nothing to . . . quite a lot of influence by a genuine and constantly pursued ambition to pull strings on behalf of other people.'
Sir John Colville's memoirs

Harry Preston was a cockney hotelier who made a fortune promoting young boxers from London's East End, and Louis thought he was just the sort of wild card who should be introduced into Albert's somewhat narrow social circle after he came down from Cambridge. He was the original Flash Harry: a chancer whose passions were bare-fisted fighting and turning a fast buck. Louis had become friends with Preston through their shared enthusiasm for the greyhound track. They were both regular punters at White City, and Louis eventually became President of the National Greyhound Society, the dogs' equivalent to the Jockey Club.

When Louis took Albert along for a night at the dogs, he found that the Prince was intrigued by this larger-than-life south-east London sports promoter, who also owned the Royal Albion and Royal York hotels in Brighton. He was a feisty, gregarious character who stood out in a crowd. A small black bowler was crammed on top of a bullet-shaped head which seemed too large for his squat figure. A tightly-buttoned, double-breasted suit stretched over his barrel-shaped frame; white spats were fitted over shiny black pumps on surprisingly dainty feet, and a Cuban cigar permanently wedged in his mouth completed the accessories for this brassy sports spiv. Exulting in his rough diamond persona, he would recount outlandish tales of his early days to the spell-bound Prince. His home had been a riverside house in Lewisham, opposite a pub called the Thieves' Kitchen that was run by a Mrs McCarthy, an old Irishwoman whose pony cart worked all day bringing in fuel for a fire. It was where 'the thieves and knaves of half London warmed themselves'.[1] When difficult or drunk customers threatened trouble, Preston would personally sort it out. 'One evening three men came in. One was a coal heaver, another a criminal, a third had come out of gaol after serving eighteen months for manslaughter. They called for beer and when they refused to pay for it, I was called. I managed to drop the first fellow with one on the jaw and fell on him. The other two piled on top of me, and in my desperation I seized the man under me by the ears and banged his head on the floor.'[2]

Preston's pugilistic presence at Buckingham Palace inevitably raised eyebrows among some of the more conservative courtiers, who wondered if Louis really was such a beneficial, mind-broadening influence on the princes as the King always maintained. Albert and his elder brother, on the other hand, relished their introduction to the wilder side of London. Louis, after all, was not trying to spark a social revolution at the Palace: it was simply that he had never been hemmed in by rigid social rules. He liked people who were energetic, amusing, brimful of character and at the centre of their particular worlds. There was, of course, kudos for Louis in being a gatekeeper to the royal princes, but it was a task that he generally performed without personal gain. Some years later, Sir John Colville, private secretary to Winston Churchill, analysed Louis's role as a fixer. 'He rose from nothing to . . . quite a lot of influence by a genuine and constantly pursued ambition to pull strings on behalf of other people. He seldom if ever pulled them for himself but he thoroughly enjoyed helping others.' Louis gained pleasure from seeing both sides benefit from his introductions. And in this instance, Preston certainly did. In his 1928 autobiography, *Memories*, which traces his path from drab Lewisham clerk to flamboyant hotel tycoon, Preston proudly reproduced a photograph of a pedestrian letter from Louis on Buckingham Palace paper, dated 15 September 1921, congratulating him on behalf of the Duke of York on the success of the Brighton boxing tournament as if it were evidence of some sort of holy grail.

Louis's introduction of the princes to boxing was proof to the irrepressible Preston that 'boxing has at last come into its own'. Preston was a passionate monarchist who relished his royal access, dropping by on Louis at his office in the palace. He even recorded elaborately in his autobiography, how Albert had rescued him from a trapped lift at the palace.

> Louis had come out with me to the lift. It turned out to be one of those press-button contrivances. I felt nervous of it. However, Louis assured me that all I had to do was to press the third button. He closed the gates on me, and with a few more cheery words, went off. I pressed what I thought was the third button. The lift refused to respond. I pressed again, hard and long, but that lift stood as still as Joshua's sun. I tried to open the door; it was immovable. What was I to do? Shout for help or wait until someone came along? In my perturbation I allowed a few hard words to escape me audibly. At that moment, a genial voice said: 'Is anything the matter, Mr Preston?' I looked through the bars and there stood His Royal Highness, the Duke of York, much amused. I explained that I seemed to be stuck. He opened the door, and covered with confusion and blushes, I emerged. His Royal Highness greeted me in his pleasant way, and we had a long talk . . . after which I was put in the lift and got my finger on the right button.

It was not exactly high drama, but clearly it meant a lot to Preston. Louis enjoyed bringing some spontaneity into the often quite dreary routine of a royal prince. George V and Queen Mary maintained a home that was stiff, formal and traditional. There were few surprises, and Preston was an unpredictable addition to Albert's circle. The promoter was particularly proud of a night when Louis managed to get him invited back to dinner with the Prince of Wales after watching a boxing match between Peter Herman and Jimmy Wilde at the Royal Albert Hall. Preston asked Louis to invite the royal party to stay for dinner afterwards. 'Back came the reply that the Prince would not be able to dine with me, but I was to dine at St James's Palace,' recounted Preston. 'I called upon Louis to explain that this was a little awkward for me, as I had already invited my guests for dinner and the fight. "Bring them all" was the laconic reply.' And so fourteen of Preston's boxing cronies, along with Louis's brother Arthur, and the author E. V. Lucas, all swung by for dinner at the palace.

Preston was almost as impressed by Louis's reputation as Scotland's former rugby captain as he was with his royal connections. 'It was Louis Greig who helped to sow the good seed of the love of sport in the King's sons,' he declared. 'His experience has been of great use to the Prince of Wales, who made a point of keeping in hard, Spartan training all the time. There is one point in common between the Prince and Louis – both have a horror of putting on flesh.' Sport played an important part in Louis's friendship with Albert and Edward. They often played racquets or tennis together, and in 1920 Louis added a dash of glamour to their tennis game by inviting 'Big' Bill Tilden, the American champion, to knock about with them on the private court at Buckingham Palace. Tilden was ranked the number-two player in America when he made his debut at Wimbledon. He won the singles title of the tournament and was idolised by the British press, who viewed the twenty-seven-year-old Philadelphia player – always dressed in eccentric woolly-bear jerseys – as a romantic Hollywood showman. That Wimbledon was the high point of his sporting career, which was to end disastrously in the 1950s when Tilden was jailed for homosexual offences against young boys. But, in the 1920s, there was no more glamorous tennis star.[3]

Albert met a great many of Louis's friends and his family, in particular his younger brother Arthur, who was a jobber in the City, and John Scrimgeour, his brother-in-law. On many occasions Louis found himself organising Albert's social life in the evening. Prince Edward often joined them, perhaps for dinner at Prince's sporting club or the Marlborough club (set up by Edward VII as an alternative to White's when he objected to their rules about smoking). The evenings were always livelier when Edward was there. One night ended with champagne being spilled down the dress of a chorus girl called Marjorie Gordon who had joined their party. More was drunk than the Greigs had bargained for judging by the hefty bill that arrived. Prince Edward afterwards wrote to Arthur insisting on paying for the drink and also any damage incurred:

> I heard from Louis 2 days ago who told me our party at Prince's cost £50. I enclose this sum as I think you have fixed it all up at Prince's!! I don't think £50 is very excessive as those stunts go nowadays & of course champagne is very expensive; but I insist on paying for everything as it was really _my_ party!! Now as regards that dress for Marjorie Gordon which I also insist on giving her as I upset a whole glass of champagne over her that night. But Louis says that he told you I wanted to do this so will you please let me know how much it will be £20, £30 or whatever it is? Only I want her to have a really good dress!! We must have another party next week when Louis & my brother come up again.[4]

Marjorie Gordon was another actress who had been introduced by Louis into royal circles. She was a minor star whose first stage appearance had been at the Court Theatre, Liverpool, in Gilbert and Sullivan's _The Yeoman of the Guard_ when she was twenty-two. Born Marjorie Kettlewell in Southsea in November 1893, she had been educated privately in Hampstead and Paris before she took her mother's maiden name Gordon as her stage name. The musical comedies in which she performed all suggest a frivolous, light-hearted side to her character, with such provocative titles as _Stop Flirting_, _Just a Kiss_, _Nightie Night_ and _Will You Kiss Me?_ She also had prominent roles in the aptly named *His Royal Happiness* and *Loves Awakening*. In the latter, she played Tonio, the mischievous son of a widowed countess. With a page-boy haircut and a flawless porcelain complexion, she was a strikingly beautiful woman, who always made the most of her pert and petite figure. She certainly added to the gaiety of the princes' lives.

Louis's friendship with Marjorie had started during the war but at about the same time he introduced Albert to Ruby Miller, one of the most celebrated Gaiety Girls of the Edwardian and post-Edwardian eras. She, too, had been a child actress who had taken to the stage in 1903 when she was just fourteen. Her ambition had always been to be a showgirl. Louis met her when she was starring in a long-running musical called *A Little Bit of Fluff*. In her autobiography, *Champagne from My Slipper*, Ruby described one farcical night when Louis and Albert took a taxi home with both actresses. During the war the royal family had given up using their own cars, except for official business, which was why they hailed a cab and were to run into trouble. No taxi drivers expected to have the King's son as a passenger.

One night an old friend, Louis Greig, equerry to H.R.H. Prince Albert, invited some of us to a small party at the Savoy, which was being given for the Prince in a private room. Marjorie Gordon and I went along after the show. It was a pleasant party, with all the men in uniform, and when supper was over a three-piece band played dance music. I taught His Royal Highness a new tango step, and the party went on until about 2am. At that hour it was almost impossible to obtain a taxi and I offered to walk to my hotel, but Prince Albert would not hear of it. Finally, Louis managed to get hold of a taxi driver who had just dropped a fare at the hotel entrance. Prince Albert, Marjorie Gordon and I got into the cab, while Louis dealt with the driver.

'Buckingham Palace,' he directed.

But the driver wasn't having any of that. ''Ere, 'ere, 'ere,' he said good-humouredly, 'none of that lark. I've got a wife and kids to go 'ome to, and it's past two in the morning. You say where you want to go to and I'll take you, but I'm too old for this larking abaht.'

Poor Louis tried desperately to convince the driver, but he was up against the Rock of Gibraltar in human form.

'You give me a proper address, ladies and gents, or else get out of my cab,' was the driver's ultimatum. He got down from the driving seat and 'stood' at us.

We were all in fits of laughter, until finally I suggested that the driver must know the Prince by sight. 'If you agree, Sir,' I said, 'to let the driver take a look at you, it might help.' Prince Albert readily agreed and Louis flashed his torch full on His Royal Highness's face.

The driver took one look and his own face was a study. 'Oh, my lord . . . my Gawd . . .' he gasped faintly. Then, shooting rocket-like back into the driving seat, he sped to Buckingham Palace as though he was on a race track. At the Palace he catapulted off his seat and stood bowing as low as he could before the Prince . . . Louis told me afterwards that he's had the greatest difficulty in making the driver accept the fare. He had protested that he could not take the money for such an honour, adding that his cab would be at our disposal for however long the war might last.[5]

A significant reason why Louis was such a powerful influence on Albert at this time was that the Prince still had surprisingly few friends of his own age. 'I do not know of any very close friends he had, except Louis Greig, who had been with him for years,' recalled his equerry James Stuart.[6] Louis and the Prince saw each other all day and every day, and sometimes again in the evening. They were an inseparable duo. It must have been difficult sometimes for Phyllis to have so much of her husband's time taken up with the Prince, although, whenever he could Louis tried to make sure that Phyllis joined them. But she was never as socially flexible as he was, and often preferred to stay at home.

Louis took on the role of a protector to Albert, sometimes reprimanding his elder brother, Prince Edward, for his more mean-spirited teasing about his stammer. No jibes are as cruel as ones made by siblings, as Louis knew only too well, having been on the receiving end of so many himself. When driving back from an engagement, where Albert had given a speech, Edward went one step too far in mocking his brother's speech impediment and Louis cut him short. 'It made Louis so angry to see Albert treated badly and he made sure that he stepped in,' a former courtier recalled.[7] Edward was a spoilt young man who was used to having his own way; almost no one opposed him except the King, and even he had failed to control his worst excesses. Old courtiers were starry-eyed about the Prince of Wales because of his rank and charm. Louis was less taken in. They played a lot of sport together, and on court he was not afraid of treating him as an equal. For instance, when Edward was losing a game of racquets against Louis, he flung down his racquet and stormed out. Louis was left alone on the court, but not before he yelled at the exiting Prince, berating him for his spoilt behaviour. Louis had a natural authority as a former rugby captain, and was used to reining in awkward players. The next day Edward sent a very handsome sterling-silver woodcock round to Louis's home with a note of apology. It was the classic gesture of a rich young man used to getting away with murder.

Louis's most exotic introduction to the Prince was another former chorus girl called Phyllis Monkman, an eye-catching singer-dancer of the London stage. Three years older than Albert, she had made her first stage appearance, at the age of twelve, as a dancer in *Lady Madcap* at the Vaudeville Theatre. She came from a well-established stage family; her father, Jack Harris, was a well-known theatrical costumier, who founded the Eccentric Club. During the First World War she had been the principal dancer at the Alhambra, and the principal lady to the Comedy Theatre, working with such leading men as Jack Hulbert and Jack Buchanan. For some people, Louis's introduction of her to Albert was one step too far. The gossip on Shaftesbury Avenue was that Albert had become extremely intimate with her – perhaps losing his virginity to her.

Monkman epitomised the fizz of the 1920s with her dark hair cut short to curl up just below her ears; a glint in her eyes hinted at a wild streak. Posing in stage costume, she delighted in making a dramatic appearance, with three rows of pearls louchely swung round her neck, ostrich feathers in her headdress and a large gemstone pinned to an ornate turban headband. Fur-fringed sleeves and a tightly cut silk dress completed the effect; she knew how to take advantage of every inch of her sensuality. She was mostly in comedies with a light and romantic theme, including the suggestive *Cut for Partners* and *Uneasily to Bed*. Very much a woman who knew how to get on in society, she had befriended Ivor Novello and Noël Coward, who described her as 'merry as a grig'.

Her reputation in the theatre was one of fearless honesty, and this was seen in the frank interviews she gave, although never on the subject of the Prince. 'Looks have never been my strong suit,'[8] she candidly wrote across the typescript of an unpublished biography of her stage career, yet her powerful presence was never in doubt. While no classic beauty, she knew how to attract men. And in 1919, when she was starring with Buchanan in *Tails Up*, according to Sarah Bradford, George VI's biographer, Louis went to her dressing room to tell her that Prince Albert wanted to meet her and would like her to dine with him, which she later did, meeting him in rooms in Half Moon Street.

What can now be confirmed from Louis's diaries is that he did go backstage to see her in the evening of Thursday, 20 February, after he had spent the morning being interviewed by the King about his future role with Albert. The King insisted that Louis stay with his second son to continue to help guide him.[9] Louis recorded simply that he 'saw Phil Monkman', establishing the link between Louis, Albert and Monkman. Further confirmation comes from the unpublished diaries of Sir Godfrey Thomas, one of Prince Edward's closest friends, who was at 'a dance at Prince's with Louis Greig & PA and the Phyllis Monkman-Jack Buchanan crowd, where we introduced HRH as "Lord Chester"'.[10] Louis adored the bright

lights and gaiety of the theatre crowd, who were both elegant
and slightly risqué. Thomas related how he attended:

> two very amusing parties at Princes when he [Prince Edward] was
> up, organised by Louis Greig and his brother Arthur. Jack
> Buchanan and Phyllis Monkman from Bubbly at the Comedy
> Theatre, 2 Caldeoli sisters from Yes Uncle. A Mr & Mrs Burns who
> were apparently giving the party, Greig's wife & sister-in-law.
> Prince A, Harry Verney & myself. We danced till an unearthly
> hour both times. The second time the party was much the same,
> the only addition I can remember was Marjorie Gordon, who is
> taking the leading role in a new thing at St James Theatre.

Louis was evidently leading his Prince on far more entertaining nights out than the old King might have expected, and
rumours were rife up and down Shaftesbury Avenue
concerning the Prince and the showgirl. Cecil Beaton was one
of Monkman's most loyal friends, right into her later years,
after her career faded. Based on her conversations, he recorded
in his diaries, written many years later in 1971, that he believed
that she provided the initiation into the opposite sex for Albert:

> The legend is that Prince Albert, later George VI, was a backward
> young man and the courtiers were beginning to worry. He showed
> no sign of the usual interest in the opposite sex, so perhaps some
> delightful, trustworthy young woman could be chosen to initiate
> the young Prince into the rites of sex. It was agreed by all who
> knew her that the well-known dancer-actress Phil Monkman
> would be a suitable person. She was attractive with dainty little
> legs & ankles, sprightly & gay & a very sound character. The
> young Prince responded as expected. Phyllis gave the young man
> a cigarette lighter & although the relationship could never be
> considered more than an affair-ette, whenever they met in public
> the Prince who became King would produce the cigarette lighter
> to show he had not forgotten.[11]

Beaton may not have been entirely accurate, or Monkman may
have made unjustifiable claims. According to letters from
Prince Edward to his mistress, Freda Dudley Ward, Monkman

was not Albert's first sexual encounter. The Prince of Wales maintained that this had occurred during the war while he was travelling in France accompanied by Louis. Writing on 26 October 1918, from the British Expeditionary Force's Canadian Corps headquarters, he told Freda:

> I'm very amused to get a letter from my R.A.F. brother this evening written from Paris where he spent a night with old Derby at the embassy on his way to the 'Independent Force' at Nancy!! But he didn't sleep at the embassy as, in his own words, 'the deed was done' though he gave me no details and perhaps just as well!! But you see darling *c'était le premier fois car il était vierge'* which is why it amuses & interests me so much! I'm longing to see him and hear all about it . . .[12]

Whatever the exact circumstances of Albert's early initiation into the opposite sex, he greatly enjoyed his friendship with Monkman. The rumour in the theatrical world was that she received a present from Albert every birthday, and that when she died, aged eighty-four, there was found among her possessions a small wallet with a portrait of him in a dark blue peaked cap with his RAF wings. It was, however, always a friendship with a hint of risk. He had always been told that actresses were socially dubious, even unsafe. The blind prejudice against them was especially evident at court, even as late as 1927, when Lord Stamfordham wrote to Lord Cromer, the Lord Chamberlain, enquiring about the criteria of eligibility for guests to meet the King at Ascot. A complaint had been made by a man whose daughters were barred from the Royal Enclosure on the orders of the King, specifically because they were actresses. 'His Majesty knew that they were performing in public in Manchester as the Sisters Ralli in a sort of Review and that HM did not consider that anyone who had joined that profession should be admitted to the Royal Enclosure.'[13] While it was all right for the two princes to consort with actresses in the evening, it was not acceptable for an actress to be seen at a court social event during the day. The twin daughters of

Major-General Lord Ruthven were also denied admission to the Royal Enclosure because they, too, were actresses; their father showed his resentment by refusing the KCVO traditionally conferred on the General Officer Commanding London District.[14] Louis took little notice of such bigotry at court. He always shared his friends, and to have a showgirl and a prince among them, and not introduce them, would have been completely out of character.

Louis was proud of bringing Albert into contact with a great variety of his friends – from City wheeler-dealers, betting sharks, old rugby lags, Brighton hoteliers, the odd duchess and a smattering of film stars. It was what the King liked about Louis, this outsider from Glasgow who had swept into Albert's life like a breath of fresh air. Louis was also increasingly interested in politics, and in particular some of the key figures in the Labour Party. Freddie Dalrymple-Hamilton, his former shipmate on the *Cumberland*, recorded his amusement at Louis hobnobbing with socialists one minute and socialites the next.

> Monday 4 April 1921: Looked into Buckingham Palace to see Louis. Found him just off to play squash with the P o W, so deferred my visit till tomorrow.
> Tuesday 5 April 1921: I went to Buckingham Palace and had a talk with Louis all about present situation [strikes] which is bad. He was v amusing about some of the Labour leaders he has met and likes most of them very much.

Dalrymple-Hamilton was conservative, conventional and not very open to the political changes occurring in Britain. When he had lunched with a Mrs Ballantine, 'an American female', he observed how she 'annoyed me by talking nonsense about the King and the British Empire generally & saying she was an up-to-date woman and that our idea of kings were old-fashioned. God preserve me from meeting such a creature again.'

Louis was far from wedded to the idea of royal service for

life, and often thought of ways to earn more money; a job in the City was an obvious possibility. When the King heard about this he asked Louis wat he could do to ensure that he remained a courtier with Albert. George V offered him the captaincy of the King's own yacht. 'He told me I could have the Alexandra but he would like me to stay on.'[15] Only later would courtiers such as Clive Wigram wonder if the King was secretly preparing for the possibility that Albert might succeed to the throne instead of his elder brother. Wigram told his son exactly that: 'He was the man who was going to shape Albert and that is why people like my father were so keen for him to be around as much as possible. There were so many rotten types around the Prince of Wales that the King wanted someone as valuable as Louis to remain around Albert. Louis put backbone into him, and that was what he desperately needed. The King saw this which was why he considered it essential for Louis to be around.'[16] The King and many of his senior courtiers despaired more and more about Edward, who led an irresponsible and egotistical life. Ramsay MacDonald was a charitable judge, but even he later was appalled by his indolence and irresponsibility. 'There never was a greater fool in the world ... one thinks of him with the inheritance of power and influence & his qualities for using it like a just steward and feels contempt for him.'[17]

But Albert was not exactly model monarch material either at this stage, handicapped as he was by his stammer and with few obvious qualities of leadership. 'In ordinary conversation he talked perfectly naturally, which proves that his impediment was a nervous affliction, born of shyness,' suggested James Stuart. He was uncertain, unconfident and still trying to find his path in life. While the Bright Young Things of the 1920s were leading a fast, fun existence, the royal children often felt cooped up. Cocktails, jazz, gambling, the Charleston, weekend parties or indeed anything modern was anathema to the tweedy King George. His idea of a social life was dinner at home, stiff and formal, often ending early at 10.30 p.m., and he expected his children to follow suit. Mabel, Countess of Airlie, a lifelong friend of Queen Mary and her lady-in-waiting, defended the King and Queen against accusations that they were 'stern unloving parents', but she did concede that 'the tragedy was that neither [the King or Queen] had any understanding of a child's mind . . . [and] they did not succeed in making their own children happy'.[18] She noted how Prince George's manner to his children (before he became King) alternated 'between an awkward jocularity of the kind which makes a sensitive child squirm from self-consciousness, and a severity bordering on harshness'.

Few people outside Albert's immediate family knew him better than Louis, and it was no surprise when he was made Comptroller of his household, confirming his role as the Prince's right-hand man. It was an important promotion which would only have been agreed with George V's specific approval. Louis had already discovered that the job of a courtier is a delicate balance between protecting and guiding a charge in the best direction and accommodating his whims and desires. His new job was not any easier, as he always had two different bosses at court; Louis was at the beck and call of the King as well as his second son.

A courtier's life was an odd existence and not to everyone's taste. The job of private secretary to the Prince of Wales, for instance, had been turned down in 1912 by J.C.C. Davidson, the future MP for Hemel Hempstead, who saw the dangers very clearly:

I was not a yes-man or a lick-spittle and I would have made a very poor courtier; nor did I like the personality of the Prince of Wales, charming in some ways as he was – and certainly to me. I made it known through my chief that I was not a candidate for the post, though I realised that it was the sort of job which, at my age, most young men would have given their eyes to have . . . I formed the judgement that he was an obstinate, but really weak man, in whose pastimes I could have no share, and whose friends, male and female, I would not wish to know intimately . . . From the earliest days I had grave doubts whether the Prince of Wales would ever succeed the throne – or that he would become an adequate King of England.[19]

But while Davidson's definition of the courtier as a syco-phantic appeaser rang true in some cases, it was not an accurate description of Louis, who was always, to some extent, an outsider at court. Most of the senior courtiers came from a small band of interconnected families who attended the same public schools and often Oxford and Cambridge. Simply by being from Glasgow, Louis was different. And he was im-patient of the petty politics and snobberies that so often dogged royal employment. Being one of the King's favourites meant that such things mattered far less to him. The old guard at the Palace liked him, but were not quite sure how to define him. They would say: 'He did well for himself'; 'He came a long way'; 'He dressed slightly differently with his rather flashy white collars on coloured shirts'. 'It was difficult not to warm to him,' remembered one courtier. 'There were few people at court that almost everyone liked and one of them was Louis,' remembered another. He was an independent spirit, which was why he never thought he would be a lifelong courtier.

Louis's closest friend at court at that time was Clive Wigram, the King's assistant private secretary, who played an important role in Louis's life, protecting and guiding him through Palace politics. Wigram was seven years older than Louis and was a calm and wise adviser to the King. He had met Louis at Sandringham in 1917, where they quickly became close. Wigram was a seasoned politician at court, and also a stickler for detail in Palace etiquette, 'acquiring the courtier's art of attaching equal weight to trivial and truly important matters'.[20] The night before the Battle of Passchendaele he pondered the great issue of whether women munition workers about to be inspected by the Queen should or should not shake hands with her. When peace was in sight he had the task of deciding the colour of the crown that should adorn a governor-general's writing paper.[21] This reflected more on the detailed social etiquette of the day than on his own over-fastidious nature.

Louis's fame as a rugby player and later as a tennis player dovetailed with Wigram's love of cricket and racquets. Wigram had won the public schools racquets championship while Louis, in 1919, had won the Bath Club Cup. They played together whenever opportunities arose, and a sense of sporting fair play was to be an important bond. Neither came from grand backgrounds, but both shared a down-to-earth level-headedness. Born in India, the son of a bureaucrat in the Madras civil service, Wigram had been an officer, first with the Royal Artillery and later with the 18th Bengal Lancers, during various stints as aide-de-camp to two successive Viceroys, Elgin and Curzon.[22] George V had first met Wigram when he served as assistant to the chief of staff during his 1905 tour of India, which led to his appointment as an equerry. On the King's accession in 1910 he became assistant private secretary, later succeeding Lord Stamfordham as Private Secretary in 1931. Then, as now, this is the most powerful post within the Court, being the eyes, ears and often the voice of the sovereign, directly wielding influence through constant intimate contact and advice on policy, personnel and politics. Both Wigram and Louis discovered they had ended up in the Palace almost by chance, and Louis was glad to have a friend at court with whom he could be totally open.

They shared an enthusiasm for reform, and would talk into the night of possible improvements at court. Wigram suggested the Palace should hire a skilled and highly paid press representative with an office in Buckingham Palace. He also wanted a greater social shift in the activities of members of the royal family, with more well-publicised visits to industrial areas. He was no soft touch where propaganda was concerned, suggesting that more teachers and clergy be invited to the Palace. 'Preachers propagate better than most people the gospel of devotion to the throne.'[23] Wigram also knew how deeply the opposition to change ran within the stultified structure of the Palace. He recounted how he faced 'the Palace Troglodytes, who shudder when any changes are proposed and consider any modification of the present Court functions as lowering to the dignity and status of the Sovereign.'[24] Aware that modernisation was needed, he suggested to the Archbishop of Canterbury that the trains and feathers worn by débutantes when they were presented to the King and Queen at court should become a thing of the past. Wigram also shared the King's view that Louis was essential to Albert because, unlike so many courtiers, he was frank, forthright and stood his ground under pressure.

Communication between the royal households was often conducted by letter. Dozens whizzed between different members of the household each day; sometimes two or three letters from one person to another on the same day. The court was bureaucratic and weighted down by protocol, which Louis often could not avoid. In August 1921, for instance, he was drawn into a dilemma facing Lord Stamfordham over the suitability of Lord Mountbatten to accompany his cousin, the Prince of Wales, on his tour of India. Stamfordham wrote to Lord Cromer about his concerns. Louis had been asked for advice because he saw a lot of the Prince of Wales, and was able to give an objective assessment to Stamfordham. 'I have written to Halsey [Rear Admiral Sir Lionel Halsey, Comptroller of the Prince of Wales's household]. Greig says that HRH is keen on taking Dick MtB and says he now has no friends on his own staff except perhaps Legh [Piers Legh] and therefore he needs a friend!! I gather that Halsey is no longer a friend!! Of course he does not include you in that category but refers only to his own actual staff. The King accepts the scheduled timetable. He has had his say & can do no more!!'[25] It is clear from his letter that the politics, in this instance, were very personal. The quietest whispers in court quickly became widely known in Palace circles. There were few secrets and plenty of intrigue. Sometimes this intrigue almost became a parody of itself as grown men worried about the way others addressed them. On 25 August 1921, Stamfordham, for instance, wrote again to Cromer about mind-numbing matters of protocol and status on the Prince of Wales's Indian trip, and in particular the correct way for Mountbatten to address the Prince in private and in public. It was a classic example of the insularity and self-absorption of the court. 'I have impressed upon him the absolute necessity for a maintenance of strict dignity on all official occasions – that said there must be a good deal of kow-towing from his Staff when on duty – The K has told him that Mt B is to call him "Sir" and HRH to call him MtBatten when on duty. I expect this particular feature of the tour may give you a little trouble but your tact & wise judgement will successfully cope with it.'[26]

In the end, Mountbatten was allowed to accompany the Prince of Wales, thereby outwitting the old men at court. Cromer was incensed by his presumption and overfamiliarity, although how he addressed the Prince on the trip is not recorded. 'We all deplore his inclusion in the Staff, as we have reasons to doubt his utility and quality of his influence, however the Prince has got round the King who has approved so there is no more to be said.' But the Palace bureaucrats, as ever, tried to make sure they had the last word. 'You need have no scruples about a very literal interpretation of the Prince's words "however small" when it comes to accommodation for Mountbatten – provided he is near and easily accessible to the Prince.'[27] If Cromer had anything to do with it, Mountbatten would be assigned a broom cupboard for a bedroom.

Form and etiquette seemed almost insanely out of proportion to their worth. Lord Stamfordham worked himself into a state over the appropriate job title for Lieutenant Campbell Tait, Prince Albert's very junior shipmate and friend from his days at Osborne. 'If Tait's not be be An Extra Equerry, and Fritz says he cannot be an Honorary Equerry because he gets pay, then I can only suggest Acting Equerry. Tait is afraid that if the

Prince left the ship and went on shore, he – Tait – would have to accompany him, but this, of course is all nonsense.'

Such matters all seemed so trivial during and after the war to anyone like Louis who had fought in the trenches. He tried not to let such distractions take up too much time, and there were plenty of interesting things at court to attract his attention. He liked the way his job gave him access to experiences he would otherwise never have had, such as the secret world of freemasonry. Never a great believer in secret societies with odd handshakes and aprons, he was amused by the whole rigmarole. He and Albert were both initiated as members of the Brotherhood in December 1919 into the Navy Lodge No. 2612, reserved for senior naval officers. It was a family tradition as far as Albert was concerned. Every British monarch since the Grand Lodge, the principal body in English freemasonry, was founded in 1717 – with the exception of Queen Victoria – had been part of what its members called the Craft, as Sarah Bradford shows in her biography of George VI. Many members of court were also masons. Sir Lionel Halsey, the retired admiral on the Prince of Wales's staff, helped them to speed through its process known as the Word, to propel them through its thirty-three degrees to the most senior ranks of masonry. In February 1921, Albert and Edward were admitted into the Rose Croix Chapter, No. 169 of the Ancient and Accepted Rite in the ceremony of Perfection, accompanied by Louis and Halsey. Louis later witnessed their rise to Exaltees in the ceremony of Exaltation, making them all members of the United Royal Arch Chapter, No. 1629. To Louis, it was all a fanciful charade, and he punctured the rather over-earnest atmosphere by referring sarcastically to his royal-propelled speedy rise through the masonic ranks.[28] He stayed a mason only as long as he was closely associated with Albert, who remained an enthusiastic devotee all his life.

The flip-side to such solemn royal duties was their increasingly glamorous social life. Louis was often out at dances and parties in his role as Albert's escort. They hunted in

Leicestershire, shot at Wilton and played racquets at the Bath Club. Always Louis was at Albert's side. He even caught the eye of Barbara Cartland, the romantic novelist and step-grandmother of Diana, Princess of Wales, who recalled Louis in her memoirs of the 1920s with somewhat overblown admiration: 'He was charming, courteous, but above all things enjoyed dancing, and while the band played he was seldom off the floor. He was one of the most interesting men who seemed to be permanently at the Café de Paris. He was perhaps the most versatile man of the period, one of the most desirable men to have at hand.'

Louis was at the heart of the court, in a privileged position with easy access to the King. A typical diary entry for 2 March 1919 reads: 'Saw the Monarch. Lunched with Cromer. Walk with PA. Dinner with Wigram at USC [United Service Club].' In these rather cryptic jottings he had covered the most powerful people at court – the Lord Chamberlain and the assistant private secretary as well as the King and his second son. The next day he had lunch with his sister Anna and went to a dance at the Cosmopolitan. On the Wednesday he 'lunched at the Palace. Tennis with Wig. Dinner with Arthur. Saw Buzz Buzz.' A few days later: 'Dined with P o W, PA. Legh at Ritz. Went to the USC & saw Wilde beat Lynch.' The next day: 'Arthur, PA & I dined at Harley Street.' And then 'Dinner BP & went to Lady Ancaster's dance.' And so it went on. It had become the norm for him to enjoy close proximity to the most senior members of the royal family and their courtiers.

Louis's world had expanded as much as Albert's. While the Prince was introduced to an earthier side of life with boxing, the dogs and an assortment of beguiling actresses, Louis was always discovering new people and places through his royal role. State banquets and diplomatic receptions were part of his routine, as were visits to industrial factories in the North. Their time together at Osborne, on board *Malaya* or even at Cranwell now seemed a narrower, more parochial existence. They had switched career together three times; from the Navy to the

RAF, from the RAF to university, and then from Cambridge to a full-blown royal life in London. Louis felt sure that Albert was finally coming into his own. The boy-prince once likened by an unkind courtier to an ugly duckling while his elder brother was the cock pheasant, was learning to take flight, and a major part of the credit for this greater assurance and confidence, in the King's eyes, went to Louis.

Chapter Eleven

> 'As you say Greig has been wonderful, he is really a
> great help not only to me but to all of us, as he has
> got such a large circle of friends & acquaintances in
> every walk of life, which counts for so much in these
> modern days.'
>
> Prince Albert writing to George V in 1923

One of the most controversial introductions that Louis made to Albert, and one that he may have regretted, was that of James Stuart. He was a dashing war hero who had fought in the Somme and been awarded a Military Cross and bar for bravery. Louis introduced them in Belgium at the time of the victory celebrations in 1918. On their return to London he had asked Stuart to come to see Albert, who consequently hired him as an equerry. At the time Stuart had nothing better to do and took the £450-a-year job at the Palace, which he described as a cross between 'an ADC and a glorified bell-hop'. Almost two years younger than Albert, this Old Etonian Royal Scots officer would have attracted little attention among Albert's circle, except that he was to fall in love with the same woman at the same time as Albert. Louis was in a highly embarrassing position, as he felt partly responsible as two of his closest friends vied for the attention of the same woman: Lady Elizabeth Bowes-Lyon.

Stuart came from one of the oldest and noblest families in Scotland. His father eventually inherited the title of the seventeenth Earl of Moray and was directly related to the elder

half-brother of Mary Queen of Scots, the bastard son of King
James V who was Regent until Mary came of age. Handsome
and armed with a coruscating wit and a mercurial tempera-
ment, Stuart was a charismatic young man whose overflowing
self-confidence made Albert seem somewhat pallid and un-
sophisticated. Stuart's ambition was to enter politics, and at
the age of twenty-six he became a Tory MP, holding the same
seat in Nairn and Moray uninterruptedly for thirty-six years.
His persuasive powers marked him out and he rose to become
Winston Churchill's chief whip from 1941 until 1951, when he
entered his Cabinet as Secretary of State for Scotland. But in
the early 1920s there was not a hint of this seriousness; his
reputation was as a smooth-talking, extremely good-looking
lady-killer. And Elizabeth appeared to enjoy the attentions of
this tall, patrician-looking officer as they danced and flirted
with each other at weekend parties throughout the social
season.[1]

According to an account of their romance in *My Darling
Buffy* by Grania Forbes, who was given unique access to
Elizabeth's private childhood papers, held by her family at
Glamis, Stuart did propose to her.[2] Some contemporaries were
convinced that they were so attracted to each other that it
might end in marriage, but others were not so sure that
Elizabeth would commit herself, or indeed if Stuart would
remain resolute in his love for her. In the end, it simply never
happened. Maybe there was parental disapproval, as Stuart
had the reputation of being a heart-breaker – he did end at least
one engagement – or maybe Elizabeth sensed there were
grander fish to fry.

Albert and Stuart were never to be friends again after
sharing an affection for Elizabeth. An indication of the cool-
ness is given in Stuart's memoirs. 'He [Albert] was not an easy
man to know or to handle, and I cannot pretend that I ever
became a close friend.' Stuart eventually found more in
common with the Prince of Wales's set, and anyway, any
chance of his romance flourishing was dashed when in 1922

he was sent to work in the oilfields of Oklahoma. Whether this was a tactful withdrawal in favour of Albert or temporary exile forced upon him is not clear, but it certainly cleared the way for the Prince. James was to remain one of Louis's closest friends.

Ironically, in this tangled triangle of romance, it was Stuart who actually introduced Albert to Elizabeth, which he recalled in his memoirs:

In the summer of 1921, the first Royal Air Force Ball was held at the Ritz Hotel and my master, the Duke of York, was guest of honour. He gave a small dinner party at the Berkeley and then we walked across to the Ritz . . . Later in the evening HRH came over to me and asked who was the girl with whom I had just been dancing. I told him that her name was Elizabeth Bowes-Lyon and he asked me if I would introduce him, which I did. It was a more significant moment than it was possible then to realise, but it is certainly true to say that from then on he never showed the slightest interest in any other young lady.

The ball, in fact, took place in 1920, not 1921, and it was on 20 May, at 7 Grosvenor Square, at a party given by Lord and Lady Farquhar. But these minor inaccuracies aside, it was how Albert's first serious romance began, although it was by no means love at first sight. This was no coup de foudre.

Born on 4 August 1900 at St Paul's Walden in Hertfordshire, Elizabeth was the ninth child and fourth daughter of ten children of the fourteenth Earl of Strathmore, and in 1920 was considered one of the most desirable young débutantes of her day. With her hair in an unfashionable fringe framing her pretty round face and intense blue eyes, she was highly attractive. Chips Channon described her as 'mildly flirtatious in a very proper, romantic, old-fashioned Valentine sort of way'.

According to Elizabeth Longford, all men fell at her feet.[3] She was petite, vivacious and full of charm and confidence. Home was principally Glamis Castle, the oldest inhabited house in Scotland, with her childhood divided between there and St Paul's Walden Bury, a Queen Anne house in Hertfordshire also owned by the Strathmores. Educated by governesses, she had an extremely happy, sheltered childhood surrounded by her large family and a tight circle of friends from similar landed backgrounds. Unlike Albert, she experienced no fearsome nannies, tyrannical parents or cold and unfriendly boarding schools. Home was a place where nanny made nursery tea and the summer seemed full of endless children's games played with her brothers and sisters and their friends. She and a coterie of girls including Lady Lavinia Spencer, who had grown up at Althorp, the Spencers' ancestral home, and Lady Katherine Hamilton, the Duke of Abercorn's daughter, called themselves the Mad Hatters. They were a privileged group who enjoyed a round of country balls, shooting weekends, fishing under the watchful eye of a ghillie, and all the other pastimes of patrician family life on a country estate.

Albert told Lady Airlie, Queen Mary's lady-in-waiting, that he realised only some time after he had met Elizabeth at that fateful ball that he had fallen in love. But his hesitation and deliberation were familiar behaviour patterns, and he joined a long line of other suitors. What Albert had forgotten was that at the age of ten he had, in fact, met Elizabeth at a children's party at Montague House, when she, aged five, gave him some crystallised cherries from her sugar cake. But in the first months of their adult friendship he failed to use even that to his advantage. History does not relate what happened on his first stay at Glamis, but clearly no great romance developed, otherwise it is likely one of them would have told one of their friends. Louis was not invited to stay, but on his return to London Albert would relate much of what had happened. Yet like many young men in the very early stages of courtship, he was reluctant to say too much in case his hopes all came to nothing. Louis was always there as a trusted confidant, to listen and encourage. Elizabeth was discreet about her feelings, but what we do know is that she did ask Helen Cecil, the future wife of the King's assistant private secretary, Alec Hardinge, to stay as a chaperone because Albert was to be a guest. 'Elizabeth is a perfect angel as usual,' Helen wrote to her mother on 15 September 1920. 'They have got the Duke of York coming here and Elizabeth specially asked me to stay and help him, though I think it is just politeness on her part and she can't want me really.'[4]

Albert's approach was slow and awkward, and when he did pluck up the courage to propose, she turned him down. No details are known of the actual encounter, but Elizabeth's mother, Lady Strathmore, was sorry and wrote to her friend Mabel Airlie, 'The Duke seems so disconsolate. I do hope he will find a nice wife who will make him happy.' Lady Airlie prophetically replied: 'I like him so much and he is a man who will be made or marred by his wife.'[5] In fact, Elizabeth was probably reluctant to exchange the freedom of her small cosy circle of family and friends for the rigid confines of George V's court and his rather Woosterish second son, Bertie, who was far less self-assured than her Old Etonian brothers and their more self-confident circle.

As perhaps the closest observer of one side of the courtship, Louis saw how deeply Albert had fallen in love, and also noted that Elizabeth would make a perfect wife: glamorous, confident, charming. More importantly she was strong-minded. Albert needed someone on whom he could lean heavily and who would offer resilience and support.

Albert took the rejection badly and went into a trough of depression – pining for rather than pursuing his girl. Louis had seen such bouts of depression before when Albert's career seemed to be going nowhere. It was a question of propping him up, listening to his woes and steadily encouraging him to start again. Louis urged Albert not to lose heart but to persist in his courtship. There were other suitors in the wings, and Louis knew that delay could be fatal to his goal of winning Elizabeth's hand. Among her other admirers was Lord Gorrell, who later gushingly recalled: 'I was madly in love with her. Everything at Glamis was beautiful, perfect. Being there it was like living in a Van Dyck picture. Time and the gossiping, junketing world, stood still. Nothing happened . . . but the magic gripped us all. I fell madly in love. They all did.'[6] Christopher Glenconner, the Scottish chemicals heir, Archie Clark Kerr, a promising young diplomat, and Lord Gage were also in the running.

Albert had been utterly captivated by the relaxed, carefree existence of Elizabeth at Glamis, where they drank cocktails, danced, picnicked by the river, listened to music, and generally behaved as they wished. What struck him was the atmosphere of lightness and ease; Albert was able to forget the stiff, formal restraint of his own family life. He impressed the house party with his tennis skills, but little else made a mark. He appeared overearnest in such relaxed and often frivolous company, as royal princes so often do. He lacked the confidence to refuse to take no for an answer and instead to persist.

Albert's hopes suffered another setback when a rumour circulated that Elizabeth was going to marry the Prince of Wales. This spread like wildfire in 1922, and the press was suddenly determined that she should be the next Queen. Chips Channon, while a guest of Lord Gage in Sussex, where Elizabeth was also staying, noted: 'The evening papers have announced her engagement to the Prince of Wales. So we all bowed and bobbed and teased her, calling her ma'am. I am not sure that she enjoyed it, but how delighted everyone would be! She certainly has something on her mind . . . She is more gentle, lovely and exquisite than any woman alive, but this evening I thought her unhappy and distrait.' But Elizabeth was not nearly as unhappy about the rumour as was Albert, who must have wondered if there was any truth in it. After all, Edward was a better catch for her, and they were friends.

Louis watched with foreboding as Albert fretted. He could not simply sit back and let this romance wither away. He

River sports: Louis and Albert at the Oxford and Cambridge boat race in 1922.

Walking tall: Louis and Albert at RAF Cranwell in 1918.

Lighting up: Louis and the Prince of Wales share a smoke.

For the ride: Louis and his son Carron, aged six and his sister Jean, in 1932 at a pony show in Barnes.

Above: At home: Louis and family at
Ladderstile, Richmond.

Right: Secret mission: Louis and Prince
George, the Duke of Kent, preparing to
fly to America in 1941.

Below: Eastern promise: Louis and
King Farouk on his diplomatic mission
in 1943.

Bow-tied and beaming: a cartoon of Louis.

Below: The fixer in his final years.

"LOUIS"

On court: Louis and Albert at Wimbledon in 1926.

Wimbledon's royal box: *from left*, Princess Elizabeth, Louis with Elizabeth Hardinge, the daughter of the King's Private Secretary Alex Hardinge and Princess Margaret in 1937.

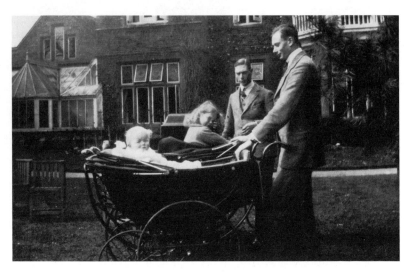

Prince Henry and Prince Albert with Bridget and Jean at Cambridge in 1920.

Below left: The Deputy Ranger: enjoying his royal residence.

Below right: Cartoon of Louis laughing with a pipe.

"I challenge You"

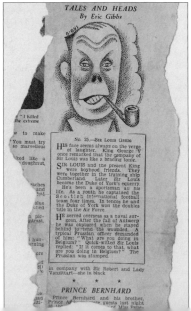

TALES AND HEADS
By Eric Gibbs

No. 25.—SIR LOUIS GREIG

HIS face seems always on the verge of laughter. King George V once remarked that the company of Sir Louis was like a bracing tonic.

SIR LOUIS and the present King were boyhood friends. They were together in the training ship *Cumberland*. Later Sir Louis became the Duke of York's equerry.

He's been a sportsman all his life. As a youth he captained the Scottish international football team four times. In tennis he and the Duke of York won the doubles title in the Air Force.

HE served overseas as a naval surgeon. After the fall of Antwerp he was captured when he stayed behind to tend the wounded. A typical Prussian officer demanded of him: "What are you doing in Belgium?" Quick-witted Sir Louis replied: "If it comes to that, what are you doing in Belgium?" The Prussian was stumped.

in company with Sir Robert and Lady Vansittart—she in black

★   ★   ★

PRINCE BERNHARD

All dressed up: Albert and Louis preparing for their flight to France in 1918.

The future King, *second on the left,* on HMS Cumberland after coaling.

Left: Acting up: Marjorie Gordon introduced to Prince Albert by Louis.

Above: Phyllis Monkman: Another gaiety girl introduced by Louis into royal circles.

Secret liaisons: The girl Albert wanted to keep quiet: Madge Saunders with Leslie Henson whom she eventually married.

decided to intervene, knowing that he was following a high-risk course. Louis was by nature always a fixer and felt Albert needed his help. The poet Robert Browning had a theory that there was such a thing as 'the good minute', and that if you did not grab it, that minute ticked by and your opportunity for romance disappeared forever. Louis felt that it was a case of now or never for Albert to use his 'good minute'. Penelope Mortimer, the Queen Mother's critical biographer, observed that Louis had by this time tried every possible form of direct encouragement; his only remaining tactic was to go for outside help. Louis was convinced that Albert was too hesitant and feeble in the pursuit of love. Bold, decisive action was essential.

Louis turned to his friend John Colin Campbell Davidson, a fellow Scot and the just-elected thirty-three-year-old MP for Hemel Hempstead. He was also parliamentary private secretary to the Prime Minister, Andrew Bonar Law, but what was important, as far as Louis was concerned, was that he had only recently got married after being turned down several times by his wife before she had accepted his proposal. Davidson had been in exactly the same situation as Albert, but had found a way to get the woman he loved to marry him.

In Louis's estimation he was the perfect man to urge Albert to persevere. Davidson was nearer his age; he was only seven years older than the Prince while Louis, at forty-one with a wife and two children, could not help being perceived in an increasingly avuncular light by his young boss. Louis made a secret telephone call to Davidson just a few days before Albert was due to lay the foundation stone of a war memorial at Dunkirk to commemorate British officers and seamen who had fallen in the First World War. He asked him to make a special point of being on the northern coast of France for the ceremony. He banked on the MP's youth, diplomacy, charm and discretion. Above all else he hoped he would be inspiring. Their rendezvous was a British ship in the middle of the Channel, safe from any prying eyes. Davidson made a note of the conversation, which became the catalyst for a defining point in Albert's life. It was recorded in a confidential memorandum, written many years afterwards, and like all documents written long after the event, memory may have cast the events in a somewhat exaggerated light:

He [Louis] was most persistent that I should make the journey, and I therefore arranged to take passage in a specially chartered ship carrying members of both Houses of Parliament from Harwich to Dunkirk. In brilliant sunshine, the Duke carried out his duties, after which we proceeded to the Town Hall, where in his parlour the Mayor proposed several toasts which we drank in sweet champagne, after which we were all escorted down to the quayside. In view of the message I loitered by the gangway and was just about to re-embark when I saw the figure of Louis Greig running along the quayside, beckoning. We went together on board the destroyer, and directly she cast off he took me down to the wardroom where I was presented to His Royal Highness, with whom I remained alone for nearly three hours . . . I had not been in the Duke's presence more than a few minutes before I realised he was not only worried, but genuinely unhappy. He seemed to have reached a crisis in his life, and wanted someone to whom he could unburden himself without reserve. He dwelt upon the difficulties which surrounded a King's son in contrast with men like myself who had always had greater freedom at school and university to make their own friends and a wider circle to choose from. We discussed friendship, and the relative value of brains and character, and all the sort of things that young men do talk about in the abstract when in reality they are very much concerned in the concrete.

He told me that sometimes the discipline of the formality of the Court proved irksome, and I sensed he was working up to something important. I felt moved with a great desire to help him if I could, he was so simple and frank and forthcoming. Then, out it came. He declared that he was desperately in love, but that he was in despair for it seemed quite certain that he had lost the only woman he would ever marry. I told him that however black the situation looked he must not give up hope; that my wife had refused me consistently before she finally said yes, and that like him, if she had persisted in her refusal, I would never have married anyone else.

To this he replied that his case was different from mine. The King's son cannot propose to the girl he loves, since custom requires that he must not place himself in the position of being refused, and to that ancient custom, the King, his father, firmly adhered. Worse still, I gathered that an emissary had already been sent to ascertain whether the girl was prepared to marry him, and that it had failed. The question was, what was he to do? He could not live without her, and certainly he would never marry anyone else.

The advice which I ventured to give him was simple. I suggested that in the Year of Grace 1922 no high-spirited girl of character was likely to accept a proposal made at second hand; if she was fond of him as he thought she was, he must propose to her himself . . . His mood when we parted was much brighter and more buoyant than at the beginning of our talk.

Davidson's words had a dramatic effect on Albert. Louis saw a new spring in his step, although at that stage Albert had no idea of Louis's Cupid role. The Prince told him he was going to head back up north to County Durham to see Elizabeth at her parents' home. Louis beamed the broadest of smiles. Albert had sprung out of his depression and was back on track to win the hand of the woman he loved. When he was staying with the Strathmores he took Elizabeth for a walk in the woods, and this time when he proposed, she accepted.

Two days after the proposal, Louis accompanied Prince Albert to Sandringham for one of the most important discussions of his life. Even aged twenty-seven, Albert was nervous of his father, who always treated his family as if he was a naval captain and they were young cadets.[7] More than anything Albert wanted his father's approval of his choice of bride. And just as he had turned to Louis for support when he needed the go-ahead from the King for his operation in 1917, he asked him to be by his side when he went to the King to seek his permission to marry Elizabeth. He need not have worried, as his family all thoroughly approved of Elizabeth, but Albert always did fret. His engagement was to be the moment when his whole life finally came into focus. More than anything else his marriage was to bring him happiness. Elizabeth was to be the magical ingredient by which he would grow and gain a greater sense of contentment and assurance. She provided a lightness to offset his more awkward and sometimes huffy standoffishness.

The engagement was reported by the King in his diary without any fanfare. In fact, before he even got round to mentioning it, he stuck to his usual habit of recording the temperature and the weather. Only then did he add: 'Bertie with Greig arrived after tea and informed us that he was engaged to Elizabeth Bowes-Lyon, to which we gladly gave our consent. I trust they will be very happy.'

The engagement caught Chips Channon by surprise: 'I was so startled and almost fell out of bed when I read the Court Circular . . . We have all hoped, waited, so long for this romance to prosper, that we had begun to despair that she would ever accept him. He has been the most ardent of wooers, and was apparently at St Paul's Walden on Sunday, when he at last proposed to her.'

Not everyone was happy, least of all Archie Clark Kerr, who had also fallen in love with her. The Australian-born Scot, ennobled as Lord Inverchapel, would later become ambassador in Moscow in the 1940s, establishing a notable relationship with Stalin and playing an important part in the 'Big Three' conferences between Churchill, Roosevelt and Stalin. He took news of the engagement between Albert and Elizabeth very badly, evidently writing to Elizabeth to confess his sadness, as she wrote back asking him not to feel sad 'as surely we can remain friends as before'.[8] Other friends tried to cheer him up, as did his mother, to whom he wrote of his great passion for Elizabeth: 'Frankly there never was a moment since my visit to Glamis when I had any real hope of success, but nevertheless I had clung to it and tried to tell myself that all things were possible. And now this has become impossible I feel tired and battered and dismal and whenever I think of it, and I think of it, even in moments of greatest crisis, my head buzzes.'[9]

What was clear was that Albert had won the hand of a very special bride. But just how he had been persuaded to make one final attempt to win her was to remain a deep secret between Louis, Davidson and the engaged couple. Davidson believed that his intervention was the critical factor in persuading Elizabeth to marry Albert. On 23 April 1948, the silver anniversary of their wedding, Davidson wrote in confidence to Louis, describing the meeting that Louis had 'made possible'.[10] The letter also mentioned the strange and doomed mission by Lord Stamfordham to Glamis to plead Albert's case to the Bowes-Lyon family. A note of desperation must have crept in.[11] The elderly courtier was hardly the most romantic envoy for this delicate task. It is not clear if it was an independent move by him or one orchestrated by the royal family. Louis can only have cringed. It may have been all right for some nineteenth-century political alliance, but Elizabeth Bowes-Lyon was a modern 1920s girl and was not going to be the subject of negotiation as if she were a mere chattel. It was a cack-handed attempt and showed little feel for diplomacy. Elizabeth had made plain that she was not to be bartered for by Palace flunkies.

It was not until she was widowed, more than thirty years later, that Elizabeth referred to the Greig–Davidson intervention and how grateful she was for it. Just three weeks after George VI had died, on 6 February 1952, Davidson had written to Queen Elizabeth, enclosing an account of the conversation that prompted the Prince to have the courage to propose. 'It has been kept in the secret recesses of my memory ever since, and I am only releasing it now because in Your Majesty's terrible loneliness I believe it may bring one tiny grain of comfort.'

Davidson told her he was convinced that in the wardroom of the destroyer *Versatile* he was 'permitted to glimpse into the innermost recesses of his heart and mind' because 'he seemed to have reached a crisis in his life and wanted someone to whom he could unburden himself without reserve'. Davidson was convinced that this was 'the greatest moment of his [Albert's] life and although from this side, the fences seemed unjumpable, if he rode at it with determination and confidence and threw his heart over it, he would land safely and win his bride. "If she accepts", I said, "go straight to your mother, and if your mother is like mine, she will square the King."'

She wrote back to Davidson to say how she was 'deeply touched' to have received an account of the talk that he had had with the King. 'I wanted to send you my heartfelt thanks for your thoughtfulness in writing so charmingly of such a personal and poignant episode . . . I must tell you that we were ideally happy, due to the King's wonderful kindness & good-ness and thought for others. I never wanted to be with anyone but him, & during the last ten terrible years, he was a rock of strength and wisdom & courage. So that in thanking you for your letter, I thank you also for the advice you gave the King in 1922.'

The engagement marked a most important turning point in Louis's relationship with Albert. It was no longer just the two of them making decisions about Albert's life and career; a very forceful Scottish wife was going to be taking over much of that role. While it was exactly what Albert needed and what Louis would have wished for him, Louis was wise enough to know that the arrival of a wife in a bachelor household often heralded changes. He had been the architect of ending his own role at court. Phyllis was always a wise counsel, and although not a great deal was said between them on this issue, they did talk of a possible career move for Louis – outside court. But in the excitement of the forthcoming wedding plans there was no time for Louis to pause for thought for long. He was swept up into the preparations.

Louis got to know Elizabeth only after the couple were engaged, and he was much taken by her sense of fun and natural ability to get on with people, and in particular by her love for Albert, and ability to draw him out. She had a wisdom and experience far beyond her years, possibly due to some tough blows early on in her life. When she was just fifteen, her brother, Fergus, was killed in 1916 at the Battle of Loos. The following year another brother, Michael, was reported 'believed dead' but was later discovered to have been taken prisoner. Louis knew it was essential for Albert to have a strong-willed and resolute wife, and Elizabeth was certainly that. 'There was a steely side to her inside the soft velvety coating. Anyone who thought she was all sweet and sugary was in for a big surprise,' observed one courtier who had worked for her. In many ways, Albert wanted mothering and guiding, and she was perfect in that role.

George V was hugely grateful for Louis's support for and friendship with Albert. Before the wedding he was once again summoned to see the King at Buckingham Palace, and in a private ceremony George V personally awarded him a CVO, making him a Commander of the Royal Victorian Order, advancing the decoration he had received in 1917. The King paid a generous tribute to Louis for all the work he had done for his family, and said he hoped he would remain with them for many more years. George V always credited Louis with 'making him [Albert] into the man he was'.[12] He did more than anyone else to promote and help his son, who had appeared so unpromising in his early days. Of all the King's children, things seemed to be working out the best for him. Edward was increasingly the least-favoured son – the King despaired of his heir.

But all such worries were cast aside as the family concentrated on the happiness of Albert and Elizabeth, who were married on 26 April 1923, at Westminster Abbey – the first time for more than five centuries that a king's son had wed there. Louis was rewarded with a prominent place during the magnificent service and the ceremonial procession. Freddie Dalrymple-Hamilton, Louis's former shipmate on HMS *Cumberland* and a close friend of Elizabeth, sat three rows from the front: 'The royal procession started about 11.30, the Queen being a magnificent spectacle in a blue and silver dress and covered with jewels etc. The Duke of York came up between the Prince of Wales and Prince Harry with Louis Greig heading his procession. We managed to catch his eye as he passed or thought we did as he half grimaced at us. I must ask some day!' he recorded in his diary.[13]

Afterwards Louis joined the couple at Buckingham Palace for the wedding breakfast: eight courses, each christened for the occasion, including consommé à la Windsor, suprêmes de saumon Reine Mary, côtelettes d'agneau Prince Albert, chapons à la Strathmore and fraises Duchesse Elizabeth. The nine-foot-high multi-layered wedding cake was donated by Sir Alexander Grant, the biscuit tycoon who had shown Albert and Elizabeth, along with Louis, around his biscuit factories in Harlesden.

The honeymoon was spent at Polesden Lacey, an imposing mansion in the Surrey countryside, lent to the couple by Mrs Ronald Greville, a rich brewing heiress with an unmatched appetite for royalty. While there, Albert wrote Louis an affectionate, appreciative letter to thank him for all he had done. He was hugely grateful and gave every indication that they would remain working together for a great many years to come. Its tone was relaxed and intimate, as Albert let him know that he was enjoying every possible aspect of his new married life.

> We arrived here safely though very tired & the sudden peace & quiet of this place was too marvellous. I must send you all my thanks for your wonderful work & half [sic] during the long & busy time which has at last come to an end. Please tell the Carruthers & Miss Heaton Smith how much I appreciated all they have done as well. It is now 12.45 & I have not had a bath yet!! Everything was plain sailing, which was a relief. You know what I mean. I was very good!!. Ever yours, Albert.[14]

The King, as always, remained Louis's greatest supporter. Three days after the wedding, he wrote to Albert and emphasised the importance of Louis's role as a guide and mentor for Albert.

Dearest Bertie.

I am indeed pleased to think that you & Elizabeth are at last having some well-earned rest after all the strains of the last three months. You are indeed a lucky man to have such a charming wife as Elizabeth and I am sure you will be very happy together & I trust you both will have many many years of happiness. We hope you will be as happy as Mama and I after you have been married for 30 years . . . It must have been with a pang that you left your home after 27 years. I miss you very much & regret your having left us, but now you will have your own home which I hope will be as happy as the one you have left. You have always been so sensible & easy to work with and you have always been ready to listen to any advice & to agree with my opinion about people and things that I feel that we have always got on very well together (very different to dear David) I trust that this state of affairs will always remain the same between us and that you will come to me for advice whenever you want it. You have got a wonderful man in Louis Greig, who will be a great help to you. I told him how grateful I am for all he has done for you when I gave him the CVO. By your quiet useful work you have endeared yourself to the people as shown on Thursday by the splendid reception they gave you. I am quite certain that Elizabeth will be a splendid partner in your work and share with you and help you in all you have to do. Wishing you and Elizabeth good luck and a very happy honeymoon. Ever my dear boy Yr most devoted Papa GRI[15]

Albert agreed with his father that Louis was an essential part of his household: 'As you say Greig has been wonderful, he is really a great help not only to me but to all of us, as he has got such a large circle of friends & acquaintances in every walk of life, which counts for so much in these modern days. May I thank you for giving him the CVO for all he has done for me since the War.'[16]

It had been a most dramatic year. Louis had proved to be a cunning Cupid as the romance faltered but then took off, ending in a fairytale marriage. Albert's hopes and dreams of securing the woman he loved had come true. Louis's position was consolidated and appeared to be unassailable at court as the newlyweds lolled around at Polesden Lacey. But always, at the back of his mind, Louis sensed that his perfect job at court would not last for ever. He was always an outsider, albeit a most fortunate and privileged one, but his intuition that this privilege was not going to endure proved to be all too accurate.

Chapter Twelve

'There is one point on which the King and I are in entire agreement, because I have often discussed the question with him. You have made PA what he is, and for the time being you are indispensable.'
- Clive Wigram, writing to Louis Greig in 1923

When Lord Stamfordham, George V's elderly éminence grise, told Louis that the court was a 'little world' it was with good reason: a royal household was often an insular and claustrophobic place in which to work. Petty politics and peevish personalities tended to loom large, and status and rank took on a disproportionate significance. To a great extent, thanks to his privileged position as a favoured courtier with the ear of the King, Louis was able to stay outside much of the rankling and rivalry. The cut and thrust of Palace politics was of little interest to him.

What also set Louis apart from most courtiers was the fact that he had known Prince Albert since his childhood, and had been hand-picked by George V to work for him. His job as the Duke of York's Comptroller was broadly to organise, guide and oversee Albert's professional and personal life, and Louis's breezy, approachable personality made him a popular figure. And of course a doctor's good bedside manner helped. He knew better than most how to put people at ease. His naval training also made him efficient and practical at solving personnel problems. His letters were short and to the point; he was simply too impatient to get bogged down in excessively detailed and elaborate protocol, or petty feuding. Louis did all he could to sidestep or ignore the jealousies, plots and conspiracies of life at the Palace, but sometimes it was impossible.

For instance, in 1924 a member of the King's household sent Lord Stamfordham an anonymous letter accusing senior officials of rudeness and snobbery.

> What a pity it is, Sir, that some of your Persons about the court are such snobs, they ought to remember in these radical days that there is responsibility attached to their positions and their manners only increase class hate. They should be more like poor Sandhurst who was always the same to every one. It may bore JHW [Hanbury-Williams], HS [Harry Stonor], PH [Philip Hunloke], FD [Frank Dugdale],to be courteous to those they think not important, but it only embitters people. We are sure His Majesty would not approve of hurting anyone's feelings.[1]

It did not directly involve Louis, but he would have been aware of such simmering discontent, and Stamfordham took the accusations seriously enough to pass the letter to the Lord Chamberlain for him to investigate the complaints. Rows often burst out over petty disputes, and a tough skin and a sense of humour were needed to survive and prosper. Lacking in both qualities was a courtier called Ralph Harwood, who had been seconded from the Treasury to work in the Privy Purse's office. Harwood had left school at fifteen to join the Post Office as a telegraphist. He went to night school after work and gained sixteenth place in the whole of England in the Civil Service Examination. He worked in the India Office, the War Office and then the Inland Revenue before gravitating to the Treasury. He was hired as an accountant at the Palace and quickly discovered that it was easy to be wrong-footed. His mistake was momentarily to forget his place in the hierarchy. When he took the initiative to try to solve a budget problem, he found himself in extremely hot water. To prevent the royal household's annual accounts from appearing in credit at the end of the financial year, he had bought £10,000 worth of wine, on behalf of the Palace, in advance of the following year's budget. Difficulties arose when he bumped into the King in a corridor in Buckingham Palace – a rare occurrence for him – and out of sheer nerves and a need to say something, he blurted out that he 'was doing his best to make His Majesty bankrupt' by purchasing gallons of wine. The problem was compounded when the nonplussed King mentioned this to Sir Frederick Ponsonby, the Keeper of the Privy Purse, who had to admit he knew nothing about the purchase. Ponsonby was livid that he had been made to look so foolishly ignorant, all because Harwood had acted without his authority. 'I told him [Harwood] frankly that while I did not wish to interfere with his work, I thought he should have informed me of his proposal to make these gigantic purchases of wine and I reminded him that the question of the balance of the Civil List was my job.' The disagreement spiralled with Harwood accusing Ponsonby of harassing him out of his job and threatening to resign. Ponsonby was then incensed by the manner of his offer of resignation. His letter was sent to Lord Cromer rather than to Ponsonby, his immediate boss. The King asked Stamfordham to draw up a report and a solution to the in-fighting: a twenty-page handwritten letter followed. The King insisted it be written out by hand, rather than typed, so that the secretaries would remain ignorant of the bust-up and not gossip about it.[2] Harwood was far from happy and sent yet another hysterical letter to Cromer: 'I do not ask for his head on a charger or anything of that sort! But I do feel that my resistance to his attack will not make him any better disposed towards me & if he has the will to do so there are a hundred ways of making my official life intolerable. Already, as I have told you, there are signs of pin-pricking me by means of his subordinates, which I view with some apprehension.' Ponsonby, in turn, told Cromer that Harwood was 'getting too big for his boots', adding that 'wine is by no means easy to choose and if at next year's functions the wine is criticised, we shall be the laughing stock of

London if it is known it was chosen by an accountant who came from the Treasury'. It was all too easy to sink into a mire of endless petty disputes in the shallow, shark-infested waters of Palace politics.

Ponsonby was so obsessed with procedure and status that he even worried about placement at lunch when there were no guests other than household staff. He really minded who sat next to whom. He wrote to Cromer on 31 December 1924, 'Glad that the King approved of you having a carriage and sitting at the top of the table. The latter was always the procedure in Queen Victoria's and King Edward's reign, but somehow it lapsed during the present reign. It was only when one of the Italians said it seemed to him so odd that the grand charges sat anywhere at the Household's luncheon that I made a mental note of it.'[3] But however hard Louis tried to steer clear of such disputes, it was inevitable that he was drawn into political wrangles on some occasions. It was simply the nature of his business.

Part of Louis's job was to be on hand during royal visits, as, for instance, in 1921 when the Crown Prince of Japan had made a visit to London and Louis was assigned to look after him and to be his link to the court while Albert and other members of the royal family entertained him. There were often unexpected perks, as Louis discovered afterwards when he was honoured by the Emperor of Japan with the 3rd Order of Merit, together with the Order of the Sacred Treasure.

Visits by foreign royals and official engagements abroad to other royal dynasties were often some of the more interesting aspects of a courtier's life, as Louis had found with his visit to Belgium and France with Prince Albert during the First World War. So when he heard that Albert and Elizabeth had been invited to Romania by their royal family it was a reasonable expectation that he too would go, as he was the most senior member of the Duke of York's staff.

The Yorks were happily settling into their new life in the first few months of their marriage when they were invited to the christening of Albert's godson, Crown Prince Peter of Yugoslavia, and also to the marriage of Prince Paul of Yugoslavia to Princess Olga of Greece, which was to take place at the same time in Belgrade. It was Albert's second trip to the Balkans. He had attended the King of Yugoslavia's wedding and the coronation of King Ferdinand and Queen Marie in Romania the previous year. This time the groom was an Oxford friend of the Prince of Wales, and the bride the granddaughter of Uncle Willy, Queen Alexandra's brother, who had been assassinated in 1913. She was also the sister of Princess Marina, who would enter Albert's life in a few years' time as the wife of his youngest surviving brother, Prince George.

On the previous trip, Louis had arranged for Captain Ronald Waterhouse, who had been Albert's private secretary and equerry, to accompany him. But he had since left Albert's household to work at 10 Downing Street as principal private secretary to the Prime Minister, Andrew Bonar Law. Louis was surprised and angry when he discovered that Waterhouse was again to accompany Albert. It was a strange and tactless decision, as Waterhouse was no longer part of any royal household. It was all the more irritating for Louis as he had not been consulted on the arrangements for the trip, which were, after all, a significant part of his job.

Waterhouse was an ambitious, bright but ultimately untrustworthy civil servant, who often pursued his own agenda at the expense of his masters. When Bonar Law resigned in the spring of 1923 after being diagnosed with cancer, Waterhouse was entrusted to take his resignation letter to the King at Buckingham Palace. Bonar Law had specifically and purposefully chosen not to recommend to the King a successor; he was simply too tired to stay in the political fray and he did not want to have to make the choice between Lord Derby, Lord Curzon and Stanley Baldwin. Waterhouse ignored this by taking along a typed memorandum recommending Stanley Baldwin and telling Lord Stamfordham that this was Bonar Law's choice. Stamfordham wrote on the

four-page memorandum, now lodged in the Royal Archives at
Windsor, that it had been handed to the King on 29 May after
'Colonel Waterhouse stated practically [that it] expressed the
views of Mr Bonar Law'.[4] This has since been proven to have
been a bare-faced lie, and shows the duplicitous and untrustworthy nature of Waterhouse, against whom Louis was pitted.
Nevertheless, he went on to become principal private secretary
to three prime ministers. His second wife, Nourah, whom he
married in 1928, published a hagiography of him after his
death in 1942, which tried to defend his honesty. It reported
various conversations she claimed her husband had had
with Bonar Law regarding Baldwin's succession, but according to Bonar Law's most recent biographer, R. Q. Adams, these
conversations, too, were figments of his and maybe also her
imagination. Lord Stamfordham also appeared to change his
views. In 1923 he addressed him affectionately as 'My Dear
Waterhouse', ending his letters 'Yours ever', but by 1926 he
was writing 'Dear Waterhouse' and ending with the distinctly
cool and less intimate 'Yours very truly'.[5]

Plans started to go awry for Louis over the Yugoslavia
trip almost as soon as the King sent a telegram to Albert on 23
September 1923, alerting him to the need to visit Romania for
political as much as personal reasons, a copy of which was forwarded to Louis by Lord Stamfordham: 'As Lord Curzon
strongly urges your going to christening at Belgrade fear must
ask you to go. Believe date ceremony is October 16th. Paul's
wedding next day. Did you know you were also his *kum*
[koom is Serbo-Croat for godfather]. Would it be possible, if
she so wished, for Elizabeth to accompany you. Her lady
would go and doubtless Waterhouse would be able to go as
before. Reply at once.'

The next day Albert wrote to Louis from Holwick Hall, the
Strathmores' estate in Teesdale in County Durham, where he
was staying, to inform Louis that he had already personally
invited Waterhouse to join him. At this stage Albert's letter
indicated that he was more concerned over the inconvenient

timing of the trip, disrupting the first few months of his married life, than the issue of who should accompany him: 'The King tells me he wants me to go to Serbia after all. Curzon is very keen about it. I have written to Ronald to ask him to come with me as before. HM told me to get him if I can. Curzon should be drowned for giving me such short notice. I have written to him for his reasons & also asked him to see me before leaving. He must know things are different now.'[6]

Louis was furious not to have been consulted about the necessity and, indeed, the propriety of taking Waterhouse. He felt more than slighted. He felt he had been squeezed out of the decision-making loop, as normally he would have arranged details with the Foreign Office and, if necessary, Downing Street. As Albert's most senior member of staff, he should have been consulted rather than presented with a fait accompli. To rub salt into the wound the Foreign Office reported directly to Waterhouse, leaving Louis completely out of the picture.

This was, at best, sloppy protocol; at worst it indicated to Louis a change in his role now that Albert was married. Was he being sidelined? Was this a sign of things to come? Palace paranoia was never lacking on these occasions. But he instinctively felt that it was not right that a Downing Street apparatchik, and a rather pompous smart-alec at that, was being sent instead of himself.

On 25 September, from his sister's house in Sussex, where he was staying, Louis fired off a telegram to Albert. 'I have heard from Lord Stamfordham that he has arranged for you and the Duchess to go to Serbia and I understand Waterhouse is to accompany you. With the latter I am not in agreement. I am now at Stedham. Writing.'[7]

Stamfordham wrote from Balmoral that same day informing Louis that the King had been made aware of his complaint and shown his letter:

Please be assured that, in asking Waterhouse to go with Their Royal Highnesses, the one idea was to help them by having a man who, through having been previously to Belgrade with the Prince, is fully 'up to the ropes', knows all the people and speaks French fluently. I quite realise your point of view that it is somewhat anomalous for Their Royal Highnesses to be attended by someone not in their Household: but at the same time the above reason, though not patent to the man in the street, *if* he concerns himself in the matter, will be recognised and understood by all who know the working of our 'little world' – for such it is – as a practical measure but one adopted without the remotest intention of, as it were, giving you the 'go by'.

The next day Albert wrote again to Louis, acknowledging his discontent but maintaining that it was the King's wish that Waterhouse go with him. This was true but not the whole truth; the King did not want Louis excluded. Albert claimed somewhat disingenuously that he was merely carrying out the King's wishes. He refused to understand that Louis felt he was being sidestepped or, as he put it, given the 'go-by'.

Waterhouse has just telegraphed he can come & I have written & told him all I know & have asked him to make arrangements on the train. Your letter has worried me a bit, I'm sorry to say as Ld S only did as he was told by the King to arrange about Waterhouse coming. I naturally wrote to him & the PM first, since then I have had so many letters from you & telegrams from the King that I did not know where or how to start writing to you. Time is so short thanks to —— Curzon making me go after my having been told I was not going. I am so sorry you don't like the idea of RW coming. I should have thought he was the one person having been there before with me and out there they won't know he is not still with me. However I have carried out my orders from my father & I could do nothing else . . . We must talk this matter of RW over when we meet as it rather worries me I'm afraid. I don't quite see your point of view.[8]

That same day Clive Wigram wrote to Louis from Windsor Castle – being careful to mark his letter 'strictly private'. Wigram was the most loyal of friends to Louis and was appalled by what he perceived to be Albert's cavalier behaviour. By this time Louis had told Wigram that he was going to resign. He had often talked of taking a more lucrative job in the City, and this seemed to be the right time to take it and move on. Wigram gave sensible advice.

Steady the buffs! My sympathies are entirely with you. You who know so much about the Duke and have been everything to him should be consulted. Especially when there is any question of a 'mystery man'. I feel the whole thing was done hastily and without meditation. I am under the impression that Lord S has been stalking his head about it for some time. Anyhow he should have had my letter yesterday morning as I sent it 'express'. My dear Louis – there is one point on which the King and I are in entire agreement, because I have often discussed the question with him. You have made PA what he is, and for the time being you are indispensable. It is difficult to have a clear vision of the future but I have a presentiment that PA will some day be King. He must then have the very best men around him and his staff without you would be incomplete. I often feel like you old man – and go to bed assuring myself that I ought to chuck my hand in as their ways are not my ways – but then I think of the history of the Royal Family and realise that things today are much better than they were, say, in Queen Victoria's reign, when the most awful enormities were committed and I hope for better things to come. Intrigues, bickering, every kind of petty recrimination were then the order of the day. Well you know my high opinion of you and how much I hold you in esteem.

I should see what PA has to say before coming to a final decision. You will be an irreplaceable loss not only to the King and PA but to your humble servant.

Perhaps some satisfactory explanations may be forthcoming – but it is annoying, I admit. It may awaken them to a sense of justice if they knew you have a more lucrative job awaiting you. Anyway go slow and don't put yourself in the wrong – above all, consult Phyllis.

Accusations and counter-accusations flew as to the correct sequence of events and the proper procedure. This was the first time Louis had run into any trouble at court; it was a shock to find himself in disagreement with any member of the family. Two days later, Wigram wrote again in support, but also to air vague insinuations about Waterhouse's un-savoury reputation.

> My dear Louis,
> I have had a very friendly answer from Lord S who says that, of course, he should not be associated with PA if these stories are really true. Before he [presumably Waterhouse] got his KCB Lord S says he made inquiries and was told that W was above reproach & most kind to his wife. Pity he did not see W's old nurse in the flat. He says he wrote to explain matters to you. I think that PA asked the King whether he could not go with him – if he did so without telling you, he was not playing cricket. However, here I am always at your service, dear Louis.

As a last-ditch effort to settle the matter, on 1 October Stamfordham wrote from Balmoral to Louis: 'I am sorry that instead of telephoning direct to Waterhouse we did not ask you to communicate with him as you would have been able to put in a question as to the expediency of W's going – But I can explain to you when we meet the rather difficult situation and the necessity for striking when the iron was hot! I write by the King's orders to F.O., saying that H.M. assumed F.O. would pay all expenses of the visit. There has not been time for a reply.'

It was too little, too late. Stamfordham failed to realise that Louis was going to resign. The row was not going to be resolved by anything being done to remedy the situation. Louis failed to find out why Albert had not been completely frank. However, on 4 October, the King personally intervened with a letter to Albert, which suggested a way forward, allowing Louis and Waterhouse both to accompany the Yorks to the Balkans. 'I am glad you are going to Belgrade, but I am sorry that Greig should think his feelings are hurt, I see no reason why you should not take both, but of course Greig would come first as he is your Comptroller. Anyway it is very stupid that the F.O. don't keep you informed through Greig.'[9]

But Albert ignored this clearly worded compromise, and the King's insistence that Louis should be his priority. On 7 October, on his return to London, Albert met Louis to thrash out the whole affair, but the prince insisted that Waterhouse alone would accompany him. Louis felt he had only one option left and resigned. It was genuinely more in sorrow than anger, but he also felt it was a good time to make a break from being a full-time courtier. He had two daughters, wanted more children and needed to make more money to educate and support his family. He was realistic about the difficulty of working for a man over whom he had been such a strong influence since his teenage years. Now that Albert was married both of them needed to make the break. It was just unfortunate that it had occurred in less than ideal circumstances.

The King and Queen learned Louis was leaving court when Albert wrote on 9 October to his mother. Louis had always been very much the King's choice as Albert's adviser and mentor, and he and the Queen were deeply upset about it. Albert downplayed any drama or suggestion of a 'row', but the King was furious that the man he had placed with his second son had been dislodged over such a footling matter of protocol. 'You may be surprised to hear that I am going to let Greig leave me as my Comptroller. He wishes to go himself, & I have been thinking of it for some time now. He has been 6 years with me now and I feel that now I am married it is better to have a change as things have not been working too smoothly and we both feel the time has come. We have had no row at all; it is quite mutual.'[10]

Louis's resignation set the rumour mongers chattering. The gossip at court was that a new broom had arrived at the Palace in the form of Albert's strong-willed wife who was sweeping out the old and bringing in new and younger staff. 'I don't care what the little duchess says but he is not going to go,' the King was reported to have told Wigram.[11] There was a widely held assumption that the Duchess had been responsible for the rift, as she wanted her own people in place rather than her husband's established, older team. And change was, of course, inevitable and understandable after their marriage. The relationship between Albert and Louis had altered with the Prince's increasing closeness to his wife, and his growing reliance on her as his new partner and guide. It left little room for a forceful figure like Louis. But there is no evidence that the Duchess pushed Louis, and whatever the King wanted, it was by now too late. Louis and Albert had both amicably agreed that they would part.

Louis's fate formally hung in the balance until 12 October, when the King and Queen tried to salvage something positive from the messy row that cost them one of their most valued courtiers. They consulted Stamfordham and Wigram to try to find him another job. Wigram wrote to Carron Scrimgeour, Louis's brother-in-law, on 12 October, as they awaited news of developments. 'Louis's fate will probably be decided this afternoon. The King and Queen are going to see him and will, I know, try to get him to stay with Prince Albert. T.M.s [Their Majesties] were furious with PA for his treatment of Louis – and if Louis goes, he will go as a hero and with right on his side – and with universal sympathy and regret.'

But Louis knew there was no going back. The relationship had come to an end in its current form. On 13 October – in a letter marked 'private' – Wigram wrote from York Cottage to commiserate with Louis, but more importantly to finesse a plan to secure him a place in the King's own household.

It's just like this. The King and Queen are miserable at the thought of your impending departure, as we all are – I call it a national tragedy. T.M.'s want somehow to keep a hold on you in the Household so that your wise judgement and wonderful experience may be at their and our disposal, when requested. If you are going into the City this will be a full-time job, I don't quite see how it would suit you to have a permanent job. The King told me I was to try to think of something. What about being an extra-equerry or extra-gentleman-usher? You would then be in the Household, and could be summoned when we were in the soup. Lord S smiles on this.

Before doing anything I thought I would let you know privately what is in the air – as naturally I don't want to do anything which might embarrass you or tie you up. Think it over and let me know privately – Don't breathe a word even to Lord S.[12]

The court was paranoid about secrecy, and Wigram added as a postscript the words: 'Tear this up.'

Albert knew that he had caused terrible upset at the Palace and he rather sheepishly tried to explain the situation away to his father by letter on 16 October. Yet he was also insistent that the split should not and would not affect their friendship. 'Directly I returned to London I saw Greig, he started the question himself & we came to the same conclusion in a most amicable way, I thought. I wish I had known what I do now about how much you liked him & all the different things he did for you. I am most grateful to him for all he has done for me, & I sincerely hope that we shall always be the best of friends.'[13]

By November the final terms of departure were agreed. Louis and Albert were to continue to work together until a replacement was found. They had by this time patched up their differences and both accepted that it was in their interests to have an amicable, professional parting. It was not the way Louis would have chosen to initiate his departure; they had known each other too long to let any disagreement fester over the role of a pushy civil servant on a two-day trip to an obscure country for a cousin's wedding. Louis was not a grudge-bearer by nature and wanted the argument to be put behind them. The King and Queen were less forgiving towards Albert. Writing from York Cottage on 14 November, Albert confessed to Louis that his parents were still livid with him: 'All seems to be going well here, though not a word has passed between the King and me with regard to anything. I expect he is still furious with me about all that has happened, and won't open the question again for discussion. I wish he would talk to me as it would make things much easier for me all round. However, I'm not going to say anything as I shall only have my head bitten off again.'[14]

The circumstances of Louis's departure were made more difficult as his replacement, Captain Basil Brooke, could not start on time owing to illness. Albert wrote: 'It is nice of you to stay on till Brooke has had the operation if he does have to have it at once. I am afraid if it does happen it will upset all your arrangements. I am sorry I did not speak about it before but the fact is I have been and still am worried over the whole matter, and then Brooke's sudden bombshell did not help at all. I hope you will understand this and not think me a beast in not asking you before.'

Louis was rather embarrassed by the volcanic eruptions that had surrounded his departure, and particularly by the personal involvement of the King and Queen and their fall-out with Albert. Queen Mary was sad and perplexed at Louis's resignation when she wrote to him from York Cottage on 23 October 1923. 'I saw your letter to Wig re Captain Brooke. Whatever happens he will not be *you* & the King & I will never cease to regret what has happened – and I *cannot* understand it at all. I was so very grateful for yr kind letter to me.'[15]

A sign of the tension between Albert and his parents is evident in the fact that Queen Mary wrote to Louis insisting that *he* meet her when she came to the Yorks' house at White Lodge in Richmond Park to check up on some pictures that she wanted removed. 'I have arranged with the Duke to lunch with them on Wed 12th Nov and asked him to arrange for you to meet me there afterwards.'[16] She wanted to make it clear that Louis was the man with whom she wanted to deal.

In the end no one came well out of the drama: neither Albert, nor Louis, nor the King. Albert was too short-sighted to see that it was a hurtful slight to his most trusted lieutenant and loyal friend to bring in Waterhouse for this Romanian trip.

George V should have stepped in with more vigour and speed to bang heads together to sort out the problem. Louis had done exactly what he would have counselled against; he had allowed Palace politics to get to him and affect his judgement. After all, at the end of the day it was just a one-off trip, and then Waterhouse would have gone back to Whitehall and never been seen again.

On 14 November 1923, Elizabeth wrote to Louis in deepest confidence, expressing her gratitude. She was well aware of the gossip that she was responsible for his departure, and she attempted to pour oil on troubled waters, telling Louis that her husband had been terribly worried about his departure. She emphasised how grateful he really was and how he had made this clear to her, telling her how Louis had been the man responsible for 'saving his life'. Elizabeth also let Louis know that Albert was being driven mad by the worry over the whole fall-out, with his parents telling him what an ungrateful fool he had been to lose such a trusted man. Elizabeth emphasised her feeling of gratitude for all his work.

Louis was never anything but loyal and admiring of Elizabeth, both privately and publicly. His departure had been a subject of much discussion between her and Albert, and in the middle of the drama she had written in exasperation to her mother, complaining that Louis had been 'very silly' but that it was too late as he had resigned. Of course, she was going to back her husband in any disagreement with someone he employed. Louis saw her as a force to be reckoned with, but felt, most importantly, that she was exactly what Albert needed in his future life.

Louis saw no point in casting blame. And the end result suited him. He was free to pursue his own career. He and Albert had an enormous fondness and respect for each other and the last thing either wanted was to change that. They had each agreed to disagree over the matter and, once it was all out in the open, like a burst boil it did not fester. Louis knew that it was the end of his royal career as the Duke of York's

Comptroller, although not the end of his connection to court.
George V had made that clear. Louis was wooed by Wigram
and Stamfordham, who emphasised his value at the Palace as
a 'wise man'.

Louis's last day as Comptroller was 29 February 1924, and
Prince Albert wrote an affectionate valedictory letter, making
it clear that their friendship remained strong.

> I was sorry not to have seen you for longer this morning, as I
> realised that it was the last day you will be with me in your official
> capacity as my comptroller. A parting between two friends is
> always a painful ordeal, but a parting between us, I hope, is an
> impossibility, even an official one. No words of mine can ever
> express my thanks to you for everything you have done for me
> since 1917. We have been through so much together and we have
> come out the right side with flying colours. I hope and trust we
> shall always be the best of friends and that we shall see something
> of each other in the days to come . . . Well good bye Louis and ever
> so many thanks for all your help. Ever yours Albert.[17]

News of Louis's departure soon leaked to the press. In the
Daily Mail, Quex, a well-sourced but anonymous social colum-
nist, interpreted the departure as a significant loss to Albert.

> It is no over-statement to say that this retirement marks a stage in
> the career of the King's second son, and not only of the Duke of
> York but of his brothers as well. For this likeable, manly, common-
> sensical ex-naval surgeon has been an influence in the lives of all
> the Princes. Even the Prince of Wales, with an experience of men
> and affairs far beyond his years, will give ear to the views of Louis
> Greig, largely because there is in them the sturdily-expressed true-
> ness of vision of an exuberantly healthy, open-air, right-thinking
> man. It is no secret that the King and Queen set high value on the
> part played by Commander Greig in their sons' upbringing.

The report emphasised the amicable nature of their parting.

> When some weeks ago Commander Greig told me he would seek
> permission to retire towards the end of the year, he explained why.

The Duke of York was now a married man; it would be better for the continued development of his character that he should be able to rule his own life; at any rate to have a comptroller of his own selecting, someone who had not 'exercised tutelary guidance since he was a boy.' He retires with the liking and esteem of every member of the Royal Family, who realise that the work he has done has been that of a sincere patriot and of an honest and fearless character.

The King was as good as his word and gave Louis a new part-time post at court. He was made a Gentleman Usher of the King's Household after George V told Wigram that Louis must be retained at court in some form.

Albert told Louis that he was glad he would still be on call in his new courtier role with the King. For many months they were still in close contact as Louis handed over the reins to Brooke. They still played tennis and racquets, but inevitably saw less of each other. The clearest evidence that they remained friends was their decision to play at the Wimbledon championships together some time after their 'fall-out'. There would have been no possibility of them agreeing to play doubles, spending hours practising and planning their Wimbledon debut if their friendship was not back on track. Louis was immensely fond of Albert and never stopped wanting to help him. Wimbledon was too good an opportunity to miss, as they were both eligible to enter the championships, having won the RAF doubles in 1920. Their first and last appearance at Wimbledon in 1926 was not the triumph for which they had hoped, but in the public's mind it indelibly linked the two men.

Louis's royal friendship was also evident when Phyllis gave birth to a son. Louis was immeasurably proud of his two exuberant daughters, but had always wanted more children, and was delighted when, on 21 February 1925, at the age of forty-five years, Phyllis gave birth to a boy. Henry Louis Carron Greig was born in an upstairs bedroom in Ladderstile, their large Edwardian house on Kingston Hill, West London, and although his first name was Henry – in honour of his godfather – he was always called Carron. It was an old Scrimgeour name, as well as Gaelic for 'rocky bottom', as in a river. Almost every member of the royal family sent messages of congratulations, and at her own request Queen Mary and Prince Henry agreed to be godparents. 'I shall be pleased to stand as godmother for your small son & am sending a small piece of silver as my Christening gift. All my best wishes & blessings. On our return from abroad I will have the silver basket engraved with my cypher,' she wrote.[18] Phyllis's brother, Carron Scrimgeour, and Mrs Hannah Gubbay were the other godparents. A cousin of Philip Sassoon, Hannah was the eventual owner of his house, Trent Park, in Hertfordshire, and was well known for her spectacular china collection.

Albert remained in Louis's life, and vice versa. For instance, when John Scrimgeour, Louis's brother-in-law, died after a short illness, Albert immediately wrote: 'I had no idea he had been ill. He will be a sad loss to the firm but I feel you will be able to carry on as before. Please tell Phiggie how sorry I am for her. I have written a line to Connie [Louis's sister], who I know will be heartbroken. John was also so kind to me in looking after my money affairs before you took them over.'[19] When Albert became a father for the first time in April 1926, he shared his good news with Louis, proudly comparing notes on their offspring: 'She [Princess Elizabeth] is very good looking, I think, and anyhow she has got a good pair of lungs. Your children taught me about them when I saw yours growing up but now I know from the beginning what it is to be a father. My wife is very well and thanks you as well.'[20] Queen Mary never altered her affection for Louis, referring to him as 'my good friend.'[21] and sharing her family's news with him. 'We are delighted with our pretty little grand-daughter. Bertie's delight is quite touching. I am so glad they have *at last* got their happiness. We did not approve of that stupid announcement, all on account of the "confounded" etiquette. We tried to stop it but it was too late.'[22] The 'stupid announcement' referred to the report in the Court Circular of the attendance of Sir William Joynson-Hicks, the Home Secretary, who 'was present in the house at the time of the birth' and conveyed the news by special messenger to the Lord Mayor. It was traditional for the Home Secretary to attend royal births, apparently to ensure verification, bizarre as it seems today. It had been a difficult delivery and the Duchess's doctors eventually released a guarded statement declaring that 'a certain line of treatment was successfully adopted' – in other words, a Caesarean.[23] Albert was delighted and wanted immediately to share his good news with Louis: nothing had fundamentally altered their friendship.

Louis was aware that departures from the Palace could be brutal, brusque and terminal. For example, Lord Brownlow discovered that he had resigned from court without knowing it. He was due to receive the Archbishop of Canterbury and introduce him to the King in his role as Lord-in-Waiting when he was told that he would not be needed. The next day he read in the Court Circular that Lord Dufferin and Ava had succeeded him as Lord-in-Waiting. Brownlow rang Buckingham Palace and was told that his name could never again appear in the Court Circular. He demanded to speak to Lord Cromer, the Lord Chamberlain, who told him 'his resignation had been accepted', though he had never resigned. 'Am I to be turned away?' he asked, 'like a dishonest servant with no notice, no warning, no thanks, when all I did was to obey my Master, the late King?' 'Yes,' was Lord Cromer's answer. His offence had been to escort Mrs Simpson to Cannes on the King's orders. Brownlow only later discovered that it was not the King who had dismissed him but a clique of courtiers who had done so without consulting the monarch.

Louis was now a semi-detached member of the court, and this situation suited him as his life took off in a number of unexpected directions.

Chapter Thirteen

'Commander Greig told me that the King had been greatly pleased with his talk with you and felt sure that you were to be of great service to the country in years to come.'

Sir Alexander Grant, writing to
Ramsay MacDonald

Leaving the Palace was a big leap for Louis after working for Prince Albert so intensely and for so long. But he was good at landing on his feet and went to work at the London office of the stockbroking firm owned by Phyllis's family, J. & A. Scrimgeour. He was hired as a rainmaker, bringing in clients to create new business.

Every day Louis drove from Ladderstile to his office in the City at No. 3 Lothbury, just next to the Bank of England. He wore the customary bowler hat and stiff collar and tie, and was something of a City swell, mixing with the 'good and the great' in an ambassadorial role to bring in the big deals. He was a figure who was noticed about town, whether it was at White's or the Beefsteak in London's clubland or in City lunch rooms and restaurants – and even at the racetrack. He started to build up an impressive network of contacts. At about this time he belonged to 'the old gang', a loose association of Scots who had left their native country and prospered. It included the developer Malcolm McAlpine and the chairman of BP, Sir William Fraser. Mixing with people from different walks of life was what he enjoyed. 'He was a man who knew the name

of every driver, mâitre d' or receptionist wherever he went,'
remembered a contemporary.[1] Scrimgeour's were delighted
with their new partner as, almost straight away Prince Albert
became a client and Louis helped to manage part of his
portfolio.

Louis's departure from court opened up many new opportunities. Sir Alexander Grant, the Scottish biscuit king, was to
provide a critical link between the worlds of commerce,
industry and politics. It was not that Louis was overtly political, but he gained pleasure from being at the centre of power.

If anyone knew the benefits of industry it was Grant, whose
life was an extraordinary rags-to-riches story. He was born in
1854 in Forres, a small town on the north-east coast of Scotland,
where his father had been a railway guard, dying while his
son was still at school. Young Sandy Grant was apprenticed
as a teenager to a baker's shop in Forres before going to
Edinburgh to work for Robert McVitie in his underground
bakery in Queensferry Street. When asked why he should be
given a job there, Grant precociously replied that he would
be able to improve the quality of their biscuits. The pay was at
first less than £1 a week, and the duties included the daily
delivery of fresh bread. He was not destined to stay doing such
a menial task for long. By the time he was thirty he was
appointed foreman of the cake department in the main
McVitie, & Price factory in Edinburgh. When Mr Price retired,
Grant became general manager, and on the death of McVitie
he acquired a controlling interest which he developed far
beyond the wildest dreams of its founders, becoming one of
the richest industrialists in Britain.

Grant made a significant difference to Louis's life by
introducing him to Ramsay MacDonald, the vain, silver-
moustached leader of the Labour Party, who had risen from
illegitimacy and poverty to become the tenant of No. 10
Downing Street. He had been born on 12 October 1866, in a
small 'but-and-ben' cottage in Lossiemouth in Morayshire, just
a few miles from Forres; his mother had been a domestic

servant on a farm and his father a ploughman. The two self-made men, or, as MacDonald described them, 'two Moray loons who came into the world in patched breeks',[2] forged a close friendship. They saw Louis as a fellow Scot also on his way up, and decided to give him a helping hand. 'Commander Greig has been very nice to me and I should like to give him this meeting [with you],' Grant wrote to MacDonald on 29 December 1923.[3] This was just after the 1923 election and by then it was clear that MacDonald would become Prime Minister (as he did a month later).

Drawn together by their shared Scottish roots, Grant, Greig and MacDonald became a close-knit trio, despite their differences in age. In 1924 Louis was forty-three, MacDonald fifty-nine and Grant seventy-one. They all bought houses within a few miles of each other in Morayshire – albeit on a very different scale. Grant purchased three large estates, Logie, Dunphail and Relugas, each with a grouse moor and beautiful stretches of the River Findhorn. Louis, by contrast, bought a small, plain seaside house in the village of Findhorn overlooking the bay, and MacDonald maintained his house in his 'beloved Lossie'. Inevitably, they were viewed as something of a Scottish mafia; they were a powerful combination, and looked after each other. MacDonald had the power, Grant the money and Louis the royal connections. The two elder men recognised and valued Louis's ability to open doors in the Palace.

Louis enjoyed MacDonald's company, finding him warm and amusing with his quirky penchant for puns, poems and poking fun. He told Grant that after their first meeting he 'came away with a strong impression of his [MacDonald's] honesty, strength & capabilities. While not agreeing with him in all his views, I believe this country is going to be governed for the first time for a long time if our friend comes in.'[4] The King had few close contacts in the Labour Party, and certainly none that he trusted implicitly. In this way Louis was a useful conduit for the Palace. In the 1920s the memory of the

Russian royal family's murder was still on the minds of their British counterparts. They were only too anxious for good relationships with any popular party of the centre left. Louis helped to strengthen that link between MacDonald and the monarchy. His connections with the Palace remained strong through Wigram and Cromer. Louis was a calming influence, brushing aside any doubts or insecurities that MacDonald and the King had about each other, sometimes passing on compliments from one to the other, often via Wigram or Grant. Early on, Louis discovered that powerful men liked to be reassured and flattered. Grant was more than willing to pass on praise concerning Louis to the Labour leader. 'Commander Greig told me that the King had been greatly pleased with his talk with you and felt sure that you were to be of great service to the country in years to come. He spoke so highly of you that I felt gratified.'[5]

Friendship was paramount to the three men as they helped each other in their different ways. MacDonald made this clear in his letters, which were at times whimsical, including this example of an imaginary dialogue in broad Scotch between Sandy Grant (S) and himself (M), discussing Louis's absence from a trip to Scotland:

We are in a fix up here of the 'to be or not to be' order as you will see by the following cogitation between Sandy & myself:

Both: A pity Greig is not up!
S: Aye, but ye see he's a faimily man an' there's Fillis.
M: Wha's Fillis?
S: Missus Greig. Didna ye ken?
M: Oh I see, I widna ca' her Fillis, ye auld dog.
S: Are ye feard o' her language?
M: Aye, an o' her dignity an' poseeshun.
S: Gae awa' wi' ye. But Lod Man she haes some o' Louis's language an' if we send for him, man he wid get it.
M: Ye dinna say so?
S: Oh Louis wid last oot. Hae ye never seen him assertin' his authority?

M: Na, an' fats mair I'm sure she never heeds it. Dinna try tae pit ill atween us. She's a nice fair-spoken, domesticated, obedient woman. If anything she gives Louis over soft a time o' it. Louis needs thwackin' noo an' again & the puir lassie hasna' the heart tae dee it. If she wid only be advised by me (though God forbid it) she wud tak the poker in her han' sometimes – nae of course tae lug it on but jeest tae threaten him by times.

S: Lord she wid dae that if we asked Louis up. Fat dae ye say? We'd better nae do it.

M: The greens are no bad, man.

S: An' the win's are ane over rock.

M: An' the sun is shining.

S: An' there's some good whisky in Bessie's charge.

M: An' he wid enjoy seeing me beat you.

S: Aye, the devil, he wid.

M: What dae ye say, then?

S: What dae ye say?

M: Say yerslef! It'll be your drink.

S: Bid your triumph at Spey Bay.

M: An' your forenichts.

S: An' my wife. Oh Fillis.

M: I gie twa sided argument. How will we get over it?

S: Just write in as ye promised.

Louis enjoyed becoming involved with MacDonald and his political world behind the scenes. With a Labour government on the verge of power for the very first time, it was a dramatic and unsettling time in politics. Change was inevitable when Stanley Baldwin, the Conservative Prime Minister, having lost his majority at the December 1923 general election, insisted on meeting Parliament. He was defeated in critical vote of confidence in Parliament by seventy-two votes after Liberals and Labour voted against him on 21 January 1924. He resigned the next day, allowing Ramsay MacDonald, by default, to become the first Labour Prime Minister, albeit heading only a minority government. Just 191 seats belonged to Labour while the Tories had 259 and the Liberals 159. The Liberals had voted against Baldwin, which created the 'safest conditions' for a Labour government to be in power, i.e. when it was handicapped by its minority status.

The day after Baldwin resigned, Louis secretly met MacDonald for a private dinner at Grant's house in Hampstead. This was no idle social visit. MacDonald wanted to use Louis to send signals to the King. Earlier that same day he had been to Buckingham Palace and had been sworn in as a Privy Councillor and asked to form a government. 'Today 23 years ago dear Grandma died. I wonder what she would have thought of a Labour Government!' George V had written in his diary that night. It was a triumphant moment for the three Scots to savour.

MacDonald used the occasion to discuss a tiresome and seemingly trivial issue perplexing the insecure and untested Labour government – the question of court dress. Inconsequential in itself, it was of considerable significance as a symbol of the new party's confidence and agenda for a new Britain. Cabinet ministers normally wore a special uniform of gold-embroidered coat with white knee breeches and silk stockings to attend an evening court, and this was seen by some republican-minded members of the Labour Party as symbolic of their class enemy. Louis passed on MacDonald's views to Clive Wigram, who, in turn, informed the King.

My dear Clive,

My dinner with Ramsay MacDonald came off last Thursday. There were only he, our host Mr Grant & myself. We dined at 7pm at Hampstead & talked hard for some hours. I came away, I must confess, much impressed. I had a long talk with him alone on the Court & Court customs. His views, e.g. on the opening of parliament in state, were that it would be better to strike a more subdued note. What seemed to get him & his followers were the long dresses of the peeresses! He agreed that as a historian, the pageantry was picturesque, but to some of his less educated followers, the ancient uniforms were a bit out of date & aroused more laughter than respect. As regards people like the Comptroller, Treasurer of the Household, one of the things he was going to ask the King was that the men, whom he appointed to these offices, might be excused dressing up on the occasions when the House of Commons is given a message from the King. RM thought perhaps some other members of the household might do this.[6]

Louis was aware of the difficulties that court dress entailed for the new Labour ministers. The cost of levée dress, as estimated by the principal Court Tailor, was £73 2s 6d, far more than most Labour members would be willing, or indeed able, to pay (around £3,000 in today's terms).

MacDonald wanted to tread slowly and to keep the King on his side, and told Louis what he would like to say to George V, knowing that Louis would pass it on to Wigram. It was a courteous message, but one foretelling change. 'I more than realise that there will be difficulties ahead of the Crown in the way of breaking a few old precedents & making perhaps some new ones, but I do want TM [Their Majesties] to know that all my efforts will be towards making these easy & acceptable & above all to keep up the dignity of the position of the Crown & that he has nothing but respect & affection for its traditions & its occupants.'

MacDonald worried that the King might view a socialist leader unsympathetically. Louis assured him that he would be treated exactly the same as any other political leader by the King, and indeed by everyone else at the Palace. He passed on to Wigram what he had told MacDonald. 'I put in some good work about readiness (as far as the little I know) of the Court to meet him & of the absolute unbiased feelings of the King as to what party produced a PM & told him one or two little examples of the King as a great sympathiser of the working man.'[7]

Louis's message went down well with the King, as Lord Stamfordham intimated, on his behalf, when he replied to MacDonald a few days later.

The press are tiresome with the headlines of the King's Democratic Revolution: Evening Dress and knee breeches etc. If they would only leave the question to be dealt with by the King and you, with

me as an intermediary, we should soon arrive at some decision!
I have heard from His Majesty who says: 'Whatever decision the
Cabinet Ministers come to I will agree to, but they must all do
the same. It would look very off at a Levée if some came in
uniform, some in evening clothes. In no case does the King wish
Ministers to get full dress coats, and if any of them do not wish to
wear white breeches and stockings they will be excused attending
Evening Function at the Palace.[8]

As things worked out, no one needed to worry for too
long about the footling issue of frock-coats as the first Labour
government lasted just 259 days before an election was called
and the Tories were back in power.

One setback to MacDonald was a controversy over a knighthood he had given to Alexander Grant, which his opponents
compared to the earlier scandal of Lloyd George's acceptance
of cash for peerages. The *Daily Mail* revealed that MacDonald
had been 'loaned' a Daimler and £30,000 in biscuit shares by
Grant. The idea was for Grant to retain the capital and for
MacDonald to gain from the interest of around £2,000. There
was little irregular about such a gift, or in keeping silent about
it, at least by the standards of public life in the 1920s. When
Churchill was Secretary of State for War, the Scottish financier
Sir Abe Bailey offered to make good the loss on any shares
bought on his advice, the profit guaranteed to Churchill. However, in the political furore that erupted, the Prime Minister
was forced to return the car and shares, plus £10,000 in other
loaned securities. The close timing of the loan and the knighthood could not have been more unfortunate, although it was
eventually considered to be more an error of naïvety than
cronyism, as it would now have been called, on both their parts.

Grant was a generous benefactor and Louis was to tap into
this for the royal family's benefit. He had given £100,000 in
1923 towards the reconstitution of the Advocates Library in
Edinburgh into the National Library of Scotland. Two years
later, Grant donated a further £100,000 for a building to house
the library. This was followed by a gift of £50,000 to Edinburgh

University to cover its building debt, and £50,000 for a new geology department. He also made substantial contributions to the National War Memorial at Edinburgh Castle and to the towns of Forres and Lossiemouth. In total, Grant gave away more than £750,000 in his lifetime – equal to about £30 million in today's money. After Albert became King, he wrote to Louis about a gift from Grant of a magnificent silver banqueting service of 4,000 pieces, weighing 18,000 ounces, for the royal family to use for entertaining at their official Scottish residence, the Palace of Holyroodhouse. He suggested that the origin of the gift should remain confidential.

It was unfortunate that Grant's knighthood was linked by politically motivated enemies of MacDonald to his donations to the Prime Minister. Several years later *The Times* declared that 'the gift was connected by certain persons with Sir Alexander Grant's baronetcy, but, needless to say, the true position was well understood, and the transaction was universally felt to be nothing but honourable to both parties.'[9] The Prime Minister was angry that his friend had been embarrassed and put under scrutiny for receiving a reward that MacDonald felt he deserved. MacDonald wrote to warn Grant of his fears about mud being flung by his enemies.

> You know that I live in a glass house & that the dirtiest & meanest things are said by political enemies. For some time I have had brought to my notice tittle-tattle about the kind help you have given me & the most offensive explanations have been given. It breaks one's heart to know how the most innocent motives get blackened by scoundrels, but such is the game of politics. In due time this will be all over the country & will appear in a certain type of paper first as an innuendo & later as a definite accusation.[10]

Labour's defeat coincided with the blistering political row which erupted when MacDonald decided not to prosecute John Campbell, the editor of *Workers' Weekly*, the official magazine of the Communist Party, who was accused of sedition after publishing an article that encouraged British soldiers to mutiny.

Another damaging factor for Labour was the intense publicity created by the publication of a letter – dated 25 October 1924 – signed by the head of the Comintern, Grigori Zinoviev, and by Arthur MacManus, the one British member of the Comintern Praesidium. They urged the British Communist Party to 'stir up the masses of the British Proletariat', to create Communist cells in the British Army, Navy and munitions factories, and to 'beware' Ramsay MacDonald and the 'bourgeois' Labour Party. Just four days after the Zinoviev letter was published (once again by the *Daily Mail*), the general election took place. Labour denounced the letter as a forgery, but it was too late. It had cast aspersions on Labour's patriotism, and the damage was terrible. It brought a landslide victory for the Conservatives, who won 419 seats. Labour won 151, the Liberals 40 and the Communists only one. MacDonald resigned, and Baldwin returned to No. 10.

Six weeks after the election, Baldwin announced that the Zinoviev letter was genuine, although it is now generally accepted as a forgery. However, it forced MacDonald to spend the next five years in opposition while Britain sank into dire economic gloom.

Although free from the Palace, Louis never stopped being a courtier. In May 1925, for instance, just six months after he had severed his professional links with Albert, he asked Grant for a donation to the Duke and Duchess of York's National Playing Fields charity. On 30 June 1925, Louis informed Grant that he had 'sent on the cheque to the Duke of York & I saw HRH this morning. He asks me to thank you with all his heart for your generous kindness to this new movement & to say that he intends to do all he can to make it a success.'[11]

Louis was always good at bringing together money and the monarchy. 'My enthusiasm for the cause of the playing fields for the people, my desire to help the Duke and Duchess of York has made me bold enough to further trespass on your kindness,' he wrote to Grant later.[12] A few days later he received a cheque for £100 and he wrote back that it was 'exactly what's wanted'. Louis had worked closely with Albert during the formation of the Duke of York camps, which he had helped to establish with the idealistic aim of easing class divisions. They brought working-class boys into direct contact with public-school boys, often for the first time in their lives. These Baden-Powell-style camps, with hearty campfire renditions of 'Underneath the Spreading Chestnut Tree', led by Albert, were funded by Grant, after Louis had invited him to Buckingham Palace in 1921 to give his views on the Duke of York 'going among the younger generation of the working classes'. Grant 'expressed the opinion that Royalty's interest in Industry was long overdue'.[13] In fact, they were not as successful as some hoped and Sir Denis Thatcher, the husband of the Conservative Prime Minister, who attended one such camp in the 1930s, remembered social apartheid in spite of the good intentions of the camp organisers.[14]

In May 1929, the dynamic political organisation of the British working-class vote secured MacDonald's return to Downing Street. This time Louis was far more confident about pulling strings, and his influence was greater since he had got to know the key players in the Labour Party better. Throughout this time he remained working for Scrimgeour's, finding the City a useful base for his many other activities. It was always beneficial for any financial house to have connections to senior politicians even though the country faced unprecedented economic, financial and imperial problems, which the Labour Cabinet was thought incapable of solving. John Meynard Keynes went so far as to describe the world slump as 'one of the greatest economic catastrophes in world history'. MacDonald and Lloyd George both conceded that the economic and political position was the greatest crisis since the 'darkest hours of the war'.[15]

Many solutions were put forward, including land settlement, tariff truces, quotas and Empire Free Trade, but the government seemed incapable of harnessing political will or producing an agreement to implement anything concrete and effective. Churchill went so far as to declare that 'democracy' was 'on trial'.[16] And, indeed, there was alarming impatience with democratic means for solving the country's problems; some even feared a slide towards dictatorship as had occurred in Italy and Germany. With a growing number of people doubting that any one single party was capable of gaining a majority or bringing about the necessary changes, the idea of a coalition government was widely aired. There was a strong feeling that the loss of the war generation had left the country under the leadership of a 'Monstrous Regiment of Old Men', unable to shake off the clothes and thinking of the nineteenth century with all its outdated factions and tribalism. The real economic issues were being ignored.

The idea of a national government had varied support. Oswald Mosley was one of the first politicians to propose a transformation of the party system.[17] He advocated a coalition with cries of 'ruthless Realism', 'soaring Idealism' and a 'thirst for action'. John Buchan, the author and Conservative MP, raised the idea of a national government in Parliament. Lady Londonderry, the Conservative political hostess and close friend of MacDonald, urged him to join Baldwin to save the country. Louis added his voice to the coalition chorus and teamed up with H. A. Gwynne, the influential high Tory editor of the *Morning Post*, the two acting as self-appointed intermediaries to try to open up an unofficial channel of communication between the Labour and Tory leaders. Louis urged MacDonald to heed Gwynne's views, or, at the very least, to read the letters which he sent him. 'He is such a real good man that I am venturing to add to your correspondence,' Louis wrote.[18] The beauty of their alliance was that Gwynne had the ear of Baldwin while Louis had MacDonald's.

By 1930 Howell Arthur Gwynne had been editor of the *Morning Post* for almost twenty years and he stayed in the job until 1937. One of the most remarkable journalists of his generation, he had first made his name as a foreign correspondent for *The Times*. Kipling was an admirer, and his intimacy with Kitchener, Haig and others who shared his political views gave his paper a greater significance than its circulation might have normally warranted. Louis admired and trusted 'Taff' Gwynne and they exchanged letters on all the pressing topics of the day, from the gold standard and Indian independence to the merits of a national government.

MacDonald welcomed Louis's invitation to meet Gwynne at 'a feast with no skeleton at it but an editor'. He enjoyed the drama and intrigue of a secret rendezvous, entering into the conspiratorial spirit with glee. He appeared more like an old actor hamming it up as a Prime Minister than the real thing, as his letters to Louis were often more like Robert Browning's baroque dramatic monologues than anything the public would have expected to have been written by the man residing at No. 10.

> We shall have wine to make us indiscreet & oysters to make us comfortable. The rest I leave to you to regulate as a doctor should. I love adventure. Must I take a pistol? Or has murder got too vulgarly common? I shall leave that to you, this time as a respectable & affluent stockbroker. But what is to happen to the MP? If a red muddy trickle runs into the blue waters of its filtered Toryism, what will the old ladies say to their maids combing their hair in the afternoon (you see how old-fashioned I am)? The wind howls outside, the sleet rattles on my window panes. 'The devil has something in his hair.' Is it this? But gracious I am tired & I have a cold & must off to bed with a hot water bottle. I shall write in a few days about a date.[19]

Louis fed Gwynne information gleaned from his conversations with the Prime Minister, sometimes even passing on the actual letters. These targeted leaks of MacDonald's views on the idea of a national government appeared to work in MacDonald's favour, as Gwynne became increasingly sympathetic towards the Labour leader, seduced by his charm and optimistic pragmatism. But then he was never the sort of socialist to scare Tories like Gwynne. This was the Labour leader who apologised to the King on their first meeting for some of his politicians raising the Red Flag at the Albert Hall when Baldwin fell from power. What made Gwynne and, indeed, the King feel safe was exactly what the more radical members of his party would later suggest had constituted a betrayal of the party. In his critics' eyes, he sacrificed his socialist principles for power. Gwynne made his appraisal clear to Louis:

> The letter from the P.M. is full of humour and imbued with a spirit of cheerfulness which I admire, I think, as much as any other quality . . . It is a curious thing that he and I should have exactly the same object in view – to ease the underdog and help the lame dog over the stile. He hasn't done it – nor have I, partly I think because we have approached the problem from opposite angles. Anyway I liked his letter immensely. I think after reading it I realise the man more than I ever did before. I return the letter with many thanks for letting me see it.[20]

As a journalist, Gwynne was, of course, only too pleased to have Louis as such a high-grade source of information. 'I am most grateful for you again acting as a telephone wire between us two. It does me good to know what is at the back of the PM's mind, and perhaps it won't do him harm to understand the workings of my mind on these matters,' he wrote to Louis. MacDonald was equally pleased. He valued Louis as a discreet and loyal go-between, introducing him loudly at a government reception to his daughter, Ishbel, as a 'great friend'.

Louis and Gwynne discreetly continued this private shuttle diplomacy between the two leaders. When Gwynne wrote to Greig, the letter was shown to MacDonald; when MacDonald wrote to Greig, it was passed on by Gwynne to Baldwin. Louis and Gwynne had the advantage of a greater freedom to manoeuvre than most professional politicians, who were constrained by party pressure.[21]

What was just as important for MacDonald was Louis's access to the Palace. It was essential for the King to warm to the idea of a coalition government; he was constitutionally responsible for the choice of Prime Minister. The King could be critically decisive in any such matter. Louis recognised this and maintained the pressure for a coalition at every opportunity. And in November 1930, Gwynne reported to Louis that their diplomatic manoeuvring appeared to be working and that Baldwin and MacDonald were coming round to actually discussing a coalition government together.

> I saw S.B. this afternoon and showed him the PM's letter and strongly advised the rapid arrangement of an interview between the two. He agreed and told me that tonight he was seeing the PM at a dinner and would suggest a time for a meeting. We two must drop out. These two men are honest men. If they can come to some agreement and arrangement so much the better for England, the Empire. If the meeting comes to nothing well, you and I can pat each other on the back for having 'tried'.[22]

Louis replied by return of post that he would let him know if RM 'gives me any indications later on'.[23]

A breakthrough occurred when MacDonald finally let Louis know of his willingness to co-operate with Baldwin: 'With SB [Stanley Baldwin] and the good honest Conservative I would co-operate in this crisis with pleasure and would be prepared to give them something. We understand and trust each other even when we disagree, and that is much.'[24]

Gwynne followed up with a long talk with Baldwin on 10 November 1930, and then passed on to Louis his understanding of how Baldwin, too, was on the verge of accepting their 'grandiose plan' for a coalition, although Baldwin saw that the political fall-out for MacDonald from his own party would be extremely damaging for the Labour leader. In all this time Louis and Gwynne were, of course, not the only influences, but they did have direct access to the leaders. At this point Baldwin was still opposed to a coalition and MacDonald had no intention of separating from the Labour Party. The discussions related to a possible future, not to definite or immediate intentions. Gwynne, however, remained optimistic in his correspondence with Louis.

> One thing was quite clear and that is S.B.'s real sympathy for the P.M. and his understanding of the difficulties which confront him. There was no bitterness such as P.M. indicates but rather a desire to give a helping hand to a good man and true, fighting for his life against strong and unscrupulous enemies. As for any co-operation with LG [Lloyd George], you can dismiss that thought. There are two men in English politics who will never work with him and they are S.B. and R.M. I gathered from S.B. that the P.M. does not realise quite the strength and the malignity of the forces working against him. He admitted that the suggestion I made to you was a good one – 'a grandiose plan' he called it – but doubted its practicality, not from any feeling of hostility to R.M. but because, as he said, 'it is a terrible thing to break away from a party one has created.' Hearing him speak with such sympathetic understanding of R.M.'s position, it occurred to me that the only thing I could suggest was that he and the P.M. should meet soon. My sole idea in making the suggestion was to disabuse R.M. of the idea that S.B. and L.G. were waiting for an opportunity of knifing him.[25]

MacDonald felt that a coalition was in the best interests of the country, but he also knew that it would make him a traitor in the eyes of many members of the Labour Party. His assessment of his political future was gloomy despite its whimsical tone.

> My Dear Louis (a gentleman in pantaloons, a trimmed beard and a 16th century air)
> Thank you for showing me the letter. It does not altogether appreciate the position. I want to enlist every man in the House, from any Party, who has the ability and drive to face with a chance of successfully handling our terrible national condition. But what prospect is there of that being a practical possibility? I am sick of the disgraceful show which parties are making, and take no delight in, and shall decline to take advantage of Mr B's difficulties or Mr Lloyd George's troubles. But the policy of both is to let

me keep the baby while they criticise its bottle, and when the moment to strike comes, they will have no scruples in knifing me. Every week they will have chances, whoever breaks away will either have to give up politics or form a new party. The first would be pleasant, the second impossible.[26]

This letter, dated 6 November 1930 is historically significant because it reveals how MacDonald was privately thinking about the formation of a coalition government at a far earlier date than had been previously realised. While there was talk in the air and discussion in the newspapers of a joint government, no one had thought that MacDonald had been contemplating such a move so seriously or so early on. Indeed in David Marquand's biography of the Labour leader, he states that on 30 November when Baldwin saw MacDonald, they talked of him possibly becoming the next Viceroy of India. No one realised that he was prepared and earnestly thinking of casting aside his party's socialist dreams and hopes of another go at No. 10 as a coalition Prime Minister, although he knew the cost to himself and his party would be high.[27] His musings to Louis concern an all-party coalition, but he clearly foresaw the potential damage to his own party.

MacDonald needed reassurance. While most of the time he displayed great confidence, there were also moments when he felt insecure. The small boy from Lossie felt that someone was telling him he had no right to be there. For instance, when the Grand Old Men of the Court had been in touch about some matter of protocol, MacDonald was momentarily unnerved. 'Queer unreal feeling about it. Sometimes I feel I should like to run away home to Lossie to return to reality & flee from these unreal dreams.'[28]

Gwynne urged Louis to persuade MacDonald that the two leaders must put their partisan politics aside for the sake of the nation.

In broad outlook and sheer capacity he [MacDonald] is far ahead of the rest of his people. As he grows older he becomes less fit to be the leader of a party because he has, for the past five years, been accustoming himself to see the broad issues of national politics and to despise the narrow disputes of the party. Stanley Baldwin is made in the same mould but MacDonald has, I think, greater energy and more driving force. Both secretly despise the tricks of party warfare and both have a supreme belief in the people.

I compare the two because these men, each of them the leader of a big party, each of them sincerely anxious about the destiny of the nation and the Empire are by the accident of politics placed face to face and expected by their followers to fight each other to the death. This is politics but is it wise or profitable that two men who might be working together to save the country from disaster should be obliged to waste their energies in opposition to each other.[29]

The King and Lord Stamfordham regarded the political situation with increased impatience as the Conservatives did not give the impression that they were more able to deal with the crisis of government than Labour. In fact, in mid-October, Stamfordham had begun canvassing opinion on 'what the King . . . ought to do if conditions go on as they are and parliamentary government becomes much more farcical'.[30] MacDonald had by then been told by Louis that the Conservatives appeared willing to make compromises to bring about a combined government initially under MacDonald's leadership. In fact, the shadow cabinet was firmly opposed to such a notion in late 1930. Consequently, MacDonald wrote pleasant things about the Conservatives in a letter ostensibly to Louis but more importantly for Baldwin's eyes. It was not until 1 December 1930, that MacDonald raised directly with Baldwin the 'possibility of a national government.' But Baldwin was not then fully convinced.

Louis's role behind the scenes unsettled politicians such as Hugh Dalton, the Labour economist, who scorned any interference by courtiers, even semi-detached ones. In his diary, he warned that this could not be countenanced.

Ben Smith* says that Wing Commander Greig, the Prince of Wales's attendant, had written to a Labour politician, who had recently held a Court Appointment, saying he had been 'working for two years' to bring about a National Government. Others about the Court, Ben says, often used to tell them that there ought to be a National Government. Let them beware of being caught in *flagrante delicto* of interference in our domestic politics.[31]

Dalton was wrong to describe Louis as the Prince of Wales's attendant, but he was correct in suggesting that Louis was a significant force behind the scenes lobbying for a national government. 'You will think I am a crank on National Government,' Louis wrote to MacDonald in early 1931. 'I only am, so long as you are to lead it. Forgive me bothering you & don't reply but I seem to have appointed myself your informant on all the wild gossip I hear & if it's any use to you, my friend, I shall go on with it for what it is worth.'[32] He continued to lobby widely, encouraging MacDonald to believe that Geoffrey Dawson, the editor of *The Times*, was waiting to endorse him, and that Lord Rothermere would also do so, if only because he hated Baldwin so much.[33]

Louis's link with the Palace and Downing Street helped in other ways, too. Godfrey Thomas, the Prince of Wales's private secretary, wrote to Louis after the Prince was misquoted in the newspapers as attacking government policies. Thomas asked Louis to tell the Prime Minister what the Prince had actually said. The word 'politicians' had been removed from the final draft of his speech about the crisis in farming, and the word 'administrators' inserted. The press had a field day after quoting from the first draft of the speech, making out that the Prince intended to criticise MacDonald's government, which was why Thomas wrote to Louis with a full version of events. 'Some day perhaps you will explain to him [MacDonald] how the mis-reporting occurred and that

* Labour MP for Rotherhithe 1922–31, 1935–46, Minister of Food 1945–6.

the actual phrase used – though it might have been better worded – was not as bad as he was led to believe.'[34]

Louis kept a steady stream of information going to and from different sources at the Palace and Westminster. For instance, he alerted Lord Stamfordham to the fact that MacDonald planned to hire the diplomat Robert Vansittart as a personal political private secretary 'as a liaison between the PM and the Labour party and to have his PS to connect with the Palace'. His advice was not always welcome, and on that occasion the elderly Stamfordham indignantly let Louis know that he was getting involved in matters that were none of his business. Usually his approach was welcomed. For instance, when staying at Sandringham he was able to iron out a minor misunderstanding between the King and his Prime Minister by pushing a note under MacDonald's bedroom door:

> I have not been five minutes here when HM was asking why you were staying such a short time & was it necessary to let the press know you were coming here before you arrived. I told him in answer to the first that you were probably very busy & also that you did not want to interfere too much with H.M.'s shooting! God forgive me. As to the second I told him that if your colleagues saw you were in London they might feel they ought to get back but if they saw you were going to S [Sandringham] they could stay away with an easy conscience. He was quite mollified, so if you can back me up, do so & if you cannot rush away too early on Friday so much the better, but don't worry if you can't manage this. Excuse bad writing but I do want you to get this before you leave.[35]

More importantly, Louis was later in April 1932 used as a stalking-horse by the King to find out if MacDonald would accept any decorations. In a forceful letter to Louis written from Chequers and marked 'very secret', MacDonald made clear he would never accept a knighthood or a peerage:

> I cannot bear the thought of coming out of this world with any reward whatever in the form of titles or decorations. I want to

die as I have lived without fuss. I quite understand how people may properly value these things as indeed I do in others – as I am the worst aristocrat of you all, but my aristocracy does not run to ribbon. Nothing would give me greater satisfaction & happiness in my old age than that I came out of all this without a badge or what the man in the street calls a 'reward'. Its moral effect in the country would be enormous and its influence no mean advantage to us. Were I to be known as Lord or even Sir, much of what has been done would be discounted. Don't forget the tribute paid to the Romans who left public achievements to contemplate in cabbage patches. How much has Snowden [Philip Snowden, 1st Viscount Snowden, Chancellor of the Exchequer 1924 and 1929-31] fallen because he was persuaded to accept a Viscountcy!

If these matters come up you can help greatly not by advocating those views which perhaps you do not share, but by letting it be known that they are held by me and held strongly, & that if I were persuaded to swerve from them by any influence, instead of adding to my peace & happiness they would only crush me & cut me off from my own real enjoyment in life.[36]

The King had appointed Louis as a Gentleman Usher to be 'on call', and that was interpreted literally in March 1932 when Louis was sent, on the King's suggestion, to Newquay to give additional medical advice to MacDonald when Sir Thomas Horder, a renowned Harley Street doctor, was treating the Prime Minister for stress and fatigue aggravated by a serious eye disorder. Horder informed the King that MacDonald's health was improving, and generously gave credit to Louis. 'The party at Newquay is a great success, chiefly of course, because Louis Greig and his wife are there. Greig is of enormous help, as you will realise, and adds to his personal experience of the patient the great advantage of medical experience. This gives me much confidence in my part of the responsibility.'[37]

Louis's loyalty to the princes never dimmed, and, in particular, he sought the Prime Minister's active support for the Duke of York camps. MacDonald responded as positively as he could. 'I am only too delighted to do anything I can to help. I really like those youths but do not want to intrude. I must not become a courtier. On the whole I thought it would be best if I wrote you a letter of an advisory kind which you can show him as it stands. Then I can be more friendly and less starchy & then it may have more warmth for the young man's heart. Let me know always if I can be any use in any way.'[38]

Louis thought the world of MacDonald and sometimes felt a little guilty about the number of letters he sent to No. 10. 'Today I have nothing of sufficient importance to waste your valuable time, but if you ever feel you need the relaxation of a cigarette & a cup of tea with any one as irresponsible as I, be sure & let me know. I have heard your praises sung by Wigram & it gave me a real thrill of pleasure,' he wrote on one occasion.[39]

Louis had, in effect, become the Prime Minister's unofficial courtier. He was summoned to Cornwall to help MacDonald recuperate after his eye operation, but found he was no easy patient. Louis privately wondered why, 'having got himself free from the Yorks he should let himself in for this'. He found the Prime Minister 'so moody, jumpy and nervous' that he momentarily wondered if the country 'should be in such hands'. MacDonald was, by 1932, hardly the committed socialist he had been in his youth. He had lost the early fire of his Fabian idealism and in talking to him Louis found his plans meant it was now 'safe for the aristocracy'. He even advocated lower income tax and the halving of death duties, two measures his party would never have advocated. This was apparently too much for his daughter Ishbel, who said, 'But father what about the redistribution of wealth,' to which the PM replied, 'Oh my dear, that is all nonsense now.'[40]

MacDonald was greatly impressed by Louis's wide contacts and ability to fix things. 'Greig is a man of the world and knows something of the common people,' he told Thomas

Jones, the Secretary to the Cabinet who acted as an adviser to Lloyd George and then successively to Bonar Law, Baldwin and MacDonald. Jones reported in his diary that he presumed that Louis was to be Lord Stamfordham's successor as private secretary to the King. It was never really likely but it was an indication of just how powerful a position he was perceived to have at court. Equally important to MacDonald was Louis's unquestioning loyalty. The Labour leader had lost many friends in battles over Labour's policies, and he greatly valued those who stuck by him. Louis made no secret of his willingness to defend him at every opportunity. In January 1932, for instance, MacDonald learned from Louis of a brusque encounter he had at a dinner with Oswald Mosley, once a MacDonald sympathiser, who would later lead the British Union of Fascists. Louis made his anti-fascist views crystal clear and confirmed that his loyalties lay with the Prime Minister.

> Me [Louis]: I told him that I was more than ever anti-fascist.
> Mosley: I have a great regard for MacDonald.
> Me: You show it in a damn funny way in your speeches.
> Mosley: I have made up my mind never to attack him personally again, only his policy.
> Me: Can I tell him that?
> Mosley: Yes, because he was very good to me.
> Me: Well, Mosley, you are more human than I thought.[41]

The material Louis passed on ranged from complicated arguments about such constitutional issues as Indian independence to insider gossip from the court and Westminster. He had the Prime Minister's ear and the potential to influence appointments, which he tried to do.

For you private ear, Lord Dudley has been going round saying that he is to be Governor of Madras. I have not any idea whether this is in your or Sam Hoare's mind, but the man is very much *persona non grata* at BP & I am certain HM would find it difficult to

welcome the appointment. The morals & reputation are not good
& before coming to any decision (if it is your mind), do have a
word with Clive Wigram. I know he entirely agrees with HM's
conception of the man. If you want any further news I shall gladly
come & put in words what I don't on paper.

Lord Rothermere, the owner of the *Daily Mail*, considered
Louis an influential lobbyist. 'I have today received an inti-
mation that Rothermere would like to meet me & so I am
lunching with Lady Hudson on the 2nd for that purpose,'
Louis wrote to MacDonald.[42] MacDonald was well served
by Louis's discreet private news service, ranging from the
Square Mile to Buckingham Palace. It sometimes included
tough assessments of key establishment figures, such as
Wickham Steed, the former editor of *The Times*: 'that somewhat
dreadful fellow. When next we meet I should like a word with
you on him, because he is inclined to say things in public which
he shouldn't & I had to take issue with him. A very nasty piece
of work I call him'.[43] Not even Churchill escaped his eagle eye.
'I had a wonderful description of a man which well applies
to Winston. Apart from his natural criminal instincts, he is
consumed with vanity, inundated with jealousy & suffers
from a superabundance of misdirected intelligence which
is the envy of true wisdom.'[44]

By choosing to persuade MacDonald of the merits of a
national coalition Louis felt he had pursued the best policy for
Britain. After all, the defining event of the Baldwin ministry
had been the General Strike, and the public wanted change. At
the beginning of 1930, unemployment in Britain stood at one
and a half million, and was to rise to two and three-quarter
million by the end of the year. The political pressure for a
solution was intense, as no one seemed able to lead a government with any conviction or confidence. Change was needed,
and fast, which was why Louis backed a coalition. It was not
exactly a magic formula, but it did keep the country united and
gave it a breathing space to regain its economic and political

confidence – despite bitter opposition from the Labour Party and the TUC.

August 1931 was an agonising time for MacDonald as his Cabinet was split about how to shore up the country's budget deficit of £170 million – £50 million more than the worst projections. Half his Cabinet refused to countenance any but the most exiguous cuts in unemployment benefit; this left MacDonald powerless to solve the nation's economic difficulties with his existing Labour government. The crisis over sterling remained the most pressing matter. A majority of his Cabinet was prepared to resign and leave the unpalatable social measures needed for the Tories to carry out.

When advised of this situation, the King did not, however, ask MacDonald to resign, but told him he would talk to the opposition leaders and 'advise them strongly to support' him.[45] Both Baldwin and the Liberals told the King they would serve under MacDonald although Baldwin had first told George V that he wanted to form a Conservative dominated government. When MacDonald reported back to his Cabinet, he found that they were split nine to eleven against the necessary financial cuts, and this was too thin a majority to continue as a ruling party. His colleagues expected him immediately to tender the resignation of the whole Cabinet, which was what he led them to believe he would do when he again went to see the King. Instead he was urged by the King to consider a coalition government. On his return to Downing Street his colleagues were shocked to learn that he was still Prime Minister, only this time of a national government. All but three resigned, but enough remained for him to have a token Labour presence to justify the formation of a coalition government. Many in the Labour Party felt betrayed, and blamed the King as much as MacDonald for emasculating their power and their chance to govern. Louis, too, would not have escaped censure, but he felt that such a deep economic crisis in Britain necessitated dramatic measures. He had no regrets.

On 7 September 1931, Gwynne congratulated Louis on his part in bringing MacDonald to the head of the new coalition government. 'You must be a proud man this day,' he declared, 'for your friend [MacDonald] has turned out trumps, and I think I know somebody who has had something to do with it.'

Chapter Fourteen

'I'll be d——d if in the next list there will be no character like Louis Greig.'
Ramsay MacDonald writing to Louis

When Louis was invited to Downing Street by Ramsay MacDonald on 23 April 1932, he thought little of it. He was used to occasionally dropping by, often on his way home from the City, to see the Prime Minister and act as an antidote to the stresses and strains of political life in Westminster. MacDonald liked to see non-political friends and, in Louis's case, sometimes just to muse about past or future trips to their houses on the Morayshire coast. Lossiemouth was always a haven for him from the political landscape. The pressures were intense in the 1930s, and he would reveal his worst insecurities to Louis. 'I seem at last to be breaking down . . . I cannot rest. I cannot sleep. But there will be a turning,' he plaintively wrote.[1] Always given to melodrama, MacDonald veered from high exhilaration to melancholic lows with alarming ease.

Louis thought that the Prime Minister might want to discuss the Findhorn Yacht Club, of which they were both founder members. The club was simply a couple of rooms in a village house overlooking the bay, where local yachtsmen gathered after their day at sea. Louis was never happier than when he was sailing round the bay in a small clinker-built vessel, known as 'the brown boat'. MacDonald had drawn up 'The

Rules & Regulations of the Findhorn Yaughtsmen's Squadron'
in a lengthy, handwritten set of faux rules, which he sent
to Louis to amuse him. ('Rule four: Yaughts made in
Lossiemouth are ineligible as Findhorn must have a chance.'
'Rule six: When the Commodore or Retiring Commodore
(Louis Greig) gets sick, all races are immediately called off.)
Louis liked to mock the Prime Minister for his lack of sailing
skills while he was teased for his failure to stop swearing and
shouting, particularly when things went wrong at sea. His
blue language could be heard echoing from one side of the bay
to the other. The elder statesman and the courtier fed off each
other's boyish humour, and MacDonald missed Louis if their
visits north did not coincide. 'You were a foolish man not to
spend your last ill-earned shilling to get to Findhorn where
Sandy [Grant] is laying all sorts of traps for you and your
"yaught",' he wrote.[2]

But that particular spring afternoon MacDonald did not
want to discuss 'yaughting' or politics; he wanted to ask Louis
to accept a knighthood. This reduced Louis to silence. He was
delighted to be offered a KBE, but at the back of his mind he
was concerned to avoid any repetition of the unfortunate controversy that had engulfed Alexander Grant when he received
his knighthood in 1924. Louis offered to forgo the honour if
there was the slightest chance of MacDonald being accused of
cronyism for a second time. The last thing he wanted was for
his proposed knighthood to cause political damage to the
Prime Minister. He had not made any financial gifts, but had
helped him to raise political funds, and he was a prominent
personal friend. Louis wrote to the Prime Minister, offering
him a let-out if he needed one.

> You must have thought me singularly unresponsive this afternoon
> but honestly I was more taken aback by the kindness of your
> thought than by the greatness of the possible honour. I am made
> of poorer stuff than you are & I cannot pretend that the honour
> would not be very acceptable but that must not stop me from
> pointing out a danger to you as it strikes me. You see, try how I

may, & God knows I have tried hard, I cannot think of any valid reason why I should get an honour & so I am afraid that you might be accused of over friendliness to a friend & that I couldn't bear. I fear I am not sufficiently high-minded to do the big & consistent thing & refuse point blank the honour if it were ever offered me. If, however, I may put it this way – I am, beyond words, eternally grateful to you for thinking of it, but if you see my point, & decide not to go further in the matter, I am still eternally your debtor.

Forgive me for adding to the labours of your overworked eyes but I feel I'd rather lose the chance of a promotion than my friend should run the risk of criticism.

But MacDonald was not the least bit perturbed and brushed aside his fears, telling Louis that the knighthood would shortly be listed in the *London Gazette* in recognition of his 'public service to many social and welfare organisations'. Louis had become involved with a number of charities, in particular the Not Forgotten Association, which raised funds to care for wounded soldiers. He was also a governor of Westminster Hospital. But both knew that the knighthood was essentially a token of the Prime Minister's gratitude for Louis's unswerving friendship.

MacDonald valued loyalty above almost everything because he had been badly hurt by so many people in the Labour Party who turned against him. In 1932, he was openly derided by a large number of senior Labour politicians for having joined with the Conservatives in the National Government. Some believed that this deprived Labour of the chance of taking power for more than a generation. Clement Attlee spoke of MacDonald's 'betrayal', and other senior Labour politicians would not even acknowledge him when he walked past in the corridor in the House of Commons. Ever since 1914 MacDonald had never lacked enemies, having split his party by boldly declaring that Britain should remain neutral in the Great War. Many members of the armed forces never forgave him for that. At the pinnacle of his career he was often a lonely figure. The King understood this, which was why, when MacDonald was ill, he sent Louis to him as 'a dose of The Tonic'.

Many people assumed that George V had given Louis his knighthood. Not everyone knew the different shades and subtleties of the honours system, with a KBE (Knight Commander of the Order of the British Empire) being a political honour bestowed by the Prime Minister and a KCVO (Knight Commander of the Royal Victorian Order) being a personal gift from the monarch. The highest decoration Louis received from the royal family was his CVO in 1923 – one level below a royal knighthood. Louis's honour bestowed on the recommendation of the Prime Minister was a political one, although when it was announced MacDonald jokily feigned ignorance in a whimsical letter of congratulation:

I have been dilatory in congratulating you upon an announcement which I saw in the newspapers on Friday morning. It came as a great surprise to me and to be perfectly honest with you I am sure none of your friends expected it. Why on earth did Pillis [sic] ever allow you to accept it? I expect she had to undergo a good deal of strong language! I am informed that the Monarch objected to the unbroken line of Nonconformist Elders which has been appearing in these lists from time to time, and that he spoke to his counsellors in these words: 'I'll be d——d if in the next list there will be no character like Louis Greig or JHT [J. H. Thomas]. Since Clive Wigram came in, the language of Buckingham Palace has become decidedly cool.' That may or may not be true but whatever the reason may be or however great the surprise, I heartily congratulate you both. I understand that Chadwick [owner of Binsness House in Findhorn Bay] is getting up a brass band amongst the cobble owners of Findhorn, and that they are going to go out into the bay and serenade you on your arrival in that God-forsaken village. Sandy Grant is talking about a new flag, and there are various other projects on foot, one of which is that Mary Grant [a Findhorn neighbour of Louis] will cross the Bar [treacherous strip of sand in the Moray Firth] in her dinghy and really get drowned at last. She says in her rather imperfect state of information – Now that Louis sits in the House of Lords the object of my life has been fulfilled and I shall give him the satisfaction of seeing me going under his very eye.

Louis also received a letter from Albert. 'Let me congratulate you . . . How does [Lady] Greig feel about it? I am so glad it has come to you. You have done a lot of good work lately for everyone.'

He became used to receiving such *jeux d'esprit* from MacDonald in the form of little poems, cards, letters, and even limericks, such as:

> *There once was a courtier called Louis*
> *Who lived upon tea and Drambuie*
> *All morning he laughed*
> *And all evening quaffed*
> *So Tommy declared he was viewy*

or verse birthday greetings:

> *A sixty-six full gun salute*
> *To you, Sir Louis, this glad day,*
> *From Findhorn to its furthest shores*
> *Echoes the Empire's loud hurrah.*
> *Gay in heart and statesman true*
> *Who lighter feels the years than you?*

When he was in an upbeat mood, MacDonald was whimsical, romantic, even fantastical. Yet when the pressure became too much, his letters and diaries verged towards melancholia or even hysteria. Louis was glad to offer emotional support, and was sometimes shocked by his friend's naked vulnerability. 'I long for Lossie and Findhorn and the other dependencies of Lossie. You are the only man who has sent news & gossip. Everyone else seems not on holiday but dead,' MacDonald wrote. With his baroque prose it was, however, sometimes difficult to know if his letters were a self-parodying cry for help or the real thing.[3]

A knighthood was not Louis's only reward. In 1932 the King resurrected for him the ancient title of Deputy-Ranger of Richmond Park, and offered him the chance to live at Thatched House Lodge, a magnificent residence in the middle of a deer park created by Charles I. The job was, in essence, a royal sinecure, carrying no salary except a yearly haunch of venison, but in Louis's case it would come with the charming eighteenth century home set in the three-thousand-acre park. The most famous past Deputy-Ranger had been Princess Amelia, George II's daughter; Louis joined a long line of tenants with royal connections, including another royal surgeon, Sir Frederick Treves. The advantage of Thatched House Lodge was that it was a large country house, practically in London. It had eleven bedrooms and extensive servants' quarters, as well as a grass tennis court, croquet lawn and swimming pool. No building had existed on the site of the lodge before 1637, when a plan of Richmond Park was made for Charles I, who had enclosed the land, forcing people to sell their property so that he could establish a private sporting estate. A tall perimeter wall was completed in 1637 to keep in the deer for the King to hunt. What had started as a modest keeper's lodge was enlarged in the early eighteenth century by Sir Robert Walpole, who lived there for many years, and who was also responsible for a summer house containing a remarkable series of murals painted by Angelica Kauffmann, the Swiss portraitist and Royal Academician.

The idea of making Louis Deputy-Ranger had originated from Lord Lee of Fareham, the philanthropist who gave Chequers, the Buckinghamshire country house, to the nation for the use of the Prime Minister. Arthur Lee had been a Tory MP in the Cabinet during the First World War whose fortunes dramatically changed after he married an American heiress. Louis had helped him mediate some administrative problems concerning the Chequers Trust, when extra money was needed for the upkeep of the house. MacDonald had been concerned about some petty regulations governing the use of the house, which were enshrined in an Act of Parliament. Was he allowed to send his children there if he was not there? Were dogs allowed? An over-zealous secretary of the Chequers Trust had suggested that MacDonald's children could not go down there without him being present. After consulting Lee, Louis had advised MacDonald to ignore all pettifogging officials and to treat it as his home, which was Lee's intention when he donated the house. Louis was a tactful middle man, getting answers without getting tangled in red tape or causing embarrassment to Lee. It was not always easy when the donor was very much alive and hypersensitive to every issue involving Chequers.

'There is one person who is ideally qualified to discharge the duties of Deputy-Ranger with the efficiency and suavity that would be requisite and that is Louis Greig,' Lee wrote to Clive Wigram[4] from White Lodge, his Crown Estate house in Richmond Park, just a short distance from Ladderstile, Louis's own home. Wigram informed the King of the proposal; he thought it a marvellous idea and immediately gave the go-ahead. George V had never stopped being Louis's most loyal backer, ever since 1917, when he had offered him a house on the Sandringham estate. He was glad to find him a more suitable property at a more opportune moment. But there was also, Louis believed, a political edge to the gift. The King knew only too well that when his reign ended there would be dramatic changes at court. He dreaded the prospect of King Edward VIII on the throne, fearing that his son's reign would be selfish and destructive. To make his gift irreversible, the King turned Thatched House Lodge into a Crown Lease property rather than a grace-and-favour house. This meant it could not be withdrawn on the whim of any future monarch. Louis was delighted with this extra safety measure, as he valued his independence above all else and he did not want his home to be permanently reliant on royal patronage, particularly under a monarch as volatile and unpredictable as the Prince of Wales was likely to be. He wanted a permanent and secure residence irrespective of his relationship with any future sovereign. But such houses were never free, and Louis worried about the rent and upkeep, even writing to MacDonald to ask his advice.

> My Dear PM,
>   I confess my own affairs at Thatched House Lodge are not easy. The Surveyor of the Crown agrees that about £1,600 is necessary to be spent on the house & the rent just almost £500. I am a bit shaken over the amount. I am very willing to put the place in order. I am not sure that I am capable of a rent of £500 a year. I have responded to Ponsonby & he is mentioning it to HM to see if a slight relief may be obtained in view of my role as Deputy Ranger. You see how honest I have become confessing my efforts to get something for less than the Crown assesses! & it's a shame to burden you with these petty troubles. So I will cease.[5]

The details of the lease were fixed by Sir Frederick 'Fritz' Ponsonby, the punctilious Keeper of the Privy Purse, who had what his mother called an unrivalled knowledge of 'all the little miseries of etiquette'. He was the consummate courtier. The second son of Sir Henry Ponsonby, Queen Victoria's private secretary, Fritz eventually served at court for more than forty years.[6] Tall and thin, this suave old Etonian was a stickler for detail. He treated with contempt anyone who strayed from the most conventional code of dress or behaviour. 'Suede shoes in a morning suit would practically cause him to cross the street in horror.'[7] In spite of his pukka credentials, Ponsonby, like Louis, was not rich. He supplemented his slender courtier's salary by writing film scripts, and had even invested in a quixotic get-rich scheme to recover the treasure of King John from the Wash.[8] He readily understood Louis's reluctance to take on such a large house if it threatened to be beyond his means.

Louis's mind was put at rest by the annual rent being halved to £250. The King wanted to be as generous as he could to Louis, to whom he was always grateful for the care of, and influence over, his second son. Louis accepted his offer with great delight, and just a little embarrassment. 'My chief regret in your scheme is that the King should be the sufferer but if his Majesty is kind enough to give up £250 a year during my lifetime I think I could manage to pay the balance of the assessed rent. It is most awfully good of his Majesty to be willing to ease what would have been an impossible burden and I do appreciate his kindness.'[9]

Accommodation on royal estates was always a sensitive issue among courtiers, who were very aware of each other's perks and privileges. And Louis's 'gift' of Thatched House Lodge was the subject of much talk at court, as yet again the doctor from Glasgow had landed spectacularly on his feet.

Louis was glad to be more independent of the court, pursuing his own career in the City. He was considerably better off financially after the minimal Palace pay, but he still liked having a toehold in court. The mid-1930s were very happy years for him as he enjoyed his new career, home and family. Thatched House Lodge allowed Louis to entertain in style with large lunch parties, tennis on his grass court, croquet on the lawn and tea in the summerhouse. It was a marvellous family home for the Greigs. Bridget and Jean loved to ride in the park, and Louis often accompanied them to local gymkhanas. The girls were taught at home by two governesses, Miss Spink and Miss Hoffman, while Carron, aged eight, was sent away to Sandroyd Preparatory School in Surrey in 1933, from where he eventually progressed to Eton. It was an idyllic retreat, and an eclectic assortment of people dropped by: Stanley Wootton, the Australian racehorse trainer, Johnny Weissmuller, the Hollywood Tarzan, Denis Wheatley, David Niven, and any number of Scrimgeours and Greigs. Louis's own family had led wildly varying lives. George disappeared in the Far East and never resurfaced, although he was rumoured to have fathered various children by local girls. Robert remained 'the pillar of the family' as a successful stockbroker, but Herbert ended up as a lift operator in a hotel in New Zealand. Louis later bailed him out of financial difficulties and gave him an allowance. Anna lived in Putney and was one of the few Greigs to retain her Scottish accent. Marjorie had married Laurence Robertson, whose Indian Civil Service career took them to India. Queen Mary was a frequent guest at Thatched House Lodge, and Albert used to bring down his two daughters. Louis and his one-time protégé always regarded each other with warmth and affection, although both had moved on from their early co-dependent days and taken divergent paths into different worlds. Yet, whenever they met up, it was as if very little had altered. Albert still liked to ask for advice, and Louis was never backward in giving it.

The King's health had never fully recovered from an infection of the lung that, in 1929, had turned to general septicaemia. 'It was his bloody guts that pulled him through,' the Labour minister J. H. Thomas had pronounced. But by the mid-1930s he had grown weary. Politically the world was dark as the shadows of a new global conflict started to loom with the emergence of the tyrannies of Mussolini and Hitler. His death was memorably signalled to the outside world by his doctor, Lord Dawson, who jotted down his final assessment of the King's declining health, in pencil, on the back of a menu card at Sandringham where George V lay in bed. 'The King's life is moving peacefully towards its close' were the moving, resonant words broadcast to the world.

On 20 January 1936, the country was plunged into mourning and uncertainty as Edward VIII was declared King. His twice-married American companion was now a potential queen, and this horrified the Establishment and cast doubts, in many minds, as to whether he had any notion of his duties or respon-sibility as sovereign. For a long time, George V had been deeply troubled by his eldest son's attachment to Mrs Ernest Simpson, the divorced, remarried woman from Baltimore with two living husbands. The historian Kenneth Rose succinctly summarised his view. 'He thought her unsuitable as a friend, disreputable as a mistress, unthinkable as a Queen.' As Edward VIII's reign began, the court was awash with gossip and rumour, with most people, including Louis, vehemently against the prospect of Wallis as Queen, or even a permanent consort to the King.

Louis greatly missed George V, who had encouraged and, at times, personally orchestrated the friendship with his second son, for more than twenty-five years. When Louis wrote to Piers 'Joey' Legh, the new King's equerry, he replied by return with a letter of condolence, edged in black to mark the court's mourning, just three days after the King had died. 'I have some idea what the late King's death must mean to you, and I would like you to accept my sympathy in what you have lost personally.' Straight away there was intense jostling for position in the new court as Edward VIII created his own hierarchy. 'I do not know what the future holds as far as I am personally concerned, but I do appreciate your kind thoughts very much,' added Legh. Change was immediate. Scarcely had he left his father's deathbed than Edward gave orders for the abandonment of Sandringham Time, the system by which the clocks were set half an hour fast to create more daylight hours for shooting. This trivial change shocked a lot of people, more for its speed than its substance. Virginia Woolf melodramatically saw it as the revenge of a man who had been 'daily so insulted by the King that he was determined to expunge his memory'.[10] The times literally were a'changing. Sir John Aird, Edward's equerry, noted in his diaries that George V had not even drawn his last breath when the plotting started.

It now seems decided that HM will die very soon & I have begun to accept it. Joey [Legh], Godfrey [Thomas], & the Admiral [Sir Lionel Halsey] discuss their prospects quite openly together & with me. I do not quite see where the Admiral fits in unless the Privy Purse is renewed, & even then Wigram may get it. Godfrey I place as PS [Private Secretary] either joint with Wigram or alone, Joey as Comptroller or Deputy. Alex Harding & Claud Hamilton are, I should say, for the sack. Joey pretends that he thinks he will not get a job, but does not really believe it & no one will be more angry if he doesn't. He said he does not want to go on as an equerry, which I can well understand but unless he gets the above I cannot think of anything else he is fit for.

Louis observed the dawn of the new era uneasily. He had little time for the rather dissolute or flippant friends of the new King such as Major Edward 'Fruity' Metcalfe, who would be best man at Edward's wedding when he eventually married Mrs Simpson. Old-timers like Admiral Lionel Halsey attributed the decline of the Prince's morals to the influence of Metcalfe – 'not *at all* a good thing for HRH . . . an excellent fellow, always cheery, full of fun but far, far too weak and hopelessly irresponsible. He is a wild, wild Irishman.'[11]

But in fact there had been early signs of the likelihood of Edward being disastrous as a monarch long before he met such inappropriate characters as Metcalfe. Louis was deeply pessimistic about the new reign. He heard dreadful reports from his friends at court, and he was more and more certain that there seemed little moral fibre to this narcissistic Peter Pan figure who had become King. He was fine as a playboy Prince of Wales, but as King-Emperor he had few admirers. Not that this was a surprise to those who had worked with him. In early April 1927, Alan 'Tommy' Lascelles, his then assistant private secretary, had allegedly told Stanley Baldwin that he considered 'the Heir Apparent, in his unbridled pursuit of wine and women and whatever selfish whim occupied him at the moment, was rapidly going to the devil, and unless he mended his ways would soon become no fit wearer of the British Crown'.[12] Lascelles then went a step further and suggested that the best outcome would be if he broke his neck in the next point-to-point race that he entered, thereby passing on his chance to be King. Baldwin's alleged response was as uncompromising: 'God forgive me, I have often thought the same.'

Louis was disheartened by Edward's cavalier approach to his responsibilities. He had seen him hailed as a boy wonder in the 1920s – bright, charming, debonair and, as far as the public were concerned, unable to put a foot wrong. He refused to grow into his role; even as a middle-aged Prince of Wales he showed few signs of responsibility or leadership. In 1936 he seemed shallow, callow and vain. The defining issue was Wallis Simpson.

Two opposite camps emerged at court in the aftermath of the King's death: those who supported Edward in his relationship with Wallis and those who fought to get her out. On this matter Edward and Albert held opposing views, which added to the polarisation at court. There was inevitably increased tension between the two brothers, and that spread to the court. Dr Stanley Hewett, who attended the King in his dying days, told John Aird 'he thought the Duke of York was the worst of the four sons & had a mean character. I should have put him just as being steady & reliable, even if dull.'[13]

Chips Channon was not much kinder, regarding the Duke of York as 'good, dull, dutiful and good-natured', and he would probably have regarded Louis in much the same light. He was too hearty and simply not interested in the rather precious social climbing and banter at which Channon was so adept. The old guard echoed George V's disapproval and despaired of Edward, but did so at the risk of being swept out of court. Louis was most definitely part of that old guard. He was also to become one of the first targets for the new King in the crossfire over the issue of his mistress.

The courtiers endlessly discussed the matter of Wallis and the changes threatened at court by Edward, who tried to sweep away those who did not fully support him. Aird, like many others, found it difficult to adjust. 'HM is so glad to have a change of staff that he is treating the new lot like he does foreigners, very nicely in that he feels superior & not equal as he did with the Admiral & Godfrey [Thomas], who knew him so well. HM has given us the impression that now he is King no one shall try to cross his path at any rate behind his back.'[14]

Wigram was equally ill at ease and told Aird that he thought 'HM was an impossible fellow to work for and he could not understand how he had been allowed to get like this'.[15] Tensions continued to rise as Aird gloomily observed that the 'trait in HM's character of showing no sign of gratitude for past work is a very nasty one'. The courtiers were not the only ones who were nervous of the new reign. Prince Albert complained to Admiral Halsey that he was not being consulted about any changes. Discontent also spread to Westminster and to the Prime Minister's office in Downing Street, where Edward's projected marriage was fast becoming a constitutional crisis as he showed every indication that he did not intend to abandon Wallis, and, more importantly, would not rule her out as his future Queen.

The new King alarmed the main political leaders by ignoring many of his essential constitutional duties, including the red dispatch boxes containing state papers. He displayed lamentable ignorance about his legal powers, almost as if he had chosen to ignore or had never learned the basic principles of being a constitutional monarch. Nothing seemed to matter except Wallis. Prearranged ceremonies were cancelled on the feeblest of excuses, such as poor weather. He turned away representatives of the Church, the City and the legal profession, who customarily presented a loyal address to a new king. Finally, when he failed to attend church regularly, as was expected of the head of the Church of England, he was criticised by one of his bishops, whose words were then interpreted as an attack on his relationship with Mrs Simpson, and after that the floodgates of criticisim opened up in the press. Edward was always able to find time for Mrs Simpson and the nation now began to wonder whether he wanted her as Queen, and also to consider the constitutional consequences of such a move. Some even felt that the entire future of the monarchy was under threat.

George V may have been limited in his approach to the

world, but he had been nothing if not duty-bound. Louis told friends that he thought that the new King was abandoning his duty for his American friend's pleasure. It was hardly an original view. In fact, it was echoed by most courtiers, but what made it different was that someone had passed Louis's views back to the King, probably in an exaggerated form. The likelihood is that it was someone like John Aird, who had no fondness for Louis. He found him too bouncy and boastful, and was irritated by how this outsider from Glasgow had become such an insider. The petty snobbery and rivalries of court life never ceased. The King was livid with Louis, and ordered Lord Cromer, the Lord Chamberlain, to fire him from his position as Gentleman Usher. But Cromer dug in his heels and refused to carry out the order. He was an honourable servant of the Crown but also a loyal friend to Louis. More importantly he was a wise and steady counsellor. He crossed the King by sending a calm, well-argued letter expressing his reservations at carrying out his orders.

> In your Majesty's interests, I am venturing to make a personal appeal for re-consideration of the case of Louis Greig, in the hope that Your Majesty may approve of his appointment as Gentleman Usher being continued until after the Coronation.
>
> My reasons for urging this are that in the eyes of the outside world, he is supposed to have been very helpful to the Royal Family over a long term of years, and, should his appointment now be terminated on the 20th July, it would undoubtedly give rise to unfavourable criticism in the many circles in which Louis Greig had managed to establish a contact, more especially in the world of sport, and also among the Labour Party. From the point of view of the Lord Chamberlain's Office, he certainly is a useful officer, and I should like to be able to summon him to the Afternoon Receptions on July 21st and 22nd, but cannot do so unless Your Majesty authorises me to inform him that his appointment will be continued until the Coronation period is over.
>
> It is the urgency of the matter in this respect which leads me to approach Your Majesty with this submission.[16]

The issue of Louis's future divided the court. Aird, for instance, thought he had got his just deserts, and told the King exactly that. 'The Admiral and Alex both agree with Wigram that it was a mistake to drop Louis Greig. I told HM I am convinced it was right. He is an unpleasant oily bounder & in the City is known as a go-between, which if not being used is a nasty thing to have about the Court. I admit to be a Gentleman Usher is not an important job but even so if he is not wanted as a spy, get rid of him & then there is a place for a new spy when required.' But Louis had no shortage of powerful supporters, including Wigram and Cromer, who regarded the King's reaction as petulant and ill advised.

For four days, Edward VIII sat on Cromer's letter, furious that his orders were not being immediately implemented. He talked to other courtiers and, of course, to Mrs Simpson, but, in the end, the King backed down, and Louis was reprieved. Cromer received a stern letter from the King promising the immediate dismissal of Louis if his 'disloyal' views were ever repeated:

> I am late in answering your letter of the 9th July because, from my standpoint, it has needed a great deal of thought. Doubtless you remember our conversation about Louis Greig, and it surprised me when you appealed for the retention at Court of a person who I had already told you had on more than one occasion been very disloyal to me. I feel so strongly that the success of the Court depends first of all on loyalty to the King, and then co-operation within that. I have, on taking over, tried to make the process of re-organisation as easy and fair as possible. You tell me that Louis Greig is supposed to have been helpful to the Royal Family. This hardly includes myself because far too often gossip of a destructive nature reaches my ears from that source. Since, however, you as Lord Chamberlain are so anxious for this re-appointment, I want your assurances that this kind of thing will cease for all time and for the good of all concerned.[17]

It was a sign of the King's lack of perspective that he even bothered to think about Louis, whose position in his household was minor, part time and inconsequential to a man who had just inherited the largest royal empire on earth. His attempt to oust Louis was no isolated incident. Edward also upset his full-time staff by trying to cut their wages and expenses in a haphazard and piecemeal way. At the same time he would pay almost anything to keep Wallis content, lavishing expensive gifts on her. His obsession blinded him to all common sense. For instance, when his head gardener at Windsor Castle proudly showed him glorious peach blossoms in the greenhouses, Edward ordered them all to be cut and sent to Mrs Simpson. The gardener was devastated that the bumper crop he had been so proud to show the King was destroyed in order that his mistress have flowers for just one day.

Louis's reaction to his spat at the Palace was to shrug it off. He knew that Queen Mary and Albert would not believe any suggestion that he had been disloyal to the royal family. It was just another example of the King's inability to act or think straight. They were just as alarmed as Louis was by the King's behaviour. But they all also knew that his mercurial mood swings and spoilt tantrums were not new. Even as a young prince, Edward had always hated the restrictive atmosphere of a royal court, and that had not changed now he was King. 'Princing,' he had told Freda Dudley Ward many years before he came to the throne, was much easier abroad: 'Guess it's because one isn't hit up with a lot of old-fashioned and boring people and conventions. One feels somehow that people are so much more genuine out of England.'[18] George V had predicted disastrous consequences for his eldest son's future, telling Baldwin that 'after I am dead the boy will ruin himself within twelve months'. George V always tried to see an alternative to his eldest son's succession, and in one of his most bitter outbursts expostulated: 'I pray to God my eldest son will never have children, and that nothing will come between Bertie and Lilibet and the throne.'[19]

George V's wishes were to be fulfilled less than a year after his death, when Edward VIII announced his intention to abdicate and marry Wallis. By taking his father's name as his title to become George VI, Albert gave a clear signal that the old order was back in place and that the hollow values of Edward VIII and his circle were finished. It was a traumatic end to a disastrous reign, but Louis, like millions of others, felt it was a blessing. He was overjoyed that the young man, over whom he had wielded such a powerful influence in his early days, was now to be King.

Chapter Fifteen

'A good and decent man has taken over, and not a
minute too soon.'

Louis writing to his brother Robert

T he year 1936 was an unsettling one for any monarchist:
it was the year of three kings. Louis had deeply mourned
the loss of George V, and disapproved of Edward VIII's
brief and selfish reign; only when George VI and Queen
Elizabeth succeeded did he feel that the monarchy was once
again secure. Few people outside his immediate family were
in a better position to judge the new King's character than
Louis. And as he sped about his business in the City, he took
every opportunity to trumpet to the world that George VI had
all the potential to be an outstanding sovereign. He felt
enormously proud that the boy, whom he had first known as
a hesitant and vacillating cadet, a quarter of a century earlier,
was now King-Emperor.

'A good and decent man has taken over, and not a minute
too soon,' he wrote to his brother. Louis was not alone in
thinking that a great threat to the British way of life had
been removed with Edward's abdication and retreat into
exile. This sentiment was echoed by John Reith, the BBC's first
Director-General, and one of Louis's friends from their early
Glasgow days: 'We felt as if a cloud of depression of which we
had been almost physically conscious had lifted. Poor Edward.
But thank God, he and his ways have passed, and there is

a new King and Queen. The effect is quite extraordinary. It seemed as if the old England was back.'[1] Alan Campbell Don, the Archbishop of Canterbury's chaplain, mirrored this thought when he wrote on the eve of the Abdication: 'Tonight there is almost everywhere, at any rate among responsible people, a sense of relief – the crisis is passed and we can now settle down to try to recover what has been lost, and I believe the new King with his Scottish Queen will prove equal to the task.'[2]

But not everyone was pleased. Some of those who had tied their colours to the mast of the last king feared they would be out in the cold, in particular the 'smart set', who had encouraged the affair with Mrs Simpson, basked in the favour of the new King, and then hurriedly claimed to have deplored the relationship all along when Edward VIII went into exile. Society's fast set had tended to back this glamorous, rake-thin Baltimore adventuress, while the Establishment old guard had mustered its forces against her.

Like everyone at Court in the aftermath of the abdication, Louis read Osbert Sitwell's 'Rat Week', the notorious piece of doggerel that denounced Lady Mendl, Lady Colefax, the fashion editor Johnny McMulen and other sycophantic hangers-on who had abandoned Edward as soon as he appeared to be on his way out. 'Rat Week' had originally been distributed to just a few of Sitwell's close friends, but they had passed copies around until the poem became widely circulated in society. A copy was among Louis's personal papers when he died. It mercilessly exposed the former King's followers as disloyal, shallow and worthless.

> *Where are the friends of yesterday*
> *That fawned on Him,*
> *That flattered Her;*
> *Where are the friends of yesterday,*
> *Submitting to His every whim,*
> *Offering praise of her as myrrh*
> *To him.*

The knock-on effect of the caustic attack was to make George VI, the new Queen and their circle appear steadfast, reliable and respectable. Albert's detractors may have cast him as safe and dull, but now that worked in his favour. The country needed someone solid to make the monarchy secure.

Sitwell needlessly worried that the new regime might look upon him unfavourably for his irreverent verse. When the new Queen was staying at Houghton, the Marquis of Cholmondely's house in Norfolk, she was lent a copy by her hostess, and devoured it with delight, immediately passing it on to the King, who gave it to Queen Mary. The question 'Are you a Rat?' was bandied about in jest, although it did highlight sharp divisions within royal circles. Out went the heartless narcissism of Edward and his American mistress. 'Thus the Court, thank God, will revert to the old well-tried ways, to the infinite relief of all concerned,' noted A. C. Don. And instead of an atmosphere of vindictiveness and petty power-play, more of a sense of forgiveness and healing prevailed. Joey Legh, Edward VIII's loyal equerry, for instance, was back in favour even though he had accompanied Edward into exile in Austria. What redeemed Legh was that he had disapproved of the Wallis–Edward liaison and had courageously made his views clear to Edward. George VI asked him to become the Master of the King's Household and stay on in a grace-and-favour house in St James's Palace. 'You've been wonderful with my brother, and I know you've done your best. I want you to come and look after me and show me the ropes.'[3] Louis, too, was back in favour, and formally invited to become a member of the new King's court with his reappointment as a Gentleman Usher, the position he had held under George V.

It was a relief to find himself no longer at loggerheads with the sovereign. The accusations of disloyalty had been hurtful. After all, if nothing else Louis was a passionate monarchist, and Phyllis even more so. When the National Anthem was played on radio or television, Phyllis would not only make sure that everyone in the room was silent but also stood up. She would defend the royal family against even the mildest criticism. And she had no time for the Rats. Of course, the feeling was mutual. The Greigs were too hearty for the effete, silver-tongued smarter set of the former regime. Phyllis was too down-to-earth and forthright for the sharp and brittle tittle-tattle of the Channons or Colefaxes. There was something of the deeply patriotic Girl Guide leader in Phyllis – fearless, outspoken, sometimes tactless, often blinkered, but always courageous – which the smart set never quite appreciated. Louis and Phyllis were more in tune with the philosophy of George V: slightly philistine maybe, but with straightforward moral values that were non-negotiable.

Emerald, Lady Cunard, the American-born society hostess, found herself one of the few people banned from court by the new King and Queen for 'disloyalty'. What she said is not known but is likely to have included snide put-downs of the Yorks, who were, it has to be said, far less glamorous than the Windsor set. Born Maud Burke in California, she had married Sir Bache Cunard, grandson of the founder of the shipping line, but her social life really took off in 1925 when she turned into a very merry widow on the death of her dull, rich, older husband. She abandoned her gloomy Leicestershire country house to dazzle London with a salon full of fast, witty cocktail chatter and society gossip. The new King told his brother, Prince George, never to see Lady Cunard, a ban supported by Queen Mary, who had been told by several people 'what harm she has done'.[4]

But overall there was no great bloodletting. The Yorks were too overwhelmed and exhausted by their new roles and responsibilities and wanted quietly to move on from the traumas of the past months. The new Queen set the tone when she wrote to the Archbishop of Canterbury, Cosmo Lang, just two days after the Abdication:

I cannot tell you how touched I am at receiving your most kind and helpful letter today. I can hardly now believe that he [Albert] has been called to the tremendous task, and (I am now writing to you quite intimately) the curious thing is that we are not afraid.

I feel that God has enabled us to face the situation calmly, and although, I at least, feel most inadequate, we have been sustained during the last terrible days by many, many good friends. I know that we may count you among them, and it means a great deal to us to know this. When we spoke together at Birkhall only three months ago, how little did I think that such drama & unhappiness was in store for our dear country . . . We were so unhappy about the loss of a dear brother because one can only feel that Exile from this country is death indeed.

We were miserable, as you know, over his change of heart and character during the last few years and it is alarming how little in touch he was with ordinary human feelings – Alas he had lost the 'common touch'. I thank you again for writing and prayers for our future. We pray most sincerely that we shall not fail our country and I sign myself for the first time & with great affection Elizabeth R.[5]

When Louis was reappointed as a Gentleman Usher, some suggested he should have been given a more senior position,[6] but Louis was, in fact, perfectly happy to be on the fringes of the court. He did not believe in pedalling backwards, and felt that a full-time job would have been a regressive step. He had moved on. Moreover, he did not fancy a pay cut, which a return to the Palace hierarchy would have required. His life was broadening out into new worlds – banking, Hollywood, racing and politics. He was gathering a lucrative portfolio of directorships that would eventually include the Dorchester, Eagle Star, Blaw-Knox, Gaumont-British, the Portland Building Society and Kodak. The year of the Abdication, he was elected chairman of Wimbledon, which would later play a very important role in his life. He valued independence above everything, and a toehold in the royal pond was all that he wanted at this stage in his life. It was enough to give him a role in the most important royal ceremonial occasions.

Louis was proud to play a part at the Coronation on 12 May 1937 at Westminster Abbey. As a Gentleman Usher, his job was to guide heads of state and other royal guests to their seats. It was an extraordinary day for Louis, and also Phyllis, who was invited to the celebrations as a guest in her own right. They saw the man they had known, almost twenty-five years earlier, as a knock-kneed, thirteen-year-old schoolboy called Bertie become the world's last King-Emperor. They witnessed his reign commence with optimism and jubilation amid the pomp and formality of the Abbey service, during which the King, with his father's inherited eye for detail, could not resist noting one or two minor glitches. On turning to leave the Coronation Chair, for instance, the King observed: 'I was brought up all standing, owing to one of the bishops treading on my robe. I had to tell him to get off it pretty sharply as I nearly fell down.'[7] It was the start of one of the most successful reigns of any constitutional monarch in the twentieth century.

After the rollercoaster ride of the previous eighteen months, Louis decided to get away from England altogether by taking his family on an eight-week tour of America and Canada. It could not have been a more dramatic change of scene as they swapped the British royal family for 'Hollywood royalty', with Tarzan as their host. The whole of the Greig family had been invited by Johnny Weissmuller, the former American Olympic swimmer and first screen Tarzan, who was a regular guest at Thatched House Lodge. Jean, Bridget and Carron idolised Weissmuller, who played his jungle role in more than a dozen films, with a variety of mates, and even more chimpanzees, between 1932 and 1947. His ululating cry was what made him most famous; it was so good that a recording of his was sometimes used when latter-day Tarzans took over the role. The Greig children were especially pleased when he agreed to demonstrate his jungle call from the top of a tree in Richmond Park. They were also rather dazzled by his wife, the spitfire Mexican actress Lupe Velez.

The Greigs set off with a mountain of suitcases for their two-month tour. Bridget was twenty, Jean eighteen and Carron twelve on this one and only family holiday abroad. As they sailed from Liverpool on the *Duchess of York* on Friday, 30 July 1937, Louis murmured to Phyllis as his children excitedly ran about the ship, 'I suppose Christopher Columbus felt as much a bloody fool as I do.' On the journey Louis would teasingly tell his two daughters that this was the perfect opportunity to find the husband of their dreams, and made them laugh with a piece of his own doggerel.

> *Oh my two girls are a couple of pearls*
> *No father could ask for more*
> *But never a sign of a couple of swine*
> *to cast them both before.*

Eight days later, and without a beau for either Bridget or Jean, they arrived at Montreal, staying for a week with Louis's niece before moving on to see such sights as the Niagara Falls, and then trekking through the Rockies to see bears and elk in the wild. The drama of the Abdication and the past few months in England seemed wonderfully distant as they moved at a leisurely pace between Louis's different friends. Austin Taylor, a sawmill tycoon, put them up in Vancouver; Helen Wills and Helen Jacobs, the two rival tennis champions, entertained them in San Francisco. But the biggest excitement was staying with Weissmuller in Hollywood. By this time, Louis had become closely identified with the new King through the saturation newspaper coverage of the Abdication and succession. Photographs of him playing at Wimbledon or accompanying the young Albert on *Cumberland*, or even to a hunt at Belvoir Castle, the Duke of Rutland's house in Leicestershire, were widely used – the press's appetite for royal news was inexhaustible. Louis found that he had become a figure of interest to the American press, which he found amusing, if a little embarrassing, as reporters greeted him off trains and requested interviews. 'Sir Louis Greig, Aide to Kings, Visits Here: Famous Flyer to be Guest of Weissmuller,' ran a headline in Vancouver's *Daily Province*.

With their English tweeds, felt hats and strident personal-ities, the Greigs intrigued the Los Angeles *Evening News*, which ran several stories during the run-up to a party Lupe Velez organised in their honour. Carron found himself elevated to the rank of a peer's son as he mused on the possible party list.

'Why not ask the lady who always wants to be alone?' suggested the honourable Carron, who is 14.

Lupe explained that Garbo does not attend cocktail parties.

The youngster frowned a minute, then brightened.

'Well then, why not ask the lady who never wants to be alone – the one who is always saying: 'Come up and see me sometime.'

The Seattle *Post-Intelligence* were equally aggrandising with their headline, 'British Nobleman and Family Arrive in City'.

When Sir Louis Greig, KBE and gentleman usher in ordinary to King George VI arrived at Canadian Pacific's Leonora Street terminal in Vancouver, he might have been an usher but it was immediately manifest that Sir Louis was in no sense ordinary. The customs gave his twelve pieces of luggage a once-over lightly, and the immigration department bowed from the waist.

'Just what do the words "in ordinary" mean,' he was asked.

Sir Louis had apparently never been asked this before. He puzzled a moment.

'Damned if I know,' he finally said.

'What does a gentleman usher in ordinary do,' he was asked.

'Well not much of anything,' said Sir Louis doubtfully.

'He shows people where to go,' suggested Lady Greig help-fully.

'Yes, and he hands out cards and things,' added one of his daughters.

And so the paper's headline was decided: 'Usher in Ordinary to the King: He hands out Cards and Things.'

Louis could not escape from his royal friendship even when he was five thousand miles away from the court. Wherever he went, he was asked about the new King. 'He is, and always will be, a fine simple fellow, easy to get on with and devoted to his wife and family. I am confident his will be a splendid reign,' he told one Hollywood paper, which ran the headline 'Royal Swans Float on Lupe's Pool'.

The one setback to their trip was the devaluation of sterling, allowing Louis only four rather than five dollars to the pound, which forced him to rein in his spending. He had only been allowed a limited amount of cash to take out of Britain owing to currency regulations. His solution to the budget cut was to put Bridget and Jean on a diet of Sun-Maid raisins ('I know what is good for you, I am a doctor,' he jauntily insisted) while young Carron was allowed chicken once a day. ('A growing boy needs his meat.') The devaluation did not affect their tour, which was mostly prepaid, and before they headed home they took in all the major sights, from the Grand Canyon to New York City, in a remarkable whistle-stop tour. But during their holiday there were warning signs that trouble was brewing back home with Germany's seemingly unstoppable pro-gramme of expansion and predatory aggression. By the time the Greigs' ship finally docked in Liverpool, it was clear that Hitler's dictatorship was firmly established. He had gained draconian powers from laws passed by a supine German parliament. On April Fool's Day, 1937, for instance, Hitler had extended the Enabling Law of 1933, which had allowed him to rule by decree for the past four years. By extending it to 1941 by a sleight of hand he had given himself a veneer of legal probity as he settled into his tyranny.

Louis was deeply worried about the Nazi spectre and its consequences, particularly for those unable to leave Germany. The twentieth century has never been free from the plight and burden of refugees and their suffering. In 1937 there were an estimated 700,000 refugees.[8] While the League of Nations was eager to solve the problem, not all governments were willing to co-operate. And in Germany, a major difficulty for those trying to flee was the issue of whether or not they were spon-sored by someone in a new host country. Many Jews tried to escape by simple means of emigration but, having no backer abroad, were destined to remain behind, and, in many instances, that was to mean facing the gas chambers. Louis helped a number of Jewish families find asylum in Britain. Joseph Oppenheimer would have found it impossible to leave Germany if Louis and Sir John Lavery, the distinguished portraitist, had not sponsored him. As a Jewish avant-garde painter, Oppenheim would have been unlikely to have survived the war without gaining asylum in Britain. He thanked Louis the only way he knew: by painting a portrait of him, and also of Phyllis. Oppenheim knew he had had a narrow escape. Hitler was determined to impose Nazi values on art and to drive out those who did not uphold and glorify the Nazi view. When an exhibition of 'degenerate art' was opened in Munich in July 1937, Hitler damned the artists involved as 'these ruffians, the lackeys and pacemakers of international Jewry'. They had, he said, 'committed crime after crime against German Art'. Hitler wondered if their 'defected vision' was congenital or acquired. If congenital, he suggested initiating steps so that 'it becomes impossible for them to pass on and thus propagate the defect'.

After the First World War Louis had been determined to do all he could to help prevent a similar global conflict ever recurring. To this end he joined the Anglo-German Association (Deutsch-Englische Vereinigung), a loosely knit group of landowners, Members of Parliament and a few writers, who had banded together in 1928, long before the rise of Nazism, to try to repair the relationship between the two countries. By encouraging contact between Germany and England, he hoped that any future conflict would be more unlikely. The association is not to be confused with the sinister Anglo-German Fellowship, which was formed later, and was used as an umbrella group by Nazi sympathisers in Germany and Britain. Nothing could have been more abhorrent to Louis than the sinister, shadowy pro-Nazi tendencies of the Fellowship. According to Professor Richard Griffiths of King's College,

London, author of *Patriotism Perverted* and *Fellow Travellers of the Right*, the Anglo-German Association was wholly innocent and bore none of the disturbing traits displayed by other similarly named bodies in the 1930s. It was a mixture of idealists and cranks, as these organisations generally are. In 1929, Arnold Bennett, John Buchan, John Galsworthy and H. G. Wells were the literary end of a membership that included a wide spread of politicians, grandees and establishment figures from Robin Barrington-Ward, the editor of *The Times* to Sir Godfrey Thomas, the Prince of Wales's private secretary. But Louis's enthusiasm for co-operation and appeasement quickly faded in the 1930s. His view of Germany had never sympathetic since he had been wounded and imprisoned in 1914. In the 1930s he voiced his views on the need to stand up to Hitler and present a message of British intransigence, rather than appeasement. In America, he had stressed the need to compete in the arms race against Germany. 'We disarmed for years, following your good example, but then others began to arm,' he told a reporter from *The Oregonian*, in Portland, Oregon. 'We are pushing our armament programmes as rapidly as we can, because in Europe as it is today we believe in the strong man armed.' Louis was a hawk when it came to dealing with the Third Reich.

In May 1939, Louis took his uncompromising message to Berlin on a private mission to assess the political situation. He had earlier come across Joachim von Ribbentrop, the ambitious and oleaginous German ambassador in London between 1936 and 1938, who was part of Hitler's inner circle. Louis was no more than a passing acquaintance, but he had been perceived as a potential agent of influence. Hitler's man in London was essentially a political lightweight and social climber who was regarded as useful by the Führer, but held in contempt by his senior colleagues. He would have known that Louis was a political fixer with strong royal links, and he may have thought he would be an easy man to influence. But even if Louis was taken in, Phyllis never let him, for an instant, forget the regime that Ribbentrop represented. In 1938, when Louis told her that a friend wanted to bring Ribbentrop to lunch at Thatched House Lodge, she was appalled. Her politics were generally more right-wing than Louis's, but always more black-and-white. While he had been supportive of Ramsay MacDonald's Labour Party, she had never wavered from voting Tory. When it came to Ribbentrop she felt he was a despicable Nazi lackey. She understood that Louis might want to hear his views, but if he came to lunch, neither she nor the children would appear at table. Carron was sent upstairs and watched from an attic window as the German guest arrived. Phyllis never set eyes on him, and liked to point out that just nine years after she refused to entertain him, Ribbentrop was hanged for war crimes.

Louis had alerted the King to his mission to Germany, and afterwards sent him a detailed report. It was a humorous but tough answer to Germany's aggression:

> I carefully told him [Ribbentrop's representative] that I was merely on a private visit, and my views would be those of the man in the street, but if he would like those, he was welcome. He started by asking me why we were mixing ourselves up with Eastern Europe. I told him that he must understand it has always been the tradition of our people to stand for a principle, and that when the average British man saw a big man bullying a small man in the street, he instinctively wished to stop it. We had always fought for this principle, and, in so far as the man in the street was concerned, would continue to do so.
>
> He then asked why we were thinking of allying ourselves with Russia, and I told him that, to return to the analogy of the street fight, one would call upon a bystander to help restore law and order. That did not necessarily mean that one would take the helpful bystander home with one, but he was useful in the common cause.
>
> He then got onto the question of the colonies, and said that naturally they must be returned. I asked him why, and he said they had laid down their arms in 1918 on condition that the colonies were to be returned. I said that our interpretation was somewhat different. To our mind they had laid down their arms because they

had damn well been beaten to a frazzle, and that they had put up a fine fight and the world had beaten them as they would beat them again . . . England's trust in the words of the Führer had received a very severe shock as the result of the Czech coup. He tried to explain that the Czechs, having been separated from the Slovaks, were becoming an acute danger to Germany. I said that we had always understood the Germans had no sense of humour, but they certainly must have some kind of humour, otherwise he could not have made such an apparently humorous remark to us.

Generally speaking the people in Germany appear to think war quite out of the question, owing to the Führer's great peace work in the way of building, and what he is doing for the working man, and I am convinced that if we could get it across to the powers that be that we are serious, there would be no war, as the public are horrified at the mere thought of it. But that is not to say that they won't fight when they are told.

Louis also passed his impressions on to Lord Halifax, the Foreign Secretary, and Horace Wilson, Neville Chamberlain's chief adviser in No. 10. Just four months, later everything Louis had learned from his time in Germany became academic, as in September 1939 Chamberlain declared war against Hitler. For the second time in Louis's life, Britain was fighting Germany in a world war. It was a conflict in which he was determined to play his part once again.

Chapter Sixteen

'I am so glad you are helping George [Kent] with his
new job. All he wants is a little help to put him on
the right track. & he must have a good man with him.
George VI, writing to Louis

L ouis was almost sixty when war was declared. He was too
old for active service, but was recalled into the RAF for
a job at the Air Ministry in Whitehall, which needed
experienced senior officers who could be trusted in sensitive
administrative posts. He was first assigned to an Orwellian-
sounding organisation called the Directorate of Plans under
the command of Air Commodore John Slessor, who kept him
busy until he was asked to work in the Cabinet War Rooms,
Britain's secret underground command centre.

This war bunker had been established in 1938, amid concern
over troop movements on the Bohemian border and general
fear of the conflict to come, and it was where the movements
of Allied and Axis troops were monitored. The government
had decided that emergency accommodation for the Cabinet
and the chiefs of staff was needed in the event of enemy air
attack on London. Dollis Hill and the West Country had been
considered as possible sites before a basement under government offices in Great George Street was eventually chosen.

Louis was given access to the all-important Map Room,
where the latest information on every war front was collected,
analysed and then presented to a small list of people including
the Cabinet, the chiefs of staff and the Joint Intelligence

Committee. Near the Map Room was Churchill's private quarters. 'This is where I'll run the war from,' he declared when first shown the underground warren. Many of his wartime broadcasts were made from the subterranean rooms, now an extraordinary time capsule, preserved exactly as they were on the day the war ended. A faded piece of paper still bears Louis's name on a list of those with sufficient security clearance to be allowed into the Map Room.

Few details of Louis's work there are documented, because he was used as an unofficial fixer. He helped to gather and co-ordinate information from the services and different government departments.[1] The advantage of using him was the absence of a paper trail; it was swift with no red tape and no fuss. He knew a great many people and was good at calling in favours to get things done. With his unstoppable optimism, persuasive charm and 'a face that always seemed to be on the verge of breaking into laughter', people found it difficult to say no to him.

Every morning Louis drove to work in his black Ford Prefect. He was a highly recognisable figure in his 'warm', an unfashionable calf-length Crombie cloth coat, and he carried a slim walking stick with a silver top. His RAF cap, a little too small with a slighter peak than was traditional, perched at the back of his head. Eccentric and stylised as his Edwardian-style uniform appeared, Louis was unselfconscious as to its effect. He simply wore the clothes that he had, and was too much the practical, careful Scot to have thought of going out to buy newer ones.

Petrol was hard to come by owing to rationing; Louis had to pull strings to obtain extra fuel for his daily journey to London. Often he would give a lift to Phyllis and his daughters, who all had wartime jobs. Jean was a captain in the ATS in the cinema corps, organising films for the troops. Bridget was in the Motor Transport Corps, often driving exiled Poles to the airport before secret missions to their Nazi-occupied homeland. She was part of SOE – the Special Operations Executive.

Phyllis was a supervisor in the Women's Land Army, as well as a commissioner in the Girl Guides in Surrey, preparing young girls for the eventuality of a German invasion. In her spare time, at a house in Lowndes Square, Mayfair, she also made string vests for soldiers sent to Finland or Norway. Carron was away at school at Eton, but even he, aged fourteen, was involved in the war effort, square-bashing with the school cadet corps and in the Eton branch of the Home Guard. At the earliest opportunity he joined the Scots Guards, training at Sandhurst, the military college near Camberley in Surrey, where he won the Belt of Honour, the prize awarded to the best cadet in his year. 'Glad to see he's a chip off the old block,' George VI wrote to Louis.[2] During the war, a belt was presented instead of a sword, which was signed by a senior general, in his case General P.A.M. Browning, the commander of the British airborne troops. (General Eisenhower later asked Louis if he, too, could sign it.) Carron spent the final year of the war in Germany as an intelligence officer with the 3rd Battalion Scots Guards. Prior to that his hand had been hurt in a training exercise when a tank barrel crushed it, but that was the only injury suffered by the Greig family. He was out of action for several weeks, and it probably saved his life as he missed D-day. 'So sorry about your poor son's injury,' a solicitous Queen Mary had written, anxious about her godson.[3]

At an early stage in the war, George VI quickly realised that Louis's job was not the grey, pen-pushing desk job that it may have appeared to the outside world. He had access to influential people and sensitive information. The King sent a handwritten letter, marked secret, asking him to pass on anything useful he picked up in the course of his duties. 'If you hear of anything which may not come my way please let me know. Quite a number of things are not told me, as people always imagine "somebody else" has told me in the ordinary course of routine, but it is not always so. In these days, if I can be of any help I must know things.'[4] The war brought many people closer together, and Louis and the King were no exception.

George VI was not a natural leader, but he was a brave and courageous one. Shyness often made him appear aloof, even bad-tempered, but he was never less than dutiful or eager to do his best. He naturally felt most comfortable with those he had known a long time, and so it was no surprise that he turned to Louis once again. Although he was in his forties and held sway over one of the greatest empires on earth, he could still be unsure of himself and quite vulnerable. Painful memories of stammering in his early days never left him. In 1939, he wrote to Louis to boast that he had successfully given a speech at the Guildhall without any hesitations. 'It was a change from the old days when speaking I felt was "hell",' he wrote.[5] Their bond never loosened, even though they saw less of each other. When they did meet up they were delighted to be the old team again. They exchanged letters throughout the war, often just snippets of information or gossip, but the link was never broken. The King, for instance, let Louis know that he thought little of Lord Beaverbrook, the ebullient press baron and Minister of Aircraft Production, and even less of the rather dull Air Minister, Archie Sinclair.[6] Louis was immensely proud that the boy who had been dismissed as a stammering semi-invalid with no future prospects in the last war had grown into the valiant leader that Louis had always believed he could become. The King rose to the challenge of the war, and, indeed, many saw it as his finest hour.

When Buckingham Palace was bombed, the sight of the King and Queen, in their formal clothes, standing in the rubble of their home, touched a popular chord. They, too, seemed as vulnerable to the German bombs as everyone else, and it made them appear courageous and undaunted. Another dramatic and lasting image was their visit to a bombed street in the East End to offer sympathy to those who had lost their homes. It was a simple and obvious gesture, but it somehow seemed heartfelt and novel for royals to share such intense moments of loss, confusion and grief. The royal family, at a stroke, seemed less formal and aloof. They were an impressive double act as Britain fought for its survival.

Yet the King's political antennae were not always so finely tuned. His loyalty to Neville Chamberlain, for instance, blinded him to the Prime Minister's failure to take a more robust stance against German aggression. In May 1940, the King had been angry at the popular dissent against Chamberlain, and felt that the country was ungrateful to an honourable man of peace. But when Labour refused to serve under Chamberlain, he was forced to resign. The King then made the error of favouring Lord Halifax as his successor, only for Churchill to point out that having a Prime Minister in the House of Lords would make it extremely difficult for him to govern. The King was a traditionalist and sentimental about rank and position; he was sorry that Halifax was not going to become Prime Minister, having already been Viceroy of India and Foreign Secretary. The King did not always find the alternative leader easy, and often tried to douse Winston Churchill's indulgences and bravado. John Colville, Churchill's private secretary, noted that the King and Queen were both 'a little ruffled by the offhand way he treats them – says he will come at six, puts it off until 6.30 by telephone, then comes at seven'.[7] The King liked to have other less formal and unofficial channels open, which was why he asked Louis to continue to be his eyes and ears.

Throughout the war, Queen Mary was isolated in her country retreat at Badminton, the stately home belonging to her niece, the Duchess of Beaufort. Louis told the MP Victor Cazalet that she was an undervalued asset, too often under-used by the other members of the royal family.[8] Louis adored her, and was practically devotional in his loyalty towards her. They corresponded throughout the war, as she too turned to him for news. But it was not the only thing she wanted. The old Queen had become hooked on watching films on a private projector at Badminton, and she wanted Louis to keep her supplied with new ones. The idea of Queen Mary glued to the screen at private viewings was the last thing many people would have imagined of this grand old lady, who always appeared so stiff, stately and Edwardian. She was living in the country for the first time in her life and needed distractions. She spent her days visiting local evacuee children, neighbouring factories and hospitals, but what she asked Louis for, again and again, was new films. 'Thank you for arranging about the films. *The Thief of Baghdad* is not available but I think I have seen it. You might let me know of any more films I may like.'[9] Hollywood films were a problem for her. 'We are still waiting for *Gone With the Wind*. Can you recommend others? The American ones are difficult to understand.' The accents were hard for her to decipher. She was grateful to Louis, 'my good friend'.[10] The war brought them even closer, too. It reminded her of the last war, when she and Louis had spent Christmas 1917 together. Then she had coquettishly admitted to taking too many pills that Louis had given her for a minor ailment, but was adamant that the old King must not know about her medication. After knowing Louis for more than thirty years, she was not shy about asking him for what she wanted. 'I was on the point of writing to ask you whether I could <u>buy</u> from the RAF farm in Regent's Pk some sausages & a ham occasionally as they are so good & we enjoyed them? They could be sent to Marl Hse to come by the bag.'[11] They both enjoyed their friendship, which for her was a nostalgic link to the old days of the late King. It also provided a window, enabling her to see what was happening in the war, throughout which she maintained a vigorous attitude towards the enemy. 'I spell germans and italians with small letters because I hate them!' she confided to Louis.[12]

In 1941, Louis left the Cabinet War Rooms to become Personal Air Secretary to Sir Archibald Sinclair, Churchill's Air Minister, with special responsibility for liaising with foreign heads of state. This job of political fixer on a grander international scale was tailor-made for Louis. If the military top brass wanted a visiting head of state to be informed un-officially on some sensitive matter, he was dispatched to nudge, wink, prod or forcefully persuade. To this end he saw a lot of the exiled leaders, like General Wladyslaw Sikorski of Poland and President Eduard Beneš of Czechoslovakia, who were both regular guests at Thatched House Lodge. After the war Louis received the Order of Orange-Nassau from Holland and from Poland the Order of Polonia Restituta 3rd class. Louis's royal access was always a useful card for him to play. 'I knew nobody else who could simply walk up to Buckingham Palace, bang on the door and be let in,' remembered Gordon Sinclair, a particularly heroic, much-decorated Battle of Britain pilot, who worked alongside him in the Air Ministry. 'He always seemed to run down King Charles Street to the Air Ministry. I never saw him still for a moment,' he recalled. Louis's contacts in high places, as usual, marked him out. 'He was socially turbo-charged, much more White's than RAC and that was useful,' remembered Joan Bright Astley, who had worked in the War Rooms.

In the early summer of 1941 Louis was summoned to Buckingham Palace to talk to the King about a proposal for Prince George to fly to America and Canada. It was a top-secret mission, as the propaganda value for the Germans, if they bombed a plane carrying the King's brother, would have been enormous, particularly as it was the first time any member of the royal family had ever flown across the Atlantic. The King asked Louis if he would fly with George to visit training schools where thousands of young men were preparing for the RAF offensive.

The King felt his younger brother needed someone like Louis to keep an eye on him. While Prince George was often considered the most talented of George V's sons, being cultured, good-looking and good company, he also had a wild streak. Seven years younger than Albert, he was less stiff and hemmed in by royal protocol and by his family's influence. Ever since his teenage years, George had found Louis an easy person to turn to for advice, particularly when he ran into opposition from his father.

George had sought out Louis in 1927 when he found that he hated being in the Navy, and when he had fallen in love with Helen Azalia 'Poppy' Baring, the twenty-six-year-old daughter of Sir Godfrey Baring, a crusty Conservative local politician from the Isle of Wight. The King objected to their romance because, in his view, Poppy was not suitable for one of his sons. This infuriated George, who wrote Louis an extremely frank letter detailing his run-in with the King. Once again Louis had taken on the role of adviser, mentor and royal fixer. It was a trusting friendship with Louis as an avuncular counsellor. He evidently did his best to intervene on George's behalf.

> Poppy wrote me that you'd been to see her & that you had been very confident about everything. I wrote to the K after I'd been gone away saying I couldn't take his no as final, & he answered that he could never change his decision & that the only reason he could give was that he didn't think it suitable (which is terribly weak). I think really he was trying to frighten me off but he hasn't succeeded. You can imagine how awful it is over here, staying with various people & at hotels in between & I feel I'll go mad before long as I feel so cut off & the people are terribly boring. Do let me know if anything more has happened & I want to thank you for being so nice & encouraging to me about it all & I can't see any reason against it nor how they can possibly stop it. I wonder if you've had a chance to say anything to the K about it. It would be marvellous if you could tell something about my not going back to the Navy as I hate it so much! Anyway I have indigestion & so I can get Weir [Sir John Weir, the doctor who introduced homeo-pathic medicine to the royal family] to say I can't possibly go back! It's all so terribly worrying & I do hope things will soon come right. I can't think what they imagine they can gain by my being away these months as they must know I'm serious & not likely to change my mind in fact it works more the other way.[13]

A month later, on 6 April 1927, when Prince George was staying at the Château de la Groupe in Antibes, he again leaned on Louis for support. By this time Louis had been to plead his case with both Stamfordham and Wigram. George wrote to express his thanks.

> I'm so sorry I've never written before to thank you for your letter telling me all that you've found out & it is marvellous of you taking all that trouble. From that it shows that they can't stop me in the end, but I suppose if I do anything now they'd stop my allowance. It is so awful being away like this & so unable to know what's really going on. They've not written me now for some weeks, as I never answered the 'famous letter' & so they're furious. I wanted to come over this week but David thought it wasn't worth it just for a day or two, as it would only stir up trouble & it wasn't worth it for such a short time.
>
> P wrote me she'd seen you again but I haven't had the letter yet telling me what you'd said but I gather things are beginning to look up a little & I only wish I could get back & help a little.[14]

There had been a lot of gossip circulating about Prince George's personal life before his marriage to Princess Marina of Greece, and Louis was a constant and staunch defender, his lavish and generous praise designed to balance some of the less appreciative reports. Queen Mary was particularly grateful. 'How kind of you to write such a delightful letter about my George. It is most gratifying to me, my brother & Pse Alice have also written pleasing accounts. I am so glad you went with him. You must have been a great help,' she replied.[15] Queen Mary was furious when other courtiers such as Alec Hardinge, the King's private secretary, attacked her favourite son. 'That ass AH always has a dig at poor G – which makes me furious. I praised G up to the skies to HM . . . I am delighted you told AH.'[16]

So when Prince George learned that Louis was to accompany him as a sort of minder for the trip to Canada, he was delighted. They flew on 29 July 1941 in a Liberator, one of the huge four-engined American bombers. The journey was far from comfortable. 'I wouldn't recommend a season ticket,' Louis joked in a letter to the King, who was grateful to have

Louis with his brother to ensure that it went well. 'I am so glad you are helping George with his new job. All he wants is a little help to put him on the right track. & he must have a good man with him. He has never had to do a job on his own & here is his chance,' wrote the King.[17] On their six-week trip they spent more than fifty hours in the air taking in thirty-three different destinations, including staying at the White House with the Roosevelts. Louis reverted to his role as the King's eyes and ears. 'May I send you a line to let you know how matters are progressing so far. The Duke of Kent has had a wonderful reception. He is sailing along on the stupendous affection & admiration which your Majesties have aroused in this country by your visit and it's all too easy. At the same time Prince George is playing up most awfully well. Nothing is too much trouble and he talks well of everyone he comes across.'[18]

The trip was to take on a far greater significance in hindsight when, less than a year later, Prince George was killed on another flying mission alongside twelve others after their Sunderland flying boat crashed in Scotland on its way to Iceland. It was only by chance that Louis had not joined him on that journey. 'I can't quite collect my thoughts over this ghastly loss we have all suffered, but I would like you to know how deep are my sympathies for the Queen & yourself,' he wrote to the King, adding, 'I had come since my trip to Canada to admire Prince George enormously. I had always adored him as a small boy, but he was developing fast into a fine leader of men & I know could have & would have been a great help to Your Majesty. He certainly wanted to be.'[19] George VI asked Louis to send a next-of-kin letter to Princess Marina. 'Thank you so much for your sympathy. The whole tragedy seems to me to be so inexplicable & so unnecessary. But weather is bad weather in those parts as we know from Scapa & it comes on so suddenly. I shall miss him & his help terribly.' Louis's heart particularly went out to Queen Mary, who had now effectively lost three sons, the first to epilepsy, the second to a life of permanent exile, and now George in a tragic accident.

After he returned, Louis's role of liaising with the heads of state brought him into contact with General Dwight D. Eisenhower, who had command of the planned D-day invasion. Ike quickly became a name on everyone's lips, capturing the public imagination as an all-American hero. He was powerful, photogenic and full of rousing soundbites, talking intensely and with visible anger about the Nazis. He would speak of someone who 'knows the score', someone else as 'a big operator'. His bosses in Washington were the 'Big Shots'. Cynicism seemed somehow discourteous in the face of his refreshing and winning approach. Louis came into Ike's life when the general let it be known that he wanted somewhere to ride. Louis offered him the use of his horses and his stables at Richmond. Early in the morning they would ride through the park together, which was the foundation for a close friendship. Eisenhower had rented Telegraph Cottage, which was close to Thatched House Lodge, which made it very easy for both men to see a lot of each other. Eisenhower sometimes used Louis's house as a place to meet people in an informal, confidential setting. He was there so much that some newspapers reported that he kept a suite of rooms there. When Mamie Eisenhower came over they would stay with Louis as his house had more room.

Louis advised Eisenhower to work the system in Britain. If his top generals came over, Louis would make sure they had a room at the Dorchester. He was a useful link between Eisenhower and the British authorities, once again on an informal, unofficial basis. Louis saw a tremendous number of people and was a useful and active fixer. 'Louis was so influential behind the scenes; everybody knew him in the upper echelons of the RAF. A lot of things were not done strictly according to the rules and he was one of the men who made things happen,' remembered Dame Felicity Peake, the first director of the Women's Royal Air Force. It was more diplomatic than strategic, but he was taken seriously as someone who could broker deals. Louis saw all the leaders of the free nations fighting the Germans when they came to London. Just as he had been devotedly loyal to Ramsay MacDonald, so Louis was an enormous admirer and eventually a close friend of the Texan general.

Eisenhower was grateful for Louis's ability to make his professional and personal life run smoothly in Britain, and in August 1945 President Harry Truman rewarded Louis with the Legion of Merit after the war. In the White House citation, President Truman noted his 'intimate and co-operative relationship served as the friendly connecting link between the Air Forces and those of the United States and the confidence inspired by him was of material aid in furthering their amicable association to the successful prosecution of the war effort'. Eisenhower gave Louis a special gold-plated Parker fountain pen, one of just nine that he had commissioned for his top commanders. Many years later, when Eisenhower was given a flat for his lifetime in Culzean Castle in Ayrshire, he asked that Louis be one of just a dozen people allowed to use it in his absence.

Perhaps the most extraordinary foreign leader with whom Louis had to deal was King Farouk. He was sent to Cairo in June 1943 to try to placate Britain's rather volatile, vain and petulant ally in the Middle East. Louis had been one of the few friends of Farouk in 1936 when the Prince had been sent to England to finish his education. His home was Kendry House, Kingston Hill, near to Thatched House Lodge, and Louis was asked to teach sixteen-year-old Prince Freddy, as he was then called, how to ride a horse. According to Sir Edward Ford, who became Farouk's tutor in Egypt, Louis was the only English friend he had at that time, and they built a considerable rapport.[20]

Louis was coaching Farouk how to jump hurdles in 1936 when a man in a black frock-coat and a red tarboosh drove up in a Daimler and Farouk was informed that his father was dead, and that he was King. 'I'll do three more rounds of jumps then I shall return with you,' he told the Egyptian messenger.

But Louis stopped him in his tracks. 'Sir, you'll do nothing of the sort. Get off that horse. We can't have two kings of Egypt dying on the same day.' Louis had seen Farouk's equestrian skills and decided that they did not merit further risk.[21]

The next time they saw each other was when Louis flew out to try to help to quell the diplomatic row over Farouk's dislike of the British ambassador, Sir Miles Lampson, in 1942. But Farouk was no longer willing to take orders, let alone advice. Yet he was thrilled to see Louis and sped him around Cairo, taking him to dine in exotic cafés and restaurants. Farouk was always a playboy sovereign and a bizarre, slightly deranged monarch. He retained his obsessive hatred of the British ambassador, who in 1943 was created Lord Killearn. To get rid of him he hatched a mad plot to send a huge box of chocolates to Buckingham Palace, with a letter hidden inside the box asking the King to fire the ambassador. Farouk used Patrick Telfer-Smollett, a young British officer, as his messenger. To get to London he had to go via neutral Lisbon, which entailed crossing the continent by way of Khartoum, Nairobi, Entebbe and Dakar. Ice was needed along the way to stop the package melting. But his main worry was getting the package to the King once he was in London. 'I explained as a junior officer I knew no one at the Palace and a few generals were of no use.' Farouk told him: 'Do not worry. Sir Louis Greig was always good to me. I will give you his address and he will help'.[22] And so, when he arrived in England, Louis was called. Telfer-Smollett never knew how, but the King was made aware of the letter, even though the chocolates never made it to the Palace. It was a small, eccentric sideshow, but one that amused both Louis and the King.

On his return to London in the Blitz, Louis maintained as normal a family life as was possible at Thatched House Lodge. Several bombs exploded in the park, lured by the decoy factories erected to try to draw the German planes away from the docks and other parts of London. 'I am sorry for the damage in the Park. Poor old quiet Richmond,' Queen Mary wrote to

Louis.[23] Aerials were secretly positioned in the park to pick up secret agents' transmissions, as Louis's house was one of the highest points in the south of England. It was a delightful oasis in London, and many friends took advantage of the Greigs' hospitality. 'It always seemed an open house with all sorts of interesting people passing through,' remembered Gordon Sinclair. John Colville, Churchill's private secretary, often came for breakfast and an early-morning ride. It was never clear who would turn up to lunch, from Queen Mary to Bertram Mills, the circus owner. 'Louis was charismatic and compelling with a great sense of fun. My father died when I was very young and I suppose I looked up to him as a sort of father figure,' remembered Gordon Sinclair who stayed with the Greigs for several months. Pamela Greig, Louis's niece, was a particular favourite. She was one of the most impressive women officers in the war, eventually becoming Deputy Director of the Women's Air Force with 180,000 women under her command. 'Louis was quite marvellous at knowing that it was a lonely business for a young woman to be in such a position of authority, and I found him a huge support. He was good at making people feel they mattered,' she said. She was one of the many unsung heroines of the war. Afterwards she found it quite a shock to get back to civilian life. When she applied for a job at Fortnum & Mason, she was asked if she could type. She pointed out that she was not applying to be a secretary but wanted a management job. The Piccadilly grocery store couldn't believe that a woman was capable of such a task; even when told that she had been in charge of more than 180,000 women they were still reluctant to take her seriously. Such were the unfair realities of a very male world.

All Louis's family survived the war. The one piece of bad news was that Bridget had broken off her engagement to a young East Surrey officer called John Armstrong McDonnell. She had written to him almost every week while he was a prisoner of war, but on his return she found their war experiences had drastically changed their preconceived notions of each other. Their parting was amicable but painful. On the more positive side Jean had fallen in love with Joseph Cooper, a delightful and extremely talented concert pianist, who married her in 1947. It was not what Louis might have expected for a son-in-law – art and music were notably absent from the Greig household. But after some initial suspicion about how a musician could make his way in the world, Joseph Cooper was warmly accepted into the heart of the Greig family. Phyllis attended all his concerts. He was later to become one of the best-known pianists in Britain, and was awarded an OBE in 1982. Wearing his deep knowledge lightly on his sleeve, he brought classical music to a huge television audience with his BBC programme *Face the Music*.

Louis and his family were most grateful for simply being alive at the end of the war. They had all survived and were free from the threat of bombs and invasion. At last, after six years of war and at a cost of twenty million lives, they could, once again, get on with the business of living rather than fighting. King George VI found himself immeasurably more popular than he had been at the start of the war. Hundreds of thousands crowded the streets to rejoice at the peace, the focal point for the celebrations being outside Buckingham Palace, where the crowd sang and cheered as King George and his queen waved from the balcony to a grateful nation. He had grown in stature and was not only a popular sovereign, but a respected international leader.

Chapter Seventeen

'Few men in the twentieth century can have had a fuller or a more varied life than he.'

The Times

When the war ended, Louis retired from the RAF, for the second time, and returned to civilian life. He was over sixty-five but far from ready to slip into retirement; he was never able to sit still for long. 'We always used to joke that he knew the back entrance of every restaurant, so that he could be on the move and onto the next place,' remembered his son-in-law, Joseph Cooper.[1] Louis directed much of his energy into running the Wimbledon All-England tennis club, where he had played his disastrous doubles match with the King almost twenty years earlier. He had been chairman since 1936, but during the war had set up a caretaker committee, and so was keen to become fully involved again. Many repairs were needed; the Germans having bombed the grounds four times because the club had been used as a civil defence base. With Louis's permission Miss Norah Cleather, the acting secretary, had also created a farmyard in one of the car parks breeding pigs, ducks, geese and rabbits.

Louis was in his element during the Wimbledon fortnight with the Royal Box practically becoming his personal fiefdom, where he loved to mix with the 'great and the good'. Harold and Dorothy Macmillan and Clement Attlee were alongside

David Niven, Ann Todd or Douglas Fairbanks Junior, as well as a good many of the royal family. In the late 1930s George VI sent his daughters along with Libby Hardinge, the daughter of the King's Private Secretary. Photographs show them sitting on Louis's knee while he pointed out the famous players on court. Every disparate thread of his life came together at Wimbledon; he became very closely associated with the club, which he ran with an old-world ease and conviviality for almost seventeen years. 'The smooth running of the Wimbledon championships owes much to Sir Louis' charming personality and indefatigable hard work,' wrote Brigadier Jackie Smyth, the *Sunday Times* tennis correspondent, in his *History of Lawn Tennis*.

Louis improved the club for the players as well as the members, changing the rules to allow former winners free tickets each day. Previously they had been jealously guarded by the increasingly elderly members. He advocated an open championship, allowing professionals to play, and argued for television coverage. He was very much a modernising, hands-on chairman. When the club feared that its wine would be destroyed in the Blitz he had it moved to his cellar at Richmond. When there was a shortage of ball-boys in the first post-war tournaments, he called a friend who ran the Barnado boys' homes, who bused in boys. He also resolved the delicate issue of how to have a male masseur in the ladies' changing room while preserving their modesty: he hired a blind one.

But his views were not always popular. He fell out with Ted Tinling, the tennis dress designer and minor Wimbledon official, over the issue of women players' frilly knickers in 1949. With his penchant for glittery gold coats, the flamboyant Tinling and bluff, clubbish Louis could not have been more different. When Tinling designed fancy, frilly lace knickers for champion Gussy Moran, they were visible under her kilt-length skirt when she reached for a shot. The whole country went mad over her underwear. The Marx Brothers, in London at the time, asked her to join their act. She was snowed under with requests to make public appearances. The incident escalated as Tinling and the Wimbledon committee clashed over the need for such fashion props. They discussed banning her knickers, and this left Louis with the unenviable task of suggesting to Tinling that they were *de trop*, and must be removed, or at least kept discreetly out of sight. Tinling, at this stage, had already parted company from Wimbledon in his role as a line judge for different reasons, but, of course, this did not stop the newspapers from linking the two issues. When the story appeared on the front page of the *Daily Telegraph*, a stuffy committee member called Alfred Stery wrote to Louis: 'I would not suggest any mention being made about Gorgeous Gussy and her under garments as the question is too common for words.'[2] Louis ignored Stery's suggestion that he write a pompous letter to the editor of the *Telegraph*. Instead he wrote privately, and jocularly, to the paper's tennis correspondent and let the matter stop there.

The nearest Louis got to relaxing in his final years was sailing his 'brown boat' in Findhorn. He had been elected a member of the Royal Yacht Squadron, but preferred to more modestly potter around the bay on his own. He would look across from the pier to the opposite side of the bay where he could see an exotic avenue of yew trees leading to a wistaria-covered house, surrounded by one of the most romantic gardens in Scotland. Binsness was the only house on the south side of the bay and had originally been, in the seventeenth century, an old sea tavern at the edge of Culbin Sands, an extraordinary expanse of undulating dunes covering more than ten thousand acres to form one of the last great wildernesses in Britain. As well as being hauntingly beautiful, it was treacherous. In 1694, a sandstorm buried the entire village of Culbin. 'A man ploughing had to desert his plough in the middle of a furrow. The reapers in a field of barley had to leave without finishing their work. In a few hours the plough and the barley were buried beneath the sand. The drift, like a mighty river, came on steadily and ruthlessly, grasping field after field, and enshrouding every object in a mantle of sand.'[3] Even the mansion house on the edge of the village was buried, never to be seen again. More than 250 years later, Carron, Bridget and Jean would find bottles, buckles, flints and other relics from the lost village in the sand. A few clumps of wild grass took root, but otherwise there were just whirling sands on the move.

The tavern had an elegant stone wing built on in the nineteenth century, but the most striking element of Binsness was its spectacular position next to the sea and its exotic arboretum planted by the Chadwick family, who travelled as far afield as Mexico and Siberia to find trees for Binsness. The centrepiece was the yew avenue of stately dark green trees tapering in size, the smallest ones being nearest to the sea, as the salt stunted their growth. More than a hundred yards long, with a strip of grass down the middle, the avenue led to the sea, which on a good day was as blue as the Aegean. The light at Findhorn is of such extraordinary translucent quality that in the 1970s an American New Age group founded the University of Light to take advantage of it. When Louis looked across the bay in the 1930s he always dreamed of owning Binsness, which appeared as exotic as a Florentine villa with its exquisite fairy-tale garden surrounded by the sands. When it suddenly came on the market on the death of James Chadwick, an expert on the lost continent of Mu, Louis bought it without pausing for thought. Carron, on duty with the Scots Guards in Germany, received a telegram. 'Am told only a poet or a madman would buy. So have bought Binsness.' It was to be Louis's Shangri-la.

The house came with 120 acres of policies, but he could not afford to buy the sands, and so made a deal with the Forestry Commission, which planted pine trees by thatching the saplings to the unstable ground, as much as a safety device as to keep the trees in place. Louis retained the shooting rights for deer and capercaillie and, of course, the wonderful house.

Louis's curiosity and energy never dimmed. He was always making new friends and contacts, always fixing something for someone. John Wayne wrote to him in 1950 after his agent had recommended that he call on Louis, who immediately invited the film star to Thatched House Lodge. Louis's circle of friends never got smaller, but there were a number of regular visitors such as Queen Mary, who remained a most loyal friend. Her curiosity never flagged, even in her eighty-fourth year, Louis told Eisenhower in a letter in July 1952. 'Phyllis had a pair of stockings with "I like Ike", on them and when Queen Mary was down yesterday she asked for one so that she could put it in her private collection of momentos which she keeps at Windsor.'[4] Princess Alice no longer needed to get the 73 bus down from Kensington Palace to Richmond, which she had done during the war owing to petrol rationing. A wartime innocence and lack of pretension always remained at Thatched House Lodge. 'It was a place of the most enormous fun.'[5] For instance, in 1950, Louis's guests and his children's friends were dragooned into a scavenger hunt. Their task was to collect twenty-five specified items, including a live American, an egg (excluding chickens), a set of false teeth, a clergyman's signature, a bloodstained cosh, a pair of corsets, a bottle of Mann's beer, a picture of King Farouk, a pair of combinations and a translation of, 'Don't pinch my leg, you bald-headed, dirty old man' into Italian. Louis was very happy dividing his time between Thatched House Lodge and Binsness. It wasn't restful, but that was never what he wanted.

Louis was kept busy with several directorships and a number of civic duties. He was a Deputy Lieutenant of London, which required him to represent the monarch at civic functions, but also had lesser posts such as that of president of the Richmond Regatta.

His courtier life took up little time, but his personal friendships with the royal family continued. The King and Queen kept in touch, although their lives were not closely entwined. George VI would bring his children down to Thatched House Lodge and occasionally his grandchildren, Prince Charles and Princess Anne. Louis told his friend, Denis Wheatley, that he could hardly believe that the young teenager who had been in his care in 1910 at Osborne, when his life had been threatened by influenza, was now a grandfather. Wheatley wrote how touched he was by Louis's interest in the King's grandchildren. 'I fully understand you can't make lunch and in your capacity of a Royal Uncle. I am sure it will be great fun for you to have the little grandson of your old friend paying a visit.'[6] Sadly, Louis never lived to see his own grandchildren. Bridget and Jean never had children and Carron married Monica Stourton after Louis's death. They had four children – Louis, born 1956, Jonathan, 1958, and the twins, Laura and myself, in 1960. Extraordinarily, from Louis and his six brothers, only one third-generation boy Greig, Louis's great-grandson, exists: my son Jasper Louis Carron, born 1998.

Only occasionally was Louis on duty as a Gentleman Usher. However he retained many friends at court, who passed on news and gossip. His closest friend was Tim Nugent, Controller of the Lord Chamberlain's Office. (He later proposed Carron as a Gentleman Usher to Elizabeth II.) Louis would lunch at White's, where many courtiers met informally, and it was there in the late 1940s that he learned that the King was seriously sick. The initial symptoms were painful cramps in his legs, which were blamed on his constant smoking. Louis remembered his old friend from the early days, so miserable at being confined to his sickbed, and his memories of tending him came flooding back. His own medical knowledge was so out of date that he could offer little practical help; it was almost half a century since Louis had trained as a doctor.

The King fought against his illness, but it was a losing battle, and in 1951 his entire left lung had to be removed after a malignant growth was detected. Louis followed every development closely, offering his support and friendship, but there was little he could do except watch and pray. The cancer had taken a grip but it was eventually a thrombosis, a blood clot to the heart, which wrestled life from the King. On the morning of 6 February 1952, after a day's shooting at Sandringham,

George VI died in his sleep. Winston Churchill caught the nation's mood in a moving broadcast on 7 February. 'During the last months the King walked with death, as if death were a companion, an acquaintance, whom he recognised and did not fear . . . we all saw him approach his journey's end.' For Louis it was the end of a friendship that had lasted almost half a century.

Queen Mary was, of course, devastated to lose another son. She was eighty-four years old and had already seen three of her sons die or disappear into exile. Louis immediately wrote, almost in disbelief that the King had died aged just fifty-seven.

> Beloved madam,
>
> Never in my life have I taken up my pen with a heavier heart for a more impossible task. It is now 46 years since I first had the honour of serving 'Prince Bertie' at Osborne and the news is a terrible shock. But when I think of all your Majesty has gone through and continues to go through my heart bleeds for a very gallant and very wonderful lady. I realise what a terrible time you must be going through. Your Majesty, I hope you realise what a rock of stability & strength you are to our people. We pray that you will take care of yourself for all our sakes as the perfect example of Queenly bearing, dignity & steadfastness which we all so need today.[7]

The little girl with the golden curls and pale blue eyes who had sat on Louis's knee at Wimbledon was now Queen, the great-great-granddaughter of Queen Victoria, who had been on the throne until 1901, when Louis was twenty-one. Louis was born a Victorian and was to die in the second Elizabethan age. Elizabeth II, just twenty-five years old, took up her duties very much as her father's daughter: valiant, dutiful and serious. It was a huge burden for such a young woman, but she appeared calm, confident and dedicated to her role. On 22 February 1952, Louis received a handwritten letter from his new sovereign, moved by a letter he had written her, and expressing

surprise that Louis and her father had been such friends for
so long.

> I was so touched by your letter. It has been a comfort to know of
> the sympathy of so many people everywhere. My father was
> indeed beloved by his subjects, who became his friends and it
> seems hard that he was not allowed to live a bit longer when he
> had made such a remarkable recovery from his operation. We can
> be thankful, though, that he died so peacefully after a day's
> shooting, doing what he liked best. It all seems so unbelievable,
> and being so far away made it much worse. I had no idea you had
> been with him for so many years – how you will miss him; like us.[8]

The friendship of Louis and Albert stuck in the minds of
a great many people, some of whom wrote to Louis, aware
of their closeness and the loss he felt. One friend of Louis's,
Philip Gardiner wrote on the day the King died to offer his
condolences.

> My thoughts are at once turned to you, Louis, on hearing of His
> Majesty's death. For I know how deeply you must feel the great
> loss which has so suddenly befallen us all. You did so much to
> make His Majesty what he became in those fourteen years and
> gave him such good advice & counsel, though please do not think
> I am minimising HM's pluck, endeavour or courage. At the same
> time I feel it was you who steered him & helped him when he was
> young.[9]

With the King dead, it was, as usual, a case of long live the next
sovereign, in this case Queen Elizabeth II. Louis was invited to
become a member of a new court, again as a Gentleman Usher.
This was the fourth and final monarch he was to serve. But
what concentrated Louis's mind more than anything else was
his own failing health. Louis, too, was diagnosed with cancer.
Doctors gave him numerous check-ups and tests, and in
November 1952 he was admitted to a nursing home, under-
going an operation in December. Louis was mostly confined
to bed and little could be done; he slowly weakened and

worsened. His secretary sent out letter after letter regretting he was too ill to attend meetings, parties and events of every kind which had filled his formerly busy life.

But his royal duties were not quite over. The Queen's Private Secretary, Tommy Lascelles, wrote to Phyllis in March 1953, when Louis was in hospital, to ask him to perform one last task for his late King: to give his memories of the young Prince Albert to John Wheeler-Bennett, his official biographer.

> The three Queens and all of us here were so very sorry to read in the newspapers how ill Louis is. You know that you have all our sympathy. May I mention something about which I was on the point of writing to you. John Wheeler-Bennett (see 'Who's Who') is going to be authorised to write a life of King George VI. I have been preparing a list of those to whom he ought to talk to about the King – particularly his early days – and Louis's name was at the top of the list.
>
> If Louis were well enough, I know that he would gladly have helped W-B in this way, and that he would have enjoyed doing so; and he is, of course, about the only man left who can give a really intimate picture of the King's life when he was Duke of York.
>
> But I have no idea whether it would be possible for him now to have even a short talk with W-B; so will you be very kind and tell us frankly? If you think it is not possible (as I quite expect you to say), I will at once explain to the Queen Mother; she is naturally, very anxious that Louis and W-B should meet, but is quite prepared to hear that such a meeting would be more than Louis can manage.[10]

Louis was able to meet Wheeler-Bennett and told him how he had 'put steel' into the young prince, but tiredness stopped him giving as much time as he would have liked. Louis hated being restricted to bed. 'Nasty and unpleasant sensation being ill but I suppose we have all got to learn sooner or later,' he wrote in December 1952 to Denis Wheatley. He loathed the tiredness, the cancellations, and more than anything else seeing his family so sad. Phyllis, whose life had revolved so much around Louis, was devastated. As he lay in a hospital bed, Queen Mary sent him an embroidered linen baby pillow to rest his head on, hoping it would make him a little more comfortable. It was the last time Louis ever heard from her and she from him, after he dictated from his sickbed a letter to her Private Secretary, Major John Wickham, on 8 December 1952. 'Please forgive the secondhand way this letter is coming to you but I would like Her Majesty to know how tremendously touched I was by the interest she has taken in my condition of health. It was so very like her, and if I may say so, deepens my affection to the nicest lady I have ever met in my life.'[11]

As Louis's last days were approaching, more and more letters and cards arrived. On New Year's Eve, 1952, the Queen and Prince Philip sent flowers. 'I am on the sick list and may be for some time,' he wrote to one friend. Jimmy Durante, Bud Flanagan, General Eisenhower, colleagues from HMS *Cumberland*, old Glasgow friends – all sent messages after his illness was reported in the newspapers. While his coming into the world was an event unnoticed outside his family circle, his final days and his death on 1 March 1953 made the pages of most newspapers. 'Friend of Three Kings Dies' was the *Daily Express* headline on the day of his death. Queen Elizabeth, the Queen Mother, sent a telegram to Phyllis: 'So deeply distressed to hear of the great sorrow which has come to you and I send you and your family heartfelt sympathy. I know how sad the King would have been and I shall always be grateful for the loyalty and friendship Sir Louis showed him through so many years.'[12]

Louis never had a triumphalist view of his own life. In his final days, he weighed up the whole of his past existence, and wrote to Phyllis, in a feeble hand in pencil on a scrap of paper, from what was to be his deathbed.

To my beloved wife – *te moriturus saluto*.
    I am moved to hold an inquest on my past fifty years, and am not encouraged. I have always regretted that coming from a family who had an incredibly gracious and religious mother, I did not develop a greater awareness of religion. True I had a philosophy,

which I suppose I held lightly but considerably. It might be embodied in the prayers I used to utter, often mechanically, but at times with an earnestness which surprised me:

> *If I live O Lord Keep me honest and upright*
> *brave and true at all times and in all places*
> *make me kindly and helpful in the ordinary ways of life*
> *so that I can cause as little unhappiness as possible*
> *and create all the happiness I can.*

This sounds all right, but I have an uncomfortable feeling that I can take no credit for this philosophy, or my small endeavours to practise it; for I hate to see people miserable but also love to see them happy. And, within my power to help them to be so – a kind of sadism in reverse – I have given up so little to satisfy it.

I have had more than my share of happiness in this life, and as I am now of an age when the Celestial Omnibus might quite fairly stop to pick me up, my philosophy at its approach develops into an attitude of mind rather than a creed. I pray that when I die I may have the courage and endurance to face pain and death; and the faith, serenity and peace to meet the unknown tomorrow. And with the certainty that God is love and therefore merciful I may cherish the hope that one day, when I have served my sentence for the sins committed on the path of life, I pray that in God's good time, I may be allowed to climb the Mountains of Atonement and see the King of heaven's worldly realms.

These were surprisingly fearful thoughts for a man who had achieved so much and led such a rich life. At his funeral in St Andrew's Church in Ham, in Surrey, all the multifarious strands of his life came together once again. The five most senior members of the royal family were represented, as was Winston Churchill, J. Arthur Rank, Catford dog track, the All-England Wimbledon tennis club and the Scottish rugby team. At the back of the church there were six waiters from the Dorchester, where he had been a director, who had taken the morning off to attend. 'Tonic was a friend to two Kings' was the *Daily Mail* headline. *The Times* called him a 'Trusted Friend of the Royal Family'. Yet his life had been so much more. He had been a rugby

international who led Scotland, a surgeon who helped save
the King's life, a naval officer, a Royal Marine, an RAF pilot, a
political fixer to presidents and prime ministers. He had been
imprisoned and wounded in the First World War and played
an influential part behind the scenes in the Second. *The Times'*
obituary declared that his life was to be envied. 'Few men in
the twentieth century can have had a fuller or a more varied
life than he. Though he was not remarkable (as he was always
the first to insist) for any outstanding intellectual qualities, he
had a personal charm, which was memorable and compelling.'

Select Bibliography

Bain, George, *The Culbin Sands, The Story of a Buried Estate*, Nairnshire Telegraph Office, (n.d.)

Bradford, Sarah, *King George VI*, Weidenfeld and Nicolson, (1989)

Bradford, Sarah, *Elizabeth: a Biography of Her Majesty the Queen*, Heinemann, (1996)

Airlie, Mabel, Countess of, *Thatched with Gold*, Hutchinson, (1962)

Alice, HRH Princess, Countess of Athlone, *For my Grandchildren*, Evans Bros, (1966)

Battiscombe, Georgina, *Queen Alexandra*, Constable, (1969)

Cartland, Barbara, *We Danced All Night*, Hutchinson, (1970)

Churchill, Winston, *The World Crisis (1911–1914)*, Heinemann, (1923)

Clark, Alan, (ed.), *A Good Innings, The Private Papers of Viscount Lee of Fareham*, John Murray, (1974)

Cleather, Norah Gordon, *Wimbledon Story*, Sporting Handbooks Ltd, (1947)

Collonette, C.L., *A History of Richmond Park*, Sidgwick & Jackson, (1937)

Colville, Lady Cynthia, *A Crowded Life*, Evans Bros, (1963)

Colville, Sir John, *Fringes of Power: Downing Street Diaries 1939–1955*, Hodder & Stoughton, (1982)

Cooper, Artemis, *Cairo in the War 1939–1945*, Penguin, (1989)

Cooper, Joseph, *Facing the Music: An Autobiography*, Weidenfeld and Nicolson, (1979)

Cunningham Reid, Alec, *Planes and Personalities*, Philip Allan, (1920)

Curjel, Captain H.E.D., 'Profile of Louis Greig', *Journal of the Royal Naval Medical Service*, vol. 59, (1973)

Dalton, Hugh, *The Fateful Years, (1931–45)*, Muller, (1957)

Darbyshire, Taylor, *The Duke of York, An Intimate & Authoritative Life-story*, Hutchinson, (1929)

Donaldson, Frances, *Edward VIII*, Weidenfeld and Nicolson, (1974)

Ferguson, Niall, *The Pity of War*, Allen Lane, (1998)

Figes, Orlando, *A People's Tragedy: The Russian Revolution (1891–1924)*, Jonathan Cape, (1996)

Forbes, Grania, *My Darling Buffy*, Richard Cohen Books, (1997)

Frankland, Noble, *Prince Henry, Duke of Gloucester*, Weidenfeld and Nicolson, (1980)

Gilbert, Martin, *Winston S Churchill, volume III (1914–16)*, Heinemann, (1971)

Gilbert, Martin, *The Twentieth Century, volumes I & II*, HarperCollins, (1997 and 1999)

Gilbert, Martin, *Winston Churchill, A Life*, Henry Holt, (1991)

Gillies, Donald, *Radical Diplomat, The Life of Archibald Clark Kerr, Lord Inverchapel, 1882–1951*, I. B. Tauris, (1999)

Godfrey, Rupert, (ed.), *Edward, Prince of Wales, Letters from a Prince*, (March 1918–January 1921), Little, Brown and Co, (1998)

Gore, John, *King George V, A Personal Memoir*, John Murray, (1941)

Hardinge, Helen, *Loyal to Three Kings*, William Kimber, (1967)

Hart-Davis, Duff, (ed.), *In Royal Service: The Letters and Journals of Sir Alan Lascelles 1920–1936*, vol. II Hamilton, (1989)

Howarth, Patrick, *King George VI*, Hutchinson, (1988)

Judd, Dennis, *King George VI*, Michael Joseph, (1982)

Longford, Elizabeth, *The Queen Mother*, Weidenfeld and Nicolson, (1981)

Massie, Allan, *Glasgow: Portraits of a City*, Barrie & Jenkins, (1989)

Macaulay, Duncan, *Talking to Sir John Smyth, Behind the Scenes at Wimbledon*, Collins, (1965)

Marquand, David, *Ramsay MacDonald*, Jonathan Cape, (1977)

McLeave, Hugh, *The Last Pharoah: The Ten Faces of Farouk*, Michael Joseph, (1969)

McLeod, Kirsty, *Battle Royal: Edward VIII and George VI, Brother Against Brother*, Constable, (1999)

Middlemas, Keith, *The Life and Times of George VI*, Weidenfeld and Nicolson, (1974)

Miller, Ruby, *Champagne from my Slipper*, Herbert Jenkins, (1962)

Mortimer, Penelope, *Queen Elizabeth: A Life of the Queen Mother*, Viking, (1986)

Nicolson, Sir Harold, *King George V His Life and Reign*, Constable, (1952)

Peake, Dame Felicity, Memoirs of the First Director of the Women's Royal Air Force, *Pure Chance*, Airlife, (1993)

Pimlott, Ben, *The Queen: A Biography of Elizabeth II*, HarperCollins, (1996)

Pope-Hennessy, James, *Queen Mary*, George Allen and Unwin, (1959)

Preston, Harry, *Memories*, Constable & Co, (1928)

Pudney, John, *His Majesty King George VI, A study*, Hutchinson, (1952)

Reid, Michaela, *Ask Sir James*, Hodder and Stoughton, (1987)

Rhodes James, Robert, *Chips: The Diaries of Sir Henry Channon*, Penguin, (1967)

Rhodes James, Robert (ed.) *Memoirs of a Conservative: J.C.C. Davidson's Memoirs and Papers 1910–1937* (Weidenfeld and Nicolson), 1969)

Rhodes James, Robert, *Undaunted: The Political Role of George VI*, Little, Brown, (1998)

Rose, Kenneth, *King George V*, Weidenfeld and Nicolson, (1983)

Rose, Kenneth, *Kings, Queens & Courtiers*, Weidenfeld and Nicolson, (1985)

Scrimgeour, Alexander, *The Diaries and Letters 1914–16*, Privately printed, (1925)

Shaughnessy, Alfred, *Both Ends of the Candle*, Robert Clark, (1978)

Smyth, J. G., Brigadier, *Lawn Tennis*, B.T. Batsford, (1953)

Steel, Nigel & Hart, Peter, *Tumult in the Clouds, The British Experience of the War in the Air 1914–1918*, Hodder & Stoughton, (1997)

Stuart, Viscount of Findhorn, *Within The Fringe, An Autobiography*, The Bodley Head, (1967)

Summersby, Kay, *Eisenhower was my Boss*, Prentice-Hall, (1948)

Symons, Julian, *The General Strike*, The Cresset Press, (1957)

Thornton, Michael, *Royal Feud*, Joseph, (1985)

Tilden, William T. 2nd, *My Story, a Champion's Memoirs*, Helman Williams Co, (1948)

Tinling, Ted, *Tinling: Sixty Years in Tennis*, Sidgwick & Jackson, (1983)

Waterhouse, Nourah, *Private and Official: Reminiscences of Sir Ronald Waterhouse*, Jonathan Cape, (1942)

Wheeler-Bennett, Sir John, *King George VI: His Life and Reign*, Macmillan, (1958)

Williamson, Philip, *National Crisis and National Government: British Politics, the Economy and Empire 1926–1932*, Cambridge University Press, (1992)

Windsor, HRH Duke of, *A King's Story*, Cassell & Co, (1951)

Ziegler, Philip, *Mountbatten*, Collins, (1985)

Ziegler, Philip, *King Edward VIII: The official biography*, Collins, (1990)

Ziegler, Philip, *Osbert Sitwell*, Chatto and Windus, (1998)

Notes

PROLOGUE

1. Muriel Spark, *The Prime of Miss Jean Brodie* (1961).
2. Interview with the Earl of Longford, 7 March 1997.
3. Conversation with Lord Callaghan of Cardiff, May 1998.
4. Diaries of Sir Bryan Godfrey-Faussett, Churchill College, Cambridge.

CHAPTER ONE

1. Interview with Nancy, Lady Maclay, June 1998.
2. Ibid.
3. Greig family papers.
4. Glasgow Academy archives.
5. Information from Sir Carron Greig.
6. Allan Massie, *Glasgow Portraits of a City* (1989).
7. Ibid.
8. Unpublished paper by Jack Fitch based on research at the PRO.

CHAPTER TWO

1. Sir John Wheeler-Bennett, *King George VI: His Life and Reign* (1958).
2. Sir Harold Nicholson, *King George V: His Life and Reign* (1952).
3. Sarah Bradford, *King George VI* (1989).
4. HRH The Duke of Windsor, *A King's Story* (1951).
5. Ibid.
6. Imperial War Museum, *Ships in a Bottle*, unpublished memoir by Captain F.S.W. de Winton, IWM 85/44/1.
7. Bradford, op. cit.

8. *Liverpool Daily Post*, n.d.

9. Ibid.

10. Wheeler-Bennett, op. cit.

11. Author's interview with Lord Wigram, June 1997.

12. Bradford, op. cit.

13. James Pope-Hennessy, *Queen Mary* (1959).

14. Windsor, op. cit.

15. Ibid.

16. Bradford, op. cit.

17. Wheeler-Bennett, op. cit.

18. Bradford, op. cit.

19. Letter to Anna Greig, 1909. Greig papers.

20. Letter from Arthur Greig to Anna Greig, 8 March 1909. Greig papers.

21. Pope-Hennessy, op. cit.

22. Royal Archive, Windsor: RA GV AA 58 134.

23. Nicolson, op. cit.

24. Martin Gilbert, *A History of the Twentieth Century*, Volume One, 1900–1933 (1997).

25. Wheeler-Bennett, op. cit.

26. Arthur Bigge writing to Louis Greig. Greig papers.

27. Author's interview with Viscount Stuart of Findhorn, August 1998.

CHAPTER THREE

1. Imperial War Museum, PP/MCR/318 reel 1/Francis Lambert.

2. Bradford, op. cit.

3. Kenneth Rose, *Kings, Queens and Courtiers* (1985).

4. Wheeler-Bennett, op. cit.

5. Taylor Darbyshire, *The Duke of York, An Intimate and Authoritative Life-story* (1929).

6. Frederick Dalrymple-Hamilton, unpublished diaries.

7. Ibid.

8. Ibid.

9. Ibid.

10. Author interview with Lord Charteris of Amisfield, June 1997.

11. *Toronto News*, 6 June 1913.

12. RA GVI diaries.

13. Wheeler-Bennett, op. cit.

14. Darbyshire, op. cit.

15. Louis Greig diaries. Greig papers.

16. RA GVI diaries.

17. Wheeler-Bennett, op. cit.

18. Martin Gilbert, *Winston Churchill: A Life* (1991).

19. Captain H. Hamilton, *Imperial War Museum RN*, MS75/41/1, n.d.

CHAPTER FOUR

1. Martin Gilbert, *Winston S. Churchill*, Volume III (1914–1916), (1971).

2. Louis Greig war journal. Greig papers.

3. Winston Churchill, *The World Crisis* (1923).

4. Ibid.

5. Gilbert, *Winston S. Churchill*, Volume III (1914–1916), (1971).

6. Ibid.

7. Ibid.

8. Major-General Julian Thompson, letter to author, December 1998.

9. Louis Greig war journal.

10. Author interview with Nancy, Lady Maclay, June 1998.

11. Churchill, op. cit.

CHAPTER FIVE

1. Louis Greig war journal.

2. *Penny Pictorial*, 25 September 1915.

3. Louis Greig war journal.

4. Bradford, op. cit.

CHAPTER SIX

1. Darbyshire, op. cit.
2. Wheeler-Bennett, op. cit.
3. Louis Greig war journal.
4. Wheeler-Bennett, op. cit.
5. Windsor, op. cit.
6. Wheeler-Bennett, op. cit.
7. Bradford, op. cit.
8. Ibid.
9. Ibid.
10. Ibid.
11. Wheeler-Bennett, op. cit.
12. Bradford, op. cit.
13. Ibid.
14. Prince Albert writing to Louis Greig. Greig papers.
15. Ibid.
16. Greig papers.
17. Greig papers.
18. Wheeler-Bennett, op. cit.
19. Bradford, op. cit.
20. Greig papers.
21. Bradford, op. cit.
22. Ibid.
23. Ibid.
24. Wheeler-Bennett, op. cit.
25. Ibid.
26. Ibid.
27. RA GV AA 60/249.
28. Author interview with Lord Wigram the son of the king's
    assistant private secretary, June 1997.
29. RA GV AA 60/251.
30. Greig papers, 20 August 1917.
31. Ibid, 1 September 1917.

32. Ibid.
33. Ibid.
34. RA GV AA 60/257.
35. RA GV AA 60/257.
36. RA GV AA 60/260.
37. Greig papers.
38. Wheeler-Bennett, op. cit.
39. Viscount Stuart of Findhorn, *Within the Fringe* (1967).

CHAPTER SEVEN

1. Rose, op. cit.
2. Greig papers.
3. Rose, op. cit.
4. Greig papers.
5. RA GV AA 64/iii/118.
6. Rose, op. cit.
7. RA GV 64/iii/119.
8. Greig papers.
9. Bradford, op. cit.
10. Kenneth Rose, *King George V* (1983).
11. Louis Greig's letter to his wife. Greig papers.
12. Greig papers.
13. Ibid.
14. Rose, op. cit.
15. Ibid.
16. Greig papers.
17. Georgina Battiscombe, *Queen Alexandra* (1969).
18. Ibid.
19. Greig papers.
20. Author interview with Lord Wigram, May 1997.
21. Rose, op. cit.
22. Ibid.

23. Battiscombe, op. cit.

24. Rose, op. cit.

CHAPTER EIGHT

1. Bradford, op. cit.

2. Nigel Steel & Peter Hart, *Tumult in the Clouds, The British Experience of the War in the Air 1914–1918* (1997).

3. Bradford, op. cit.

4. RA GV AA 60/280.

5. Ibid.

6. RA GV CC 10/273.

7. RA GV AA 60/292.

8. RA GV CC 10/278.

9. Wheeler-Bennett, op. cit.

10. Greig papers.

11. Draft BBC script, 7 April 1952. Greig papers.

12. John Pudney, *His Majesty King George VI, A study* (1952).

13. Greig papers.

14. Ibid.

15. Bradford, op. cit.

16. Ibid.

17. Ibid.

18. BBC script, op. cit.

19. Steel & Hart, op. cit.

20. Ibid.

21. Squadron Leader R.B. Caswell, *History of the RAF*, unpublished lecture given at Royal Naval Staff College, Greenwich (1937). PRO AIR 1 682 2/13/2215.

22. Greig papers.

23. Ibid.

24. *The Times*, obituary, 3 December 1957.

25. Edward, Prince of Wales, *Letters from A Prince (March 1918–January 1921)*, edited by Rupert Godfrey (1998).

26. Ibid.

27. Prince Albert writing to Queen Mary, 20 June 1918. RA GV/CC 10/284.

28. Author's interview with Lady Margaret Colville, June 1997.

29. PRO Air 2 90.

30. Wheeler-Bennett, op. cit.

CHAPTER NINE

1. RA GV AA 60/362.

2. Wheeler-Bennett, op, cit.

3. Ibid.

4. RA GV AA 60/373.

5. Louis writing from the Palais de Bruxelles. Greig papers.

6. Alec Cunningham Reid, *Planes and Personalities* (1920).

7. Wheeler-Bennett, op. cit.

8. Edward, Prince of Wales, op. cit.

9 Ibid.

10. Ibid.

11. Ibid.

12. Rose.

13. Edward, Prince of Wales, op. cit.

14. Ibid.

15. Ibid.

16. Greig papers.

17. Greig diaries.

18. Bradford, op. cit.

19. PRO AIR 1 1/21/15/1/103.

20. Ibid.

21. Bradford, op. cit.

22. Ibid.

23. Wigram, op. cit.

24. Wheeler-Bennett, op. cit.

25. Greig diaries.

26. RA GV CC 11/15.

27. RA PS/GV/O 1595/1.

28. Noble Frankland, *Prince Henry, Duke of Gloucester* (1980)

29. Wheeler-Bennett, op. cit.

30. Ibid.

31. Ibid.

32. Wigram, op. cit.

CHAPTER TEN

1. Harry Preston, *Memories* (1928).

2. Ibid.

3. William T. Tilden 2nd, *My Story, A Champion's Memoirs.*

4. Susan Greig papers.

5. Ruby Miller, *Champagne from my Slipper* (1962).

6. Viscount Stuart, op. cit.

7. Private information.

8. Bradford, op. cit.

9. Greig diary.

10. Sir Godfrey Thomas, unpublished memoir.

11. Cecil Beaton diaries, unpublished extract.

12. Thomas, op. cit.

13. Lord Cromer papers.

14. Rose, op. cit.

15. Greig diaries.

16. Wigram, op. cit.

17. MacDonald papers, PRO 30/69 1753/2.

18. Mabel, Countess of Airlie, *Thatched with Gold* (1962).

19. Robert, Rhodes James (ed.), *Memoirs of a Conservative: J.C.C. Davidson's Memoirs and Papers 1910–1937* (1969).

20. Rose, *King's, Queen and Courtiers.*

21. Ibid.

22. Rose, *King George V.*

23. Rose, *Kings, Queens and Courtiers.*

24. Ibid.

25. Cromer Papers.
26. Ibid.
27. Ibid.
28. Bradford, op. cit.

CHAPTER ELEVEN

1. Author interview with Viscount Stuart, 15 August 1997.
2. Grania Forbes, *My Darling Buffy* (1997).
3. Elizabeth Longford, *The Queen Mother* (1981).
4. Bradford, op. cit.
5. Ibid.
6. Ibid.
7. Windsor, op. cit.
8. Donald Gillies, *Radical Diplomat, the Life of Archibald Clark Kerr, Lord Inverchapel, 1882–1951* (1999).
9. Ibid.
10. Letter to Louis Greig. Lord Davidson papers, House of Lords.
11. Ibid.
12. Wigram, op. cit.
13. Dalrymple-Hamilton, op. cit.
14. Greig papers.
15. RA GV AA 61/156.
16. RA GV AA 61/157.

CHAPTER TWELVE

1. Cromer papers.
2. Ibid.
3. Ibid.
4. R.J.O. Adams, *Bonar Law* (1999).
5. Private papers.
6. RA ADY 103.
7. Ibid.
8. Greig Papers.
9. RA GV AA 61/187.

10. RA GV CC 11/49.
11. Wigram, op. cit.
12. Greig papers.
13. RA GV AA 61/188.
14. Greig papers.
15. Ibid.
16. Ibid.
17. Ibid.
18. Ibid.
19. Ibid.
20. Ibid.
21. Ibid.
22. Ibid.
23. Ben Pimlott, *The Queen: A Biography of Elizabeth II* (1997).
24. Channon diaries.

CHAPTER THIRTEEN

1. Author interview with Joseph Cooper, September 1998.
2. Laing family papers.
3. MacDonald papers, PRO 30/69.
4. Laing family papers.
5. MacDonald papers, PRO 30/69, 19 March 1923.
6. RA PS/GVO 1908.
7. Ibid.
8. MacDonald papers, PRO 30/69 197, 1 February 1924.
9. *The Times*, 22 May 1937.
10. Laing family papers.
11. Ibid.
12. Ibid.
13. Ibid.
14. Author conversation with Sir Denis Thatcher, 29 April 1998.
15. Philip Williamson, *National Crisis and National Government: British politics, the economy and empire 1926–1932* (1992).

16. Ibid.

17. Ibid.

18. MacDonald papers, PRO 30/69 1441.

19. Greig papers.

20. Ibid.

21. Williamson, op. cit.

22. H. A. Gwynne papers, Bodleian Library, Dept of Western Manuscripts.

23. Greig papers.

24. Ibid.

25. Ibid.

26. Ibid.

27. David Marquand, *Ramsay MacDonald* (1977).

28. Ibid.

29. H. A. Gwynne papers.

30. Williamson, op. cit.

31. *The Political Diaries of Hugh Dalton 1918–1940, 1945–1960* edited by Ben Pimlott, (1986).

32. MacDonald papers, PRO 30/69/678.

33. Greig papers.

34. MacDonald papers, PRO 30/69/678.

35. MacDonald papers, PRO 30/69/679.

36. Greig papers.

37. Thomas Horder's letter, 6 March 1932, RA GV K 2344 14.

38. Greig papers.

39. MacDonald papers, PRO 30/69 680.

40. Thomas Jones, *Whitehall Diary*, Volume II (1969).

41. MacDonald papers, PRO 30/69/1444.

42. MacDonald papers, PRO 30/69/680.

43. MacDonald papers, PRO 30/69/679.

44. MacDonald papers, PRO 30/69/1444.

45. MacDonald papers, PRO 30/69.

CHAPTER FOURTEEN

1. Greig papers.
2. Ibid.
3. Ibid.
4. Ibid.
5. MacDonald papers, PRO 30/69/754.
6. Rose, *Kings, Queens and Courtiers*.
7. Ibid.
8. Ibid.
9. Greig papers.
10. Philip Ziegler, *Edward VIII* (1990).
11. Bradford, op. cit.
12. Duff Hart-Davis (ed.), *In Royal Service: The Letters and Journals of Sir Alan Lascelles*, Volume II, 1920–1936.
13. Sir John Aird, unpublished diaries.
14. Ibid.
15. Ibid.
16. Cromer papers.
17. RA GV EE 10/2921.
18. Ziegler, op. cit.
19. Airlie, op. cit.

CHAPTER FIFTEEN

1. Bradford, op. cit.
2. A. C. Don's diaries, Lambeth Palace.
3. Alfred Shaughnessy, *Both Ends of the Candle* (1978).
4. Bradford, op. cit.
5. Queen Elizabeth, letter to Cosmo Lang, Archbishop of Canterbury, copied out by A. C. Don, Lambeth Palace.
6. Private papers.
7. Rose, *Kings, Queens and Courtiers*.
8. Martin Gilbert, *A History of the Twentieth Century*, Volume Two, 1933–51 (1999).

CHAPTER SIXTEEN

1. Author's conversation with Sebastian Cox, Air Historical Branch, Ministry of Defence.
2. Greig papers.
3. Ibid.
4. Ibid.
5. Ibid.
6. Ibid.
7. Rose, op. cit.
8. Victor Cazalet diaries.
9. Greig papers.
10. Ibid.
11. Ibid.
12. Ibid.
13. Ibid.
14. Ibid.
15. Ibid.
16. Ibid.
17. Ibid.
18. RA PS/GVI/C 342/G/13.
19. RA PS/GVI/C 342/6/45.
20. Author interview with Sir Edward Ford, April 1998.
21. Hugh McLeave, *The Last Pharaoh: The Ten Faces of Farouk* (1969).
22. Patrick Telfer-Smollett, letter to Sir Carron Greig. Greig papers.
23. Greig papers.

CHAPTER SEVENTEEN

1. Author interview with Joseph Cooper, September 1998.
2. Greig papers.
3. George Bain, *The Culbin Sands*.
4. Greig papers, 14 July 1952.
5. Author interview with Lady Margaret Colville, June 1997.
6. Greig papers.

7. RA GV/CC 47/2590.
8. Greig papers, 22 February 1952.
9. Ibid.
10. Ibid.
11. Ibid.
12. Greig papers, 1 March 1953.

Index